"Andrew Chandler's perceptive study of Bishop George Bell makes extensive and insightful use of Bell's vast archive and shows his courageous contribution in defending the cause of Christian unity during the war-torn years of the last century. He praises Bell as a lone prophetic figure in the Church of England. This book is a valuable contribution to the cause of ecumenical church history."

— JOHN S. CONWAY
University of British Columbia

"George Bell was one of the most outstanding leaders of the Church of England in the twentieth century, with an unrivalled breadth of vision and a courageous willingness to speak out against injustice. In this outstanding biography Andrew Chandler paints a brilliant portrait of a many-sided figure who helped to define the Church of England's ecumenical policy and who was in turn defined by his very public, and frequently unpopular, commitment to defend the victims of Nazi oppression."

— JEREMY MORRIS
University of Cambridge

GEORGE BELL
Bishop of Chichester

Church, State, and Resistance
in the Age of Dictatorship

Andrew Chandler

WILLIAM B. EERDMANS PUBLISHING COMPANY
GRAND RAPIDS, MICHIGAN / CAMBRIDGE, U.K.

Published 2016 by
Wm. B. Eerdmans Publishing Co.
2140 Oak Industrial Drive N.E., Grand Rapids, Michigan 49505 /
P.O. Box 163, Cambridge CB3 9PU U.K.

Printed in the United States of America

22 21 20 19 18 17 16   7 6 5 4 3 2 1

Library of Congress Cataloging-in-Publication Data

Names: Chandler, Andrew.
Title: George Bell, Bishop of Chichester:
church, state, and resistance in the age of dictatorship / Andrew Chandler.
Description: Grand Rapids, Michigan : Eerdmans Publishing Company, 2016. |
Includes bibliographical references and index.
Identifiers: LCCN 2015038505 |
ISBN 9780802872272 (pbk.: alk. paper)
Subjects: LCSH: Bell, G. K. A. (George Kennedy Allen), 1883-1958. |
Church of England — Bishops — Biography. |
Anglican Communion — Bishops — Biography. |
Church of England — History — 20th century. |
England — Church history — 20th century.
Classification: LCC BX5199.B355 C43 2016 |
DDC 283.092 — dc23
LC record available at http://lccn.loc.gov/2015038505

www.eerdmans.com

For Eric Adams

Blessed is the man that hath not walked in the counsel of the
      ungodly, nor stood in the way of sinners
    and hath not sat in the seat of the scornful.
But his delight is in the law of the Lord
    and in his law will he exercise himself day and night.
And he shall be like a tree planted by the water-side
    that will bring forth his fruit in due season.
His leaf also shall not wither
    and look, whatsoever he doeth, it shall prosper.

Psalm 1:1-4, Book of Common Prayer

Contents

Preface

This study in many ways represents an unfolding reflection of some twenty-five years on a man I first glimpsed as a boy, on the dust jacket of a book, while browsing in a second-hand bookshop in the little English town of Devizes with my father. Here was a striking face, belonging to a quite different world, looking firmly but benignly, with almost translucent eyes, into the lens of Howard Coster's camera. Needless to say, it was only my father who read the copy that was carried home. It is a mark of his generosity that twenty-five years after he lent it to his deplorable younger son he has not once asked for it back.

Jasper's 1967 biography of Bell was commissioned by Henrietta Bell, who took the greatest interest in the work as it unfolded. For an author to work in such a personal context must surely have been both an opportunity and a difficulty. Jasper had, in fact, inherited the task, for Norman Sykes, eminent as both church historian and ecclesiastic, had first begun a biography and died before much had been accomplished. Sykes had known Bell well, and it is tantalizing to imagine what he might have made of him on paper. At all events, an air of disappointment has hung over Jasper's work since its appearance in 1967; and Jasper himself placed it no higher than an "Upper Second" in class. But even if it does not quite capture the elusive properties of Bell's character and struggles to find the best way to organize a great weight of intricate material, it is a book of genuine substance, achieving a very great deal on its own terms and providing a solid, indispensable foundation for all subsequent assessments. If Jasper was more happily and successfully the biographer of Bishop Headlam, surely far more is owed to him for his life of Bell.

The name of George Bell — and the existence of his immense archive at Lambeth Palace Library in London — next occurred in my life in an undergraduate seminar at the University of Birmingham, led by Professor John A. S. Grenville. John was one of those British historians who, like Ian Kershaw, knew the significance of Bell in that other, German landscape. It was characteristically generous of him to turn me in such a fruitful direction, and he remained a great presence in my work. It was then under the direction of Professor David M. Thompson at Cambridge that I first came to study for myself what would once have been called the literary remains of this striking bishop of the Church of England who had so perseveringly labored on behalf of Germans caught up in the destructive crisis of Nazism in Germany between 1933 and 1945. I was fortunate to do so at a time when Melanie Barber, the archivist responsible for the organization and cataloguing of the great archive that Bell had bequeathed, was there to guide and encourage me. Writing this book has shown me again how very much I came to owe to her.

Without these influences the figure of Bell would surely have never been more than an obscurity to me. Since then, my sense of what he stood for in the world, and what he sought to do for it, has evolved by degrees and gained some intensity in many different landscapes, not least in the context of the George Bell Institute, which came to life in Birmingham in the autumn of 1996, and which found a home in 2007 in Chichester itself. For the creation, life, and work of the institute I must above all thank Eric Adams, former Director of the Barrow Cadbury Trust. In this surprising context I also owe much to the late Charles Cadbury, and to his widow, Jill.

During the very last stage of preparation of this book, the Church of England issued a startling press release on 22 October 2015. This disclosed that an out-of-court settlement had taken place concerning allegations that sexual offenses had been committed by Bishop Bell, from the late 1940s to the early 1950s, against an individual who was at the time "a young child." Quite unforeseen, this revelation provoked consternation, at home and abroad. It need hardly be added that this has also presented the author of this book with a painful and difficult situation. But while a contemporary history of the controversy provoked by this statement is becoming feasible — for there are public articles and letters appearing in the British press by the week — no consideration of the substance of the allegation itself is possible. Quite simply, whatever materials exist remain secret. "The result," as an editorial in the *Church Times* observed on 4 December 2015, "is that Bell now rests uneasily in some sort of moral limbo."

The purpose of this book is to examine, and assess, the profound contributions that George Bell made to the age in which he lived. He remains one of the very few English church leaders of the twentieth century to achieve a genuine significance in international history. That significance arises from what is thoroughly documented and openly available to scholarship; in short, from what we have reason to feel can be known. It was a work of many decades. It came to touch, and even to influence, the great narratives of at least three continents and to encompass the lives of far greater numbers than we can realize: the writers, composers, and artists who sought, often with so little encouragement, to offer their gifts to the church; the many harassed Christians who lived under tyranny in other lands; the Jews of Germany and then all Europe who faced persecution and then destruction; the refugees who sought sanctuary in countries where they might be safe from such terrors; the civilians of enemy states caught up in the maelstrom of what came to be known as a "total" war. The context in which all of Bell's diverse works transpired was a rich, vivid vision of the universal church, in which all Christians could find each other and labor for justice, not merely as members of different confessions but together, as brothers and sisters.

These days, short biographies that allow some space for a more personal reflection, perhaps like Evelyn Waugh's study of the tragic Jesuit, Edmund Campion, are not much in vogue: instinctively we tend to feel a greater confidence in vast, dispassionate ones. Bell, as his admirer Donald MacKinnon saw, certainly had in him the stuff of a great Life. Perhaps the present work will mark a step toward such a study. But one must also think of what the market will bear, and while it may be said that the figure of George Bell deserves a revival, such things are difficult to predict or engineer. I am truly grateful to Bill Eerdmans for having the conviction and confidence to publish such a book as this, and to Jenny Hoffman, who has dealt so patiently and efficiently with the text and its author. I also owe much to the admirable Norman Hjelm.

The origin of this particular venture lies in an early, extended essay produced to commemorate the fiftieth anniversary of Bell's death, in 2008. The thanks that I offered then still stand: to the Very Revd. Nicholas Frayling, Canon Peter Kefford, and Canon Anthony Cane at Chichester Cathedral; and to Rachel and Michael Moriarty, in whom I have found the patience and kindness of friends. Since then the papers gathered at the anniversary conference have been published as *The Church and Humanity: The Life and Work of George Bell, 1883-1958* (Ashgate, 2012). I have drawn gratefully from this. It should also be noted that much of what happened in 2008 owed much to the late Professor Paul Foster, the Great Commemorator of Chichester, whose precious Otter Memorial Series saw the publication of two titles devoted to Bishop Bell and one on Hans Feibusch. I am grateful to Keith Clements, a distinguished ecumenist and historian; Frank Field, MP, whose noble commitment to George Bell has remained conspicuous and constant throughout his own, busy public life; E. C. John, theologian and historian of Bangalore; and Alan Pardoe, in the security of whose judgments I have come wholly to trust. I acknowledge gladly the continuing kindness of staff at the Lambeth Palace Library, particularly Rachel Cosgrave, and Janet Carter and Wendy Ellison at the library of the University of Chichester. My colleague in the George Bell Institute, Charlotte Hansen, has offered steadfast help and sympathetic friendship, often from the cathedral library. Ferdinand Schlingensiepen has been an astute and gracious critic; very seldom, I imagine, has an author been so fortunate in such a reader. Any mistakes will surely be mine alone.

I continue to owe much to my father and mother, Eric and Janet Chandler. My sons, Joel and Reuben, have brought constant reassurance and happiness in times of great upheaval. To my wife, Alice, I owe far more than words can convey. For wholly without realizing it, she has made me want to write such things as books again.

True, Love finally is great,
Greater than all, but large the hate,
Far larger than Man can estimate.

W. H. Auden, chorus from
"The Ascent of F6"

The Little Blue Notebook

The reading room of Lambeth Palace Library in London is for some scholars of church history as much an intellectual home as an immense archive of papers and a repository of books. The little volume now held in my mind, bearing the bland title "Bell Notes, Volume 275," barely measures more than ten centimeters by seven. It could easily have been slipped into a jacket pocket. Very likely it was, and often retrieved so that the owner could write something new inside, something to be acted upon soon or remembered later. The blue notebook seems at first to answer to no very clear scheme. But it is not merely private, for the scribbles that are gathered here turn out to be both intensely personal and purposefully public. The name "Bishop of Chichester" is written firmly on the flyleaf. There is a scheme of daily prayers, for "Hettie," for his mother and father, for two brothers long ago killed in the Great War, for the schools of the diocese of Chichester, for the unemployed, for the League of Nations, for the peace of the world. There follows one list of names after another, framing a cycle of prayer lasting twenty-eight days. There is a long quotation found in a letter from the English poet, the Roman Catholic Gerard Manley Hopkins, seeing in the life and character of Christ "that chastity of mind which seems to lie at the very heart and be the parent of all other good." On the next page falls a stray fragment of an argument: "Tendency to regard Church as an end in itself, for the sake of its members"; on another is a budget for a New Housing Association; on another a list of Russian and Hungarian names; on another an extensive list of statistics recording the demobilization figures of German troops in July 1946. Then there follows a further list of names and addresses, "People to ask for," in the cities Düsseldorf, Münster, Kiel, Hamburg, Hanover, Berlin. A few pages on there is the sketch of an idea for a sermon referring to Shakespeare's *Measure for Measure*: "Man proud man. Power. See Hitler. See Science. Nothing above."[1]

No great claim has been made on behalf of this little blue notebook. It offers little to distract the historian busily searching for other things. The book is indeed almost buried in a vast archive, duly listed near the end of a long catalogue defined by heavy portfolios of speeches, sermons, memoranda, and thousands of letters, public and private. Even so, this practical, discreet, and unassuming book expresses a world of life, work, and worship. It captures a mind and a soul in perpetual motion in the world: attentive, enquiring, pursuing. It is a testament of Christian life in the middle twentieth century, wrought out of the turmoil of politics, war, persecution, calamity. It is a proof of one man's decision to take his place in such a world, and to do so as a faithful Christian. Before we view the little blue book too lightly we should remember that such a man need not have done so. Indeed, some felt that it would have been by far the better for him if he had stayed at home. What could an English bishop think he was up to, drawing up lists of German names and chasing about in Continental cities?

History is not much the fashion among theologians these days. Their eyes are turned toward the preoccupations of the present day. Meanwhile, those who organize the life of the church might throw a dutiful backward glance into the past, or allow themselves an introductory historical paragraph in a report or memorandum. But, by and large, they do not allow it to detain and distract them. We cannot flatter ourselves that we can govern the past — it is filled with people unlike ourselves who are quite unaccountable to us and who cannot be changed by us — and we can certainly congratulate ourselves on appearing to organize the present, even if the skeptic observes that most people seem to carry on regardless of all our campaigns. But history still makes its claims upon us because it reveals humanity, not simply here and now but in its length and breadth, its richness, its costly wisdom, its surprises. What matters to the historian is not that men and women die and disappear but that they live and labor. What is fundamental to all of this is the acknowledgment that we are all somehow caught in a common responsibility together.

Although George Bell once excited, and has continued to attract, condemnation or praise, my purpose in this book is neither to criticize nor to eulogize, but rather to seek to understand why he thought and acted as

---

1. London, Lambeth Palace Library, Bell Papers, vol. 275, "Bell Notes" (various pages).

he did. Furthermore, while Bell became conspicuous as an individualist who persevered in his own opinions, often against severe odds, he was also in some measure a representative figure, whose life and work spoke of the possibilities that lay within a particular religious culture at a certain time in history. It is also important to see why this English priest came to matter so profoundly to a striking number of men and women in different countries whose lives have, in the eyes of historians, come to define the age in which he lived. Even when the things that Bell actually did are duly acknowledged and weighed by scholarship, it may be that the significance of what he represented to such contemporaries remains his enduring contribution, both to history and to the life of the Christian church.

Scholarship converts lives into subjects. The historian, of course, must at first corner the subject himself in a library and an archive. While the great weight of the collection of papers that Bell left behind is today a glory of Lambeth Palace Library, the library of the Archbishops of Canterbury, scholars have still done little more than skim the surface of what it contains. There is a broad catalogue to offer a guide, connecting periods of activity with particular themes. The themes are as follows: the ecumenical movements (Life and Work before 1939 and the World Council of Churches after 1948), the names of countries, the German churches, the refugees, the World War. Our current enthusiasms, theological or ecclesiastical, are not represented by this. Although there are sermons, the reader who hunts for a volume of spirituality will go unrewarded. If anything of the kind is to be found at all it will be found in different places. So we come again to the little blue book — perhaps of all the heavy tomes in the archive the smallest and least inviting. In the turning of these obscure pages comes the opening of a door onto a vast, tumultuous world, which fell silent long ago, but which is now suddenly illuminated, and made vivid, by a shaft of clear, bright light.

CHAPTER ONE

Beginnings, 1883-1914

George Kennedy Allen Bell was born, on 4 February 1883, into a world that may now seem to us very remote indeed. The Victorian era had transformed the British Isles into something far richer and grander than even the boldest imagination could once have conceived: a vast enterprise blazing a relentless progress through half a century. This was a society characterized by the devices and designs of industrial capitalism with all its gains and costs; by a mood of national confidence boomed abroad by an army of diplomats, engineers, politicians, and entrepreneurs; and by an empire that dominated a quarter of the habitable globe. But these bold claims had been achieved at a price. It was quite as much a society riven by divisions, frustrations, disease, and squalid poverty. In politics, it had been Britain's achievement to attach monarchy to representative government, and to see the emergence of mass democracy. In the realm of the arts, its tastes were often epic and always diverse, for it was an age that could read Trollope with satisfaction, praise the Brownings (husband and wife) and the Arnolds (father and son), eulogize Tennyson, the poet laureate of forty years, revere the wisdom of Ruskin, and queue to see the stagy frivolities of Gilbert and Sullivan; an age in which a bishop of Wakefield could (allegedly) read Thomas Hardy's *Jude the Obscure* and then burn it; an age that could laud Oscar Wilde to the very skies before locking him up in Reading Gaol. The child is, of course, father to the man, and many of the assumptions and expectations that we carry through life are ours in the days of our schooling. It is as well to observe that Bell was already a young man when Queen Victoria died. As an Edwardian student and a Georgian priest, he carried the baffling richness, the complexities and adventures, of Victorian life in the very fabric of his quiet personality. He knew well its reasons for confidence and its apprehensions of doubt.

Though historians continue to ask whether this astonishing age was also one that witnessed a "crisis of faith," it is hard to deny that the Church of England occupied a firm place within the statuesque world of public authority and amid that wider, popular bustle of national life. Fearful that such a combustible society would leave religion behind, the Victorians had built churches and chapels of all traditions across the country to assure the population of a place in their pews. Yet, for all this, the strengths of Christianity were not absolute; indeed, they could look rickety in a country parish or even feeble in a northern industrial slum.

In his birth, then, George Bell took a little place in a small fraction of this order. For the future bishop of Chichester, who was born at Hayling Island on a clear day within sight of the spire of Chichester Cathedral, was the first child of James Allen Bell, the vicar of Hayling Island, and his wife, Sarah Georgina (née Megaw). The Bells were a family of farmers and businessmen; the Megaws were bankers from the north of Ireland. It was the kind of secure, comfortable middle-class clerical home that produced many of the bishops of the church in the twentieth century. With his father, the young lad appears to have had a particularly close and affectionate relationship. When, in his student days, George Bell was asked why he was a Christian, he acknowledged the debt simply, replying, "First, I was born one."[1] There is little evidence that he ever resisted the gift.

From the south coast, the Bells moved by stages northward; first to Southampton, then to Pershore in Worcestershire, and from there to Balsall Heath in Birmingham. By 1903 they were to be found in Wimbledon, in London. Throughout his early boyhood George Bell endured a succession of schools. At one of them, Temple Grove, his teachers found him "so terribly shy and inarticulate that it is very difficult to get him to do justice to himself."[2] He was rarely placed above average in his classes, and in French and German he failed even to reach the standard of "poor." But stability came in 1896, when he was awarded a place at Westminster School. The school was then, as it is now, an imposing pile, located beside the great Abbey and adjacent to Dean's Yard. This was a decisive step upward: a place at Westminster School represented, consciously, a privilege and a

1. R. C. D. Jasper, *George Bell, Bishop of Chichester* (London: Oxford University Press, 1967), p. 1.
2. All the reports are gathered in the Bell Papers, vol. 184 (various pages).

preparation for the world of authority. When Bell was a pupil there a young working-class lad, who had become by his own prodigious efforts a copyist in the Whitehall civil service, observed this environment closely, but as an outsider: "Just past the half-hidden entrance to the Little Cloister lies the way into Westminster school-yard. Passing as it were from the dead to the living, I watched enviously the top-hatted, tail-coated boys rushing hither and thither, for in those days the school was to me a glorious mystery, a certain entry for chosen people to the land of heart's desire."[3] The very stones of the place were eloquent with the poetry of history. Bell, sensitive and receptive, evidently absorbed their lessons gladly, and at Westminster he managed a modest flourishing. There were at least two foreshadowings of future enthusiasms: he wrote a poem of seventeen stanzas, "Auri Sacra Fames" ("the holy lust for gold," a phrase taken from Virgil), and even joined the cast of a production of *The Adelphi,* with the young A. A. Milne.[4]

Oxford

In 1901, the year in which the new Edwardian age dawned, George Bell went with a number of his Westminster peers to study at Christ Church, Oxford. It was a second formative step. Christ Church, the largest of Oxford University's colleges, was one of its most statuesque, harboring the cathedral church of the city, its high walls frowning across open fields and down to the river. Here, again, Bell enjoyed a secure place in the heart of an orderly world, carefully laid out for the cultivation of elites. It was a rich realm of learning and seeking, of conversations, books, and friendships. A recently discovered photograph captures him standing outside the porter's lodge, serene in a straw boater and college jacket.[5]

There was a good deal of Christianity to be had in Oxford, but not a great deal. The movement of the English middle classes away from religion was already well under way. Here, at first, Bell's religious beliefs were, in his own words, "suspended."[6] But he did not lose his belief in God. When he

3. Albert Mansbridge, *The Trodden Road: Experience, Inspiration and Belief* (London: J. M. Dent, 1940), p. 26.

4. Bell Papers, vol. 184, fols. 77-81.

5. The photograph was reproduced in a commemorative booklet privately published by Paul Foster to accompany an exhibition of portraits of Bell in the House of Lords, November 2008.

6. Jasper, *Bell,* p. 17.

looked at himself he found he was not a youth much given to speculations, abstractions, and doctrines; he was drawn instead by the holiness of great souls. The essentially humane quality of his intelligence was confirmed in this distinctive setting, and it matured. Oxford was no great home to radicalism, either. But in Bell's day it saw the steady cultivation of social and educational reformists of various kinds, and even an occasional flurry of controversy or campaign of righteousness. A tutor thought Bell the student "a man of both industry and taste."[7] Here he shone academically, securing a First Class in the first part of his degree, Moderations, in 1903. He looked for a time to be set for another, in the second, Greats. But he also rejoiced in lively company and struck up a friendship with the young Irish poet Oliver St. John Gogarty, whose amiable profanities are not quite easy to attach to the company of this young soon-to-be-priest of the Church of England. There is even a hint that he traveled with Gogarty to Ireland to keep company with William Butler Yeats and other creative spirits. Indeed, Bell liked poetry above all, and the affinity would always be a significant one. Oxford was quite the place to offer him early opportunities in the art. Soon he was busily editing no less than five anthologies for the publishing house Routledge (newly acquired by the father of a friend). One of these was *Poems of Patriotism;* another was *Poems of Love* (which he dedicated to his mother and father). An equal glory came when in 1904 he won a celebrated university prize, the Newdigate, for a long, ripe rhapsody of 276 lines, entitled *Delphi. Delphi* invoked a lost mythical world as rich as a mellow arcadian evening, crumbling at last to the onward march of time and leaving behind a landscape deserted and bereft:

> Pitiful vale, O widowed Delphi, mourn,
> Thy rites abandoned and thy shrines forlorn
>
> . . . .
> With alien lips I greet thee, alien eyes
> Imagine the dim glories of olden times;
> For now no taper column heavenward climbs,
> Or votive pillar glistens: only I
> Hear the lank eagles crying up the sky. . . .[8]

7. Jasper, *Bell,* p. 10.

8. Published in *George Bell, Poems 1883-1958* (printed for private circulation, Brighton, 1960; new edition, Chichester: Bishop Otter memorial paper 24, *Humanitas* subsidia series 3, 2008), pp. 9-16.

Gogarty, a defeated competitor, acknowledged a poet in those "lank eagles," and saluted him wryly.

The Newdigate was happy compensation, perhaps, for the disappointment of a narrowly missed First Class degree at the end of his final year, and it is not difficult to sense how proud the young Bell was of this achievement and what enduring confidence was built upon it.

Ordination

Somewhere in the midst of all this George Bell had moved, almost imperceptibly, toward ordination in the Church of England. Evidently, it was no dramatic dawning, but rather the steady unfolding of something within himself, already long known. "My father was a clergyman," he once remarked, late in life, "and it was what I wanted to be ever since I can remember."[9] But it was not to Oxford that he now turned. In April 1906 he went for a year to a little theological college in the west country city of Wells. It was here, in what were perhaps the quietest circumstances, that the young ordinand made a decisive connection. He met Canon Tissington Tatlow, the English pioneer of the student ecumenical movement. The excitement that this vision of Christian life could spark in an idealistic mind that was ready to seize upon something new and visionary is hard to exaggerate. For Bell, this was something very like a revolution. Here lay the universal church, the creation and gift of God, the body of Christ, yet broken by centuries of human strife, glimpsing at last the argument of its essential and effective unity. Such a quest set down an immense task for this new generation to accomplish, and many rallied to the cause. It was even heard that this was an ecumenical "awakening." Ecumenism became almost at once a great cause for Bell, too. Soon he was leading weekly services in the college to pray for the unity of the church.

Another dimension of contemporary religious life fashioned the young George Bell. It was the duty of all Christians to work for the coming of the Kingdom of God. Like so many of his peers, he inherited the accumulated wisdom and achievements of two generations of Christian social enterprise. By now the very term "Christian socialist" was venerable, even if few knew what it meant. The generation that had brought Frederick Denison Maurice, Charles Kingsley, Octavia Hill, and John Malcolm Ludlow had yielded a new

9. Jasper, *Bell*, p. 376.

generation that had set up university settlements in poor areas, launched missions to the poorest quarters of society, established the Christian Social Union, and found its new prophets in bishops like Brooke Foss Westcott (who had done much to resolve a mining dispute in Durham), Joseph Lightfoot, Henry Scott Holland, and Charles Gore (the architect, and first bishop, of the new diocese of Birmingham, in 1905). This "socialism" united Christians, too: it connected a cautious archbishop of Canterbury like Randall Davidson to a public lion like the Baptist John Clifford. It was no rare thing to read an article by a priest or minister pleading that capitalism was an error because it thrived on competition when Christianity preached the contrasting virtue of cooperation. Bell inherited it all. At such a time it would have been no surprise to see an idealistic young ordinand heading purposefully off for the industrial north. This is what George Bell now did. He was ordained deacon in Ripon Cathedral in 1907 and then priest a year later in Leeds parish church. It was in Leeds, too, that he served his curacy, encountering the austerities of urban working-class life and labor and sharing them ardently, the young men he taught in evening classes viewing him kindly, even protectively. But within months his health began to suffer; he began to miss meals; he very nearly caught pneumonia.

Friends feared that Bell was wearing himself out in Leeds. He returned to Christ Church, first as a tutor and lecturer and then as a student in October 1910. It was the year of the great international missionary conference in Edinburgh, in which many would see the dawn of a new era of international ecumenical movements. Did Bell feel its influence then? Whatever the case, Leeds had left its mark upon him: every now and then he still disappeared with groups of students up to Leeds and Liverpool. His commitment to social justice was ripening in the company of the indefatigable public educator Albert Mansbridge, who years before had glimpsed the top hats and tails of Westminster schoolboys through the gate by Little Cloister; the greatest Anglican Christian Socialist of his generation, Henry Scott Holland (by now also at Christ Church); and a brilliant young fellow of Queen's College, and son of an archbishop of Canterbury, William Temple. Bell lectured for the University Extension Movement and supported a number of socially concerned local bodies. He helped to found an Oxford University cooperative society. His home, above the junior common room, became a center for vigorous discussion, "as living a 'cell,'" recorded a friend, provocatively, "as would have contented the reddest communist."[10]

10. Jasper, *Bell*, p. 13.

Yet theological disputes, of which there were many in the Oxford of his day, did not much draw him. Intellectually, he had already found where he belonged. A very full letter to his friend Dick Rawstorne yielded an uncharacteristically lengthy statement of faith. All were capable of receiving the teachings of Christ. The word of God was "alive, quick and powerful." "To me," wrote Bell, "'faith' in the New Testament suggests something very living, moving, creative, rather than something settled and deposited once for all." Steady, ongoing prayer was fundamental to the Christian who sought simply to be led by God. But more than this: "Christianity is a life before it is a system and to lay too much stress on the system destroys the life."[11] It is a remark so lightly accepted that the real force of it can too readily be overlooked. But in this single sentence lay the key to the future of George Bell.

11. Jasper, *Bell*, pp. 16-18.

CHAPTER TWO

To Lambeth Palace, 1914-1924

Randall Davidson has been viewed, at least once, as "the last Victorian" archbishop.[1] This was, in certain important ways, true. His rise was far more a story of the workings of a confident royal establishment than of the widening compass of Downing Street politics. The admired court chaplain of Queen Victoria's later years, Davidson had quietly cultivated a gift for pragmatic wisdom that had become highly prized at Buckingham Palace and Balmoral. He duly arrived at Rochester as its bishop and rose to be bishop of Winchester before succeeding Archbishop Frederick Temple at Canterbury in 1903.

Davidson offered this role a circumspect character. Neither a reactionary nor a progressive, he knew how to weigh contrary arguments and seek credible common ground in times of dispute. But he also achieved an undemonstrative revolution of manners, cultivating the friendship of Free Church leaders and doing much to inaugurate a new consensus between churches, hitherto often divided by arguments about the privileges of establishment, education, and politics at large. Davidson insisted that the Church stood at the heart of national life. He was almost as much to be found at the House of Lords as in his study at Lambeth.

It is often heard that 1914 marked the passing of a time-worn era, resting for decades on its old assurances, privileges, and principles, and the dawning of a new and terrible world of trenches, casualty lists, and public grief, a world soon saturated with disillusionment and longing for change. History is rarely so tidy, but for George Bell the year did mark a

---

1. David Edwards, *Leaders of the Church of England, 1828-1944* (London: Oxford University Press, 1971), pp. 223-56.

turning point. In that year Archbishop Davidson required a new domestic chaplain, and when the discreet oligarchies that maintained affairs at the summit of the Church of England chattered of candidates, Bell's name was to be heard. The invitation was made. With characteristic caution, Bell himself hesitated, sought advice, and accepted. A friend accused him amiably of "monstrous flagrant treachery to the Working Man, supposed, wrongly, alas, to be the apple of your eye!"[2] This would be the first of the three public roles that would define George Bell's career, and he would make it his own, growing in confidence and watching the world of institutional responsibility minutely in what became almost at once an age of international conflict.

It is likely that both Davidson and Bell knew, instinctively, how to value each other. Certainly, the archbishop allowed his new chaplain plenty of creative scope. The historian David Nash has observed how Bell now lost no time in stirring up a serious debate about the moral character of this Great War.[3] When Bell ventured to suggest to Davidson that church leaders of all traditions be invited to Lambeth to discuss the crisis that was now upon them, Davidson thought such a gathering could only be a good thing and stipulated merely that it should be unofficial in character and claims. That said, Bell was left to organize the affair himself. No less than fifty representatives duly turned up. By December 1914 the new Lambeth chaplain had published a ripely poetic repudiation of another poet, A. E. Russell, who had argued that a Britain that fought Germany should invoke not the example of Christ but the spirit of Thor and Zeus.[4] The instigator, organizer, and poet promptly turned into editor. Bell saw that there was a need to present an affordable and intelligent Christian view of the war to the reading public. Under his aegis a collection of essays by different authors was soon under way. Bell himself was firm that the crisis was a humiliation to all Christians and urged that they show how the church might "realise her prophetic Office."[5] In 1915 *The War and the Kingdom of God* appeared. A certain amount of his own introduction shows how many

2. R. C. D. Jasper, *George Bell, Bishop of Chichester* (London: Oxford University Press, 1967), p. 19.

3. For a valuable discussion see David Nash, *Christian Ideals in British Culture: Stories of Belief in the Twentieth Century* (Basingstoke: Palgrave Macmillan, 2013), pp. 82-89.

4. See "Our Rightful God," *The Commonwealth* 19, no. 228 (December 1914): 383. The principal voice of the Christian socialists, the journal was edited by Bell's Christ Church friend, Henry Scott Holland.

5. Nash, *Christian Ideals in British Culture,* p. 83.

of the ideas by which Bell would come to be known in his maturity were already forming within him. Patriotism was a high virtue, but Christians were called to proclaim another, greater Kingdom. A war may be just, but war itself remained "incompatible" with the Kingdom of God.[6] Though now obscure, this book earned a lasting respect.[7]

In what ways Davidson and Bell influenced one another is, inevitably, harder to judge. When it came to controversy, Davidson was a man most at home in an undemonstrative *via media*. But this war found him protesting when poison gas was adopted, interceding (albeit unsympathetically) on behalf of conscientious objectors, and condemning military action that could be regarded as simple "retaliation" against civilian targets. Bell's maturing loyalty to Davidson soon contained an element of devotion. For now, the assiduous Lambeth chaplain was ready to immerse himself in his service to a great figure and a great institution — indeed, such a combination of backroom endeavors and public authority appeared to suit him perfectly. Davidson would later acknowledge that over time this relationship had become something far richer and greater, and something far more creative, than a mere collaboration between the occupant of a public office and his deputy:

> You and I for all these tempestuous years worked together, and it is our joint work, and not *my* work in any narrower sense, which has had such degree of effectiveness as belongs to it. . . . [Y]ou have by sheer effectiveness and resourcefulness of work, got into a position in central Church affairs which is markedly your own. Quite apart from myself, people look to you and don't look in vain.[8]

This curious station of archbishop's chaplain certainly yielded all kinds of responsibilities — and novelties — in the run of a day's work. But it also placed Bell squarely in the path of new and scintillating company, wending its way to Lambeth from all corners of the world on all kinds of surprising missions. It is to the historian Muriel Heppell that we owe the

---

6. G. K. A. Bell, ed., *The War and the Kingdom of God* (London: Longmans & Green, 1915), p. 6. For the whole introduction see pp. 1-13.

7. Of all such books produced to justify the war to the public, Stuart Bell finds Bell's collection the most significant. See Stuart Bell, "The Church and the First World War," in *God and War: The Church of England and Armed Conflict in the Twentieth Century*, ed. Stephen G. Parker and Tom Lawson (Farnham: Ashgate, 2012), p. 44.

8. Jasper, *Bell*, p. 30.

story of one of Bell's early international friendships. He met the young Serbian priest Nikolai Velimirovic over a meal at an Indian restaurant in London in 1915, when the latter was visiting England as a propagandist for the Serbian Relief Fund. It was natural that the chaplain to the archbishop of Canterbury should, in the line of his duties, do business with such a figure. Yet there was evidently something more to share with this personable, intellectual young Serb. By February 1917 the two were clearly getting along famously.[9] Jeremy Haselock has drawn our attention to a second significant rapport struck in these years with a French monk, Lambert Beauduin. While Bell and Velimirovic seldom exchanged theological insights, in Beauduin Bell found a persevering ecumenist and a reforming liturgist. This, Haselock finds, was a "rapprochement des coeurs."[10] There were far, far more. A diary entry of November 1922 finds a grand duchess from Russia perched on Bell's sofa, recounting her experiences of life under the new Soviet state, "nervously, brilliantly, dramatically."[11]

The Great War cost the young Lambeth chaplain two of his brothers: Donald and Benedict Bell were killed within days of each other in the spring of 1918. In what was, evidently, a close family, the impact can only be imagined. Meanwhile, for George Bell himself life had just taken a fundamental new turn. It was at Lambeth, and under Davidson's aegis, that he had met Henrietta Livingstone. On 8 January 1918 they were married. Davidson saw clearly that what now mattered was not simply the life that his chaplain might live, but the work to which he and his wife would be called together. For it would be, he predicted, "a joint life."[12] The daughter of Canon R. J. Livingstone and sister of the Oxford classicist Richard Livingstone, Henrietta possessed the self-assurance and the resolution that she needed to face the world with such a husband. She would soon cut an authoritative figure with the guests who would come to the homes they would create over forty years of marriage. The well-loved son of a close-knit family, Bell now found himself the husband of a woman who knew how to value his gifts and how to place them within the security of

9. See Muriel Heppell, *George Bell and Nikolai Velimirovic* (Birmingham: Lazarica Press, 2001).

10. See Jeremy Haselock, "George Kennedy Allen Bell, Bishop of Chichester and Pastoral Liturgist," *Studia Liturgica: An International Ecumenical Review for Liturgical Research and Renewal* 35 (2005): 192-93.

11. Bell Papers, vol. 256, pp. 111-12.

12. Jasper, *Bell*, p. 13.

a steadfast devotion. At home they were only to have each other; there would be no children.

It is no easier to judge this marriage than any other. Those who observed the Bells at close quarters over the years acknowledged that Henrietta was a powerful presence but found theirs a relationship wholly integrated, wholly admirable. Perhaps an age that expected to find a defining form of conventional order in matrimony was too lightly assured by a firm maintenance of outward appearances? What intensities lay beneath this surface and even outside its apparent coherence, acknowledged or unacknowledged, is quite impossible to know. The historian encounters Bell in his public hours, not his private ones, and even the curious have often been left to acknowledge the achievement of privacy. Bell would always hold a high, indeed sacramental, view of marriage. It was, he would later write, "the happiest of all human experiences for the man or the woman who enters into it with the right partner in the right spirit."[13] It is difficult to believe that Bell would have written these words if he had not known such happiness himself.

Oud Wassenaar and the Phenomenon of Archbishop Söderblom

The war, at last, ended. At Lambeth, Bell's ecumenical concerns took a bold new turn. In the autumn of 1919 Davidson had decided that his chaplain should go as part of a delegation representing the Church of England to Oud Wassenaar in Holland to view the beginning of the new, post-war World Alliance for International Friendship through the Churches. The speed with which this gathering was convened was striking, and also significant.

Only one man, the archbishop of Uppsala, Nathan Söderblom, could have made such a thing happen and in such a way.[14] Once a lawyer, and in many shades a politician, Söderblom was simply a tremendous figure; all of him was busy intent, activity, ambition. To many who encountered the archbishop of Uppsala, he looked very like an implacable, unstoppable force of nature. A prodigious correspondent, he was even glimpsed

13. *Christian Marriage: A Pastoral Letter from the Bishop of Chichester to Those Who Desire to Be Married in Any Church or Chapel of the Church of England in the County of Sussex* (Chichester, 1931).

14. For further studies of Söderblom, see Dietz Lange, *Nathan Söderblom und seine Zeit* (Göttingen: Vandenhoeck & Ruprecht, 2011); in English see Bengt Sundkler's still admirable book, *Nathan Söderblom* (London: Lutterworth Press, 1968).

now and then dictating to his secretary while he strode through the city streets.[15] Söderblom was a practical man in earnest, one who had no intention whatever of burying himself prayerfully in a remote cloister while the world around him tumbled toward new disasters. It was characteristic of Söderblom that the agenda at Oud Wassenaar comprised no vague incantations, no theological rhetoric, no pious platitudes. Indeed, Söderblom left the sixty men who gathered there nowhere to hide at all. He wanted committed, pragmatic, and constructive discussion about Bolshevism, war guilt, and the blockade of Germany. Furthermore, he looked to the future with a view to creating a great international conference in which Christians could set to work on the great questions that the world now faced. Oud Wassenaar itself was near to the Hague, which possessed many of the attributes of a seat of international law. In sum, what Söderblom sought was a form of progressive Christian internationalism that could contribute to the new age of the League of Nations, to international arbitration, and to social progress. His appeal to the churches was an appeal both to reason and to idealism. By hook or by crook he would somehow carry all these trembling clerics with him and show this wretched, fumbling world that the Christian faith in every land and every tradition might unite to affirm the righteousness of God. He was too sage to hope for much, if anything at all, from Rome. But he did look with hope to Canterbury.

Quiet men and women are not often taken for idealists. Bell was most certainly one, and he was susceptible to idealistic men, principles, moments, and movements wherever he found them. He must have gone to Holland with wide eyes and open ears. He would one day recall that Söderblom was "a totally different person from what we had expected — very vivacious, alert, full of knowledge. He caught everyone, addressed them, was here and there and everywhere; not a dignified and distant figure, but in the stir and turmoil of everything and everybody."[16] Söderblom was also impressed by Bell, urging his friend Albert Schweitzer to visit him when visiting England, in March 1922. He would later write of the young priest in affectionate terms that would become well known:

To Oud Wassenaar in 1919 the Archbishop of Canterbury had sent a man who was then his private chaplain and whose name was Bell. The

---

15. See Dietz Lange's splendid *Nathan Söderblom: Brev — Letteres — Briefe — Letters; A Selection from His Correspondence* (Göttingen: Vandenhoeck & Ruprecht, 2006).

16. Jasper, *Bell*, pp. 59-62.

largest hall of the hotel was the room for our divine service, where also our meetings took place at a horseshoe-table. He was sitting just opposite to me. He uttered scarcely anything without having been asked. Then, after reflection, he gave a notable answer which always proved reliable. His countenance is dominated by two large round eyes, glowing with the soul's fire and disclosing a rich inward life.

It is my opinion that nobody is more important to the future of the ecumenical revival than this silent Bell. This Bell never rings for nothing. But when it does ring, its tune is silver-clear. It often seems to travel from another sphere and make itself heard. It reaches farther than any shouting voices. He never begins to speak without having something to say. The strong spirituality of his nature characterizes everything he does.[17]

This admiration of Söderblom, the great Christian statesman, for Bell, the Lambeth chaplain, is profoundly significant because it comes as rare praise from a high place. For such a man as Söderblom had a continental richness, a range, even a vastness of mind and character, which was barely known in public office or university study in Britain. All his life Bell would know the kindly appreciation of a handful of truly great international figures, while finding his qualities undervalued and overlooked by conventional Englishmen, however eminent in office, who could not see anything in him beyond modesty, tenacity, and inconvenience.

The conference at Oud Wassenaar proved to be no easy occasion: the wounds of war were still open. The French delegation sought to extract from the German representatives an acknowledgment that their country had been to blame. Much was owed to one of the Germans, the theologian Adolf Deissmann, for offering words of reassurance on their behalf. The consequences of it all were at first quiet, but they soon gathered momentum. To onlookers — sympathetic, critical, or simply baffled — the ecumenical movement looked very like a juggernaut rushing forward to claim the future, billowing committee papers and conferences as it went. At these the Church of England was not at first represented. Davidson, no doubt with Bell in the room, insisted that a merely Protestant conclave could not merit the title "ecumenical": there must be invitations to Rome

17. I have chosen a version published by Franz Hildebrandt as a preface to *"And Other Pastors of Thy Flock": A German Tribute to the Bishop of Chichester* (Cambridge: Cambridge University Press, 1942).

and to the Orthodox. If they were turned down, then at least the claim to be intentionally, openly, and truly ecumenical would still be merited. Sufficiently reassured that this would be done, the Anglicans jumped on board.

The Lambeth Conference of 1920

It was in 1920, at the sixth Lambeth Conference, that Bell won particular renown among the leading episcopal lights of the Anglican Church. The reverberating shocks of war had not yet ceased; peace was still young. Across the church itself ecclesiastical controversies hovered uninvitingly, over theological latitude and doctrinal formulation, over marriage, over the ministry of women, over the reunion of churches. There were known conservatives and avowed liberals. What would they make of each other? Gathered opinion might divide in almost any matter; there might even be schism. "I dread the Lambeth Conference," wrote Bishop Gore to the archbishop, "and its consequences."[18] Davidson himself could see the risks all too clearly, but he was sure that the time for this conference was now.

Certainly, the 1920 Lambeth Conference generated a vast amount of paperwork. No fewer than 252 guests turned up, from the United States, Canada, India, China, and elsewhere. Bell observed and studied them as he oiled the machinery and turned the wheels: the bishop of Zanzibar, Frank Weston, he found an "extraordinary mixture of generosity and menace";[19] a guest, the metropolitan of Demotica, made a particularly vivid impression. Davidson, suffering a bout of lumbago and encumbered by rugs and what Bell later called "a hot water apparatus,"[20] needed all the help he could get. For two weeks numerous committees scratched about, examining a variety of concerns. When he visited them Davidson found that at least one of the most important, the Reunion Committee, hardly knew what to say. Yet it was this committee that suddenly achieved a revelation. There should be a Letter to All Christian People, decided its chairman, the archbishop of York, Cosmo Gordon Lang. This hit the mark. There was a quiet flurry of little meetings, discussions, drafts. The idea of a letter grew into that of a bold appeal. The bishop of Zanzibar unexpect-

18. G. K. A. Bell, *Randall Davidson, Archbishop of Canterbury,* 3rd ed. (London: Oxford University Press, 1952), p. 1004.
19. Bell, *Davidson,* p. 1010.
20. Bell, *Davidson,* p. 1011.

edly became its ardent advocate, and suddenly there was an unmistakable sign of momentum. That this should be an appeal not to "churches" but to "Christian people" was not the least of its purposeful innovations. For Christians everywhere held to a belief in Scripture, in the Nicene Creed, and in the sacraments of Baptism and Holy Communion. They should seek not the absorption of some churches by others, but unity "in a new and great endeavour to recover and to manifest to the world the unity of the Body of Christ for which He prayed."[21] Episcopacy they commended to the whole Church, not as a dogma of church order, but as an expression and an instrument of visible unity.

This great statement provoked the opposition of only four delegates. A further resolution yielded important ground in actualities: any "general schemes of intercommunion or exchange of pulpits" must incur disapproval — but because of the new, hopeful atmosphere that now existed between the churches at large, an individual bishop might give "occasional authorization to ministers, not episcopally ordained, who in his judgement are working towards an ideal of reunion such as is described in our Appeal, to preach in churches within his Diocese, and to clergy of the Diocese to preach in the churches of such ministers."[22] Furthermore, it was for a bishop to decide himself if confirmation in the Anglican Church must remain the condition for admission to communion in that church. When he looked back on this in later life Bell still found it "almost unbelievable" and "a great blow struck for the Reunion of Christendom."[23]

This sixth Lambeth Conference was a great accomplishment. Everybody who was there knew that the archbishop's chaplain was busy at the heart of it all. Indeed, his capacity for unglamorous, exacting labor was strangely conspicuous. His reputation was not yet a public one, but in this oligarchic, clerical world it was something more valuable. George Bell was seen to have a future.

21. Bell, *Davidson*, p. 1014.
22. Bell, *Davidson*, p. 1014.
23. Bell, *Davidson*, p. 1014.

CHAPTER THREE

The Canterbury Deanery, 1924-1929

A Lambeth chaplaincy was often seen to augur well for an eminent career in the Church of England, and Bell's abilities were both confirmed and extended by his role there. Moreover, although he was reticent, Bell was also seen to be confident — even too confident. A waspish visitor to Lambeth Palace in these years observed him to be "bustling, eager, almost too obviously ambitious, and entirely self-assured."[1] In 1924 the prime minister of the first Labour government, Ramsay MacDonald, offered Bell the deanery of Canterbury and he accepted it. He was now forty-one. His predecessor, the illustrious Dean Henry Wace, had been eighty-seven. To Canterbury Bell brought change: encouraging visitors, writing guides, and abolishing fees. The broadcasting of services by the BBC was encouraged and became regular. Visiting preachers from different traditions appeared in the pulpit. His sense of Christian worship was reverent, orderly, and beautiful in language. He took advice from choirboys on the length of services and confronted those who resisted change with a quiet tenacity. He set up the first association of cathedral Friends.

The international landscape of the 1920s had become bleak and increasingly pessimistic. Abroad, almost all the monarchies that had governed Europe before 1914 had crumbled and disappeared. The Versailles settlement had sought to steer the Continent on a course governed by the principles of self-determination and democracy, but the word on everybody's lips was "Revolution." The new, Bolshevik Soviet Union had changed utterly the consciousness of the political world. In 1922 Italy fell

---

1. An anonymous "Unknown Layman," quoted by David L. Edwards in his *Leaders of the Church of England, 1828-1944* (London: Oxford University Press, 1971), p. 340.

into the hands of Mussolini's fascists. Germany was in turmoil. At home, the Representation of the People Act had widened the franchise and given women over thirty the vote, but those who had longed for a new movement toward social justice were thwarted by the calculations and compromises of the politicians in Parliament, as the Liberal party divided and the Conservatives went off into an unremarkable coalition with Lloyd George and his remaining allies. Industrial relations were querulous and liable to blow up. The threat of a general strike loomed over everything. For their part, the churches were not acquiescent: in 1924 a grand Conference on Christian Politics, Economics and Citizenship took place in Birmingham, attended by 1,500 men and women from across the traditions, debating twelve reports on matters ranging from the Relations of the Sexes to International Relations and War. All of this Bell simply observed from a distance. But beyond the cathedral close in Canterbury, he worried about the austerities of the East Kent coalfields, where men were poorly paid and life itself could seem precarious. Meanwhile, much of the internationalism of Lambeth came to Canterbury with him. A letter of November 1925 from Nicholas Berdyaev, busily at work in the new Russian Theological Institute in Paris, welcomes an offer from the dean of Chichester to assist in the editorial work of his new journal *Put.*[2]

Provincial English life might well have looked glum. As the Bells settled into their new address, the state of public theater was frankly depressed (one in the town had just closed). But responsible now for the life of a great cathedral, Dean Bell found that he was free to put his love of literature and art to good effect. At Lambeth he had already been pressing for a new entente between the church and the arts. Here at Canterbury the possibilities were surely immense, and by now the church at large was awash with bustling new enterprises that looked for a lead. Little societies and companies of players were breaking out to perform wherever they could: the Pilgrim Players, the British Drama League, the Religion and Drama Association, the Canterbury Old Stagers, the Canterbury Amateur Dramatic Society, and the Christopher Marlowe Society. Plays written by Laurence Housman had already been performed by the Glastonbury Players. Here was much to work with. To Housman, Bell wrote, "If you want a Patron (I expect you abhor such things, and so should I) I am prepared to be one."[3]

2. Bell Papers, vol. 75, entry for 16 November 1925.
3. Bell Papers, vol. 153 (various pages).

Housman was a kindred spirit, but the fruitful connection now lay with the popular John Masefield, whom Bell first contacted with a telegram in July 1927. Consequently, Masefield's play *The Coming of Christ* was performed not in a theater but in the cathedral itself; indeed, it was widely — though mistakenly — judged to be the first dramatic performance to take place in an English cathedral since the Middle Ages. The historian Peter Webster has observed that although the production was "not quite as ground-breaking as has been suggested, the play was nonetheless an audacious venture in a charged polemical climate."[4] There were protests from evangelical Protestants who feared that the Gospel was becoming entangled in dubious company. Some feared that plays were inappropriate during Lent. The National Church League complained to the Chapter of the cathedral, detecting a "serious abuse" and deploring a resort to "pagan methods."[5] One correspondent of the dean lamented this "profanation" of the cathedral of Canterbury.[6] Bell himself was not prepared to allow entire freedom to his emerging geniuses. He had to ensure the maintenance of orthodoxy, and this involved him in some quiet measure of editorial participation, which the gentle Masefield accepted graciously.

The Coming of Christ was not perhaps a great work of literature (T. S. Eliot grumbled that the poetry was "pedestrian"[7]), but as an occasion it was a triumph. "On that day," Bell later recalled fondly, "history was made. In a moving and enchanting form, the Poet and the Artist together re-entered the Church. They had only to be asked."[8] Not least striking in this achievement was the music, composed by Gustav Holst, and the costumes, designed by Charles Ricketts. £800 was taken in donations — and it provided the funds for future ventures, which continued to appear even after Bell had gone to be a bishop. In sum, the Dean of Canterbury had entered wholeheartedly into a rambling, vibrant bustle of artistic idealists and vigorous volunteers. If anything, he appeared inordinately happy to be keeping such company. In time he would encourage the work of young, or more mature, writers whose productions would come to be seen to characterize the culture of the age: Eliot himself, Charles Williams, Dorothy

---

4. See Peter Webster, "George Bell, John Masefield and *The Coming of Christ:* Context and Significance," in *The Church and Humanity: The Life and Work of George Bell, 1883-1958,* ed. Andrew Chandler (Farnham: Ashgate, 2012), p. 48.

5. Bell Papers, vol. 154, fol. 42.

6. Webster, "Bell, Masefield," p. 51.

7. Webster, "Bell, Masefield," p. 54.

8. Webster, "Bell, Masefield," p. 47.

Sayers, Christopher Hassall, and, later, Christopher Fry. The many fruits of these associations would often be splendid.

Meanwhile, in the more orderly patterns of the church at large, Bell was making his way dutifully and steadily. He duly made his presence felt at the Lower House of Convocation. Since 1921 there had also existed the Church Assembly, the first synodical body by which the Church of England achieved a substantial, though not final, measure of self-government. The consequences of the 1920 Appeal to All Christian People were still working themselves out, and Bell had a place in this. With W. L. Robertson he edited a collection titled *The Church of England and the Free Churches.*[9] When the new Prayer Book of 1927 "crashed" (as he later put it[10]) in Parliament, he watched it all happen bleakly and was left to commiserate with his old master, the now beleaguered Archbishop Davidson.

It was this crisis that converted many who had supported the establishment of the Church of England to doubt that a state church could be just or free. Bishop Henson, ardent in most things, performed a superb *volte face,* turning almost at once from a champion of establishment to a prophet of disestablishment. In Bell's case, the calamity did something to prod a new book into life, *A Brief Sketch of the Church of England,* in 1929. A survey, the book was safe, sound, and essentially practical. Some years later he would settle to the task of picking up the pieces left by the debacle in Parliament by joining a new commission on church and state. It would not report until 1935, and then little came of it.[11] Bell himself was clearly disappointed, but by the middle 1930s Davidson's successor, Archbishop Lang, saw other, more pressing things with which to contend.

Stockholm, 1925

At Canterbury, Bell's international ecumenical work was soon maturing, indeed flourishing. In 1924 he published the first of a series of books presenting documents concerned with Christian unity. "It is hoped," he ventured, "that the collection thus brought together will prove practically useful to those who may be called upon to take part in negotiations or

9. G. K. A. Bell and W. Robertson, eds., *The Church of England and the Free Churches* (London: Oxford University Press, 1925).

10. *George Bell, Poems 1883-1958* (Brighton: privately published, 1960), p. 31.

11. *Church and State: A Report of the Archbishops' Commission on the Relations between Church and State* (London: National Assembly of the Church of England, 1935).

in conversations leading towards Church unity, and may itself contribute to the development and increase of that interest in the subject which is already so abundantly manifest."[12] But it was as part of the Anglican delegation to the Life and Work conference in Stockholm, in 1925, that he truly became an established presence in the lively counsels in a great conclave of 500-odd Christians from thirty-seven countries. The absence still of the Roman Catholic Church was not allowed to dampen this vivid sense of a high moment: it had been said that such a conference was impossible — a remark, if anything, all the more likely to galvanize Archbishop Söderblom. Now enthusiasts pronounced that this was the greatest ecumenical gathering since the Council of Nicea. And here was the Dean of Canterbury in the very thick of it, speaking about "co-operation" and "federative efforts," immersed in conversation and keeping high company, joining the Greek Archbishop Germanos, the French pastor Wilfrid Monod, the American Presbyterian William Adams Brown, the Danish Bishop Ammundsen, the Scottish Presbyterian A. E. Garvie, and the German Friedrich Siegmund-Schultze. Together they set about the business of a Conference Message to the world, straining for the right words, striking balances, and worrying over proofs and corrections late into the night.[13] This message proved to be a great success, and no one could doubt that it was in part Bell's achievement. When he was asked to speak on the last day, the conference found him a firm disciple of Söderblom, pointing to the power of a faith that could bring together so many people otherwise divided by nationality and politics. They had a heavy task placed upon them, and they must surely press on with it in all the many forms it had by now come to assume. Söderblom looked to the foundation of a great international council. Bell knew that some quivered at such a notion, but he would stand by it. This speech was seen to count.

In the wake of Stockholm there came to life a new Continuation Committee. Bell was on it. When it was agreed that there should be published two conference reports, one in English and the other in German, it was Bell who undertook the former. Stockholm was, in certain ways, the crowning moment of Söderblom's international career. For him, time was

12. G. K. A. Bell, ed., *Documents on Christian Unity, 1920-24* (London: Oxford University Press, 1924), pp. vii-viii.

13. For the Stockholm conference at large, see Bengt Sundkler, *Nathan Söderblom: His Life and Work* (London: Lutterworth Press, 1968), pp. 330-82; for Bell in this context see R. C. D. Jasper, *George Bell, Bishop of Chichester* (London: Oxford University Press, 1967), pp. 60-65.

now running out. But that same time was carrying Bell into the fullness of his vocation. For him Stockholm was not quite the beginning, but it certainly established beyond question his crucial place in the unfolding future of the movement.

Writing, Editing, and Publishing

In the academic year of 1926-1927 Bell was invited to give a series of lectures on pastoral theology at the Divinity Faculty at Cambridge, and the upshot was a book, *The Modern Parson,* which appeared in 1928. Here he was determined to explore not merely the individual qualities of a priest of the church but the ways in which they might emerge in response to the shifting contexts of a new and challenging age. But the claim to realism went further. Bell saw, all too sharply, that congregational numbers were declining. Religion no longer gave society even its outward form. Instead it presented a spectacle of rival responsibilities and attractions. Yet Bell was sure that people wanted more than they so often found in this complicated life, and perhaps even yearned for God. The modern parson, he wrote, must find his way into the schools, the charitable and social organizations, the factories and offices. In his parish, he must resist anything that made material gain the heart of all, anything that trivialized or debased. It was not his place to impose new designs but rather to cooperate in the building of the Kingdom of God with the men and women with whom he had come to live. The shortage of ordained ministers was no bad thing if it meant that the laity did more for themselves. The modern parson must think, preach, and teach ("to tell the truth, the clergy, like other people, are apt quite suddenly to stop thinking, in the large sense, altogether"); he must frame a public worship that was founded squarely on the Book of Common Prayer, but still be imaginative, inclusive, and participatory. It was, in sum, the task of the parson to be "the true *pontifex,* or bridge-builder, and also the true 'opener of doors,' the doors between the classes, the doors between nations, the doors of friendship with men and of communion with God."[14] In this book he acknowledged an ongoing allegiance to the social Christianity of his father's generation at large and to one of its greatest figures, Samuel

---

14. G. K. A. Bell, *The Modern Parson* (London: Student Christian Movement, 1928), various, but particularly pp. 43-66.

Augustus Barnett, the founder of the most famous social settlement in the poor east end of London, Toynbee Hall.

The Anglo-German Conversations

Out of the many ecumenical connections that Bell had busily cultivated at Lambeth it was those with German church people that remained to him most precious. In important respects he was not well qualified for this. He had no command of the German language. His understanding of German scholarship was as weak as that of most Anglican priests of his generation (the ministers of Free Churches in this respect fared far better, and the Scots better still). But what he had was worth something far more: a quiet power to attract sympathetic and steadfast friendship among men who often saw the world too deeply in forms of arguments, schools, and categories. Bell knew the value of intellectualism at large, whatever his own merits in that particular realm. This gave him a detachment from intricacies that he could not match and a patient, almost kindly, appreciation of all kinds of personalities, even if they were found to be in a state of loud conflict with each other.

The quiet gentleness of Bell, so often observed by contemporaries, could have been overdone. These much-lauded, self-consciously august professors and pastors would surely not have valued that quality very highly for itself. Bell had self-confidence. He could reconcile deference with initiative, generosity with conviction. This also made him a reliable editor: people were ready to write for him, and clearly they trusted him to hold their opinions together in a coherent whole inside two clothbound boards. And Bell undoubtedly enjoyed these Germans, too. He knew they were figures of stature, and he must have sensed the privilege of time spent in their company. It was Bell who proposed at Stockholm that "a group of representatives of different countries and Churches might meet together for some common intellectual task under the shadow of his cathedral." An alliance with Adolf Deissmann, the chairman of the new theological commission, brought thirteen men to the first British-German Theological Conference in Canterbury in April 1927. Their theme, very much a Stockholm one, was "the nature of the Kingdom of God, and its relation to human society."

In 1928 it was the turn of the German theologians to be the hosts. The historical eloquence of Canterbury they matched with a week of Christology in Wartburg, near Eisenach, in August. Here they were joined by the Danish bishop Ammundsen and by Söderblom himself. Bell sent a rather laconic note to Davidson that showed him to be relaxing happily in such a worthy enterprise. Reports were subsequently published jointly in English and German, the former in the pages of the Anglican journal *Theology* and the latter in the German *Theologische Blätter*. The year 1930 yielded a book, *Mysterium Christi* (a title that worked equally for English and German editions). It was not, Bell insisted, a representative document, still less a manifesto, but more a meeting of minds in which each contributor took responsibility only for himself. The book did possess genuine weight; here Bell and Deissmann could be found in company with the cream of scholarship in both lands: the Germans, Gerhard Kittel, Paul Althaus, Hermann Sasse, and Heinrich Frick; and the British, Sir Edwyn Hoskyns, J. M. Creed, J. K. Mozley, A. E. J. Rawlinson (all Anglican) and C. H. Dodd and Nathaniel Micklem (both Congregationalists).

Bell modestly placed his own contribution, "The Church and the Theologian," at the end of *Mysterium Christi*. It is a characteristic piece, a little short on inspiration, but sensitive and sanguine, urging that the body of the church surely stands too firmly on the ground of Truth to have anything to fear from the freedom of the individual theologian in his study. The church needs to be led by the inspiration and exposition of the thinker just as the studies of the individual theologian need to be rooted in the life of the church and the world of ordinary men and affairs. This was now, and more than ever, a world of science, education, and discovery, and the teaching of religion must comprehend and integrate all of this if the Christian faith were to breathe and flourish: "It is in the realm of thought that the Christian conflict is raging to a peculiar degree today."[15] If there were abrasions, and even mischief, in such was the assurance of life.

For Bell, the theologian should be set at liberty to think and write as he wished. The church should not censor or denounce: the truth would out in the end: "The Church has no reason to be afraid; and Church authorities have, alas, often only made themselves foolish by violent and unthinking attack on some new thing. . . . Often the new opinions die without trouble, for they have no permanent force, but sometimes they become the correct opinion, the orthodoxy, of tomorrow. It is, I am convinced, worthwhile to take risks." As for the new idea, "time and reason will show just where it fits

---

15. G. K. A. Bell and Adolf Deissmann, eds., *Mysterium Christi: Christological Studies by British and German Theologians* (London: Longmans, Green & Co., 1930), p. 278.

in." But these were rights to be maintained only by those whose theology still fell within the bounds of the fourth century. Indeed, the theologian owed duty to the church: "the fundamental faith to which the creeds give witness must be his. The experience of life in Christ which is so real and so indisputable he will recognise to the full. . . . He theologises as a debtor to Christ, as a servant of the Church." For Bell, the church must affirm to the world a "bold and fearless theology." It was the task of the theologian to provide it. He should not merely be tolerated, but honored, supported, and rewarded.[16]

A New Archbishop of Canterbury

When Archbishop Davidson retired, few were surprised to find Cosmo Gordon Lang named as his successor. The Dean of St. Paul's in London, Ralph Inge, had mused as to what it would be like if the seat of St. Augustine passed now not to the Archbishop of York but to the young Dean of Canterbury. It was an attractive speculation, but an idle one.[17]

Because Davidson and Lang had for so long collaborated closely and effectively, Bell already knew the new, ninety-fifth Archbishop of Canterbury well. It fell to the Dean and Chapter of Canterbury to manage the enthronement. It was perhaps the summit of Bell's achievement there to oversee the diplomatic intricacies that arose in the passage of preparation for this service and at last to make this immense occasion something both stately and brilliant in the eyes of all who attended. Lang himself would later recall how the dean took "infinite pains with all the arrangements. He had given full play to his vivid imagination in order to make the ceremony symbolic, not only of ecclesiastical life but of national life, including 'the Arts.' Never certainly had any previous Archbishop been enthroned on a scale of such colourful and symbolic magnificence."[18]

It was December 1928. At Canterbury, Archbishop Lang had entered into the last, full period of an imposing ecclesiastical career. The dean of that cathedral, meanwhile, now stood on a different threshold.

16. Bell and Deissmann, eds., *Mysterium Christi*, pp. 280-82.
17. Although Inge was not quite alone in this view. See Jasper, *George Bell*, p. 53.
18. J. G. Lockhart, *Cosmo Gordon Lang* (London: Hodder & Stoughton, 1949), p. 313.

CHAPTER FOUR

Chichester, 1929-1932

In 1929 a bishop of the Church of England still had some reason to think himself a figure of substance beyond the church itself and across society. When he wrote a letter to the *Times,* it was more likely than not that what a bishop said would be published there. The most senior bishops and those longest in their positions sat in the House of Lords. At the summit of the episcopal structure, Archbishop Lang was resented by some for his apparent courtliness, his susceptibility to prestige, and his reluctance to favor public campaigns. But he was in fact a considerable presence, a humane, melancholic man of duty who knew his world almost too well. Bell's Oxford contemporary William Temple had quickly become bishop of Manchester (whereupon he resigned his membership of the Labour party) and was now cutting a famous figure as the Archbishop of York, no less.

The other bishops could seem a stern and frosty lot: Arthur Foley Winnington Ingram of London had gone there when young and now seemed determined to stay there as long as possible, even as his diocese disintegrated around him; Herbert Hensley Henson of Durham was brilliant, even glorious, but austere and often caustic; Arthur Cayley Headlam of Gloucester was at the height of his formidable powers as an ecumenist, erudite but rigid, vigorous in conservativism but often teetering on the verge of crusty reaction; Bertram Pollock of Norwich was intractable in his views and, evidently, immovable. Norwich was for many years known as "the Dead See."

In 1929 Bell, like his friend Temple, represented a new generation. This was not held against him: he was surely a ripe candidate for the House of Bishops. He had stacked up a pile of notable achievements at Canterbury itself, within the church at large, and across the oceans. His credentials as a dean, a diplomat, and an ecumenist were unimpeachable. He had supplied evidence of thought that possessed genuine rigor, even creative worth. Apparently, in none of this had he offended anybody. But the apostolic succession is a difficult matter to orchestrate, however the oligarchs of the church might huddle together in colloquy, sketch their designs, and canvass (and disown) their ambitions. It was still not common for a bishop to retire; the preferred method of exit was simply to die in office. This placed the whole system on a basis that was wholly unpredictable. If Bell was to become a bishop, too, it was impossible to know which See might come his way because it was impossible to know which bishop would be carried off first.

In February 1929, death came for the bishop of Chichester, Winfrid Burrows. Dean Bell received his summons this time from a new prime minister, Stanley Baldwin. But he did not rush at this. Davidson, Lang — all but one of his friends, in fact — urged him to accept. They saw another Lambeth Conference coming and thought that he could do more for that as a bishop than as a dean. But his friend and successor as chaplain to Archbishop Davidson, Mervyn Haigh, also told him that if he accepted, it must be because, above all, he wished to be a diocesan bishop. Bell at first drafted a letter of decline, while also sensing the awkwardness of resisting. In the end he accepted. A touching letter from his father offered a kindly, and sane, remark: "No one today would wish to exchange such a position as yours for the office of a bishop." But watching attentively from Norwich, his parents were sure that this was a call that must be answered.[1]

On 11 June 1929, George Bell was consecrated ninety-ninth bishop of Chichester in Canterbury Cathedral. Directly, the Bells arrived at their new home, a modest but elegant city with its mellow cathedral, its Georgian streets, and its ancient walls. The enthronement in Chichester Cathedral followed sixteen days later. He came, he said, "as a brother not a prelate, as a servant not a lord, as a disciple and by God's grace a Father in God."[2]

Chichester and the World

Britain was a society divided in politics between a robust Conservative party, which was wary of too bold an expansion of the role of the state,

---

1. R. C. D. Jasper, *George Bell, Bishop of Chichester* (London: Oxford University Press, 1967), pp. 54-55.

2. Jasper, *Bell,* p. 70.

and a growing Labour party, which had displaced the Liberal party as the principal opposition to the Conservatives in Parliament and which had now occupied, briefly, the corridors of government. Chichester rested in the western corner of a diocese that then, as now, rolled far into the southeast of England. It was comfortably provincial, not to say conservative, by character. But the dean of the cathedral, A. S. Duncan-Jones, cut a powerful figure; he was an internationalist and, broadly, a man of progressive leanings who had once stood as a Labour candidate and now refused to avoid shopkeepers whose sympathies were known in the town to lie with the Left.

There was much in the world at large for a public-spirited bishop and dean to watch anxiously, even from a place like Chichester. In Russia, the Soviet state had maintained itself in power in conditions of unthinkable persecution and suffering. Democracy in Germany was hostage to economic fortunes that swung from moments of stability to long bouts of chaos. The United States had retreated from the high claims of Wilsonian internationalism and had withdrawn into itself. The international economy was volatile and soon to sink into depression.

Set in such a vast, tumultuous world, Chichester preferred the steady patterns and comfortable obscurities of provincial English life. But it still gave its new bishop much to do; and, in return, Bell set to work with a will. When he wrote for the *Chichester Diocesan Gazette,* which he effectively refounded as editor in 1930, he framed his thoughts as "From the Bishop's Window." The illustration that prefaced each article at least hinted at a room full of books and occupied by a workmanlike desk. Over the years the books and the papers would mount ever higher. One of his chaplains, Lancelot Mason, came to observe a contrast between the bishop's "extremely orderly and compartmentalised mind which enabled him to pass easily from one matter to another and back again without losing his way" and a desk that presented daily an infuriating spectacle of "clutter and confusion."[3]

In his maturity, the bishop of Chichester had become more than familiar with the humdrum committees, meetings, resolutions, and campaigns that came and went with the years. But his private and public lives had by now almost completely intertwined. Not even his home was very

---

3. Lancelot Mason, "A Portrait of George Kennedy Allen Bell," in *Bell of Chichester, 1883-1958: A Prophetic Bishop,* ed. Paul Foster (University of Chichester, Otter Memorial Paper No. 17), p. 20.

much his own. Two guest books held by the library at Chichester Cathedral show how the Bishop's Palace in Chichester received a constant stream of visitors, testifying to the breadth of his sympathies and commitments. Bell himself can hardly have known any more than they on what road they were traveling. On one page falls the signature of Paul Petit, a young French journalist who would one day resist the German occupation of his country and die for what he wrote. The Bells must have regarded the Bishop's Palace as something very like a bastion in a volatile world — and they knew how to use it on behalf of their loyalties. Here piety, work, and pleasure were found by the Bells' many guests to be held in humane balance. The building contained a little medieval chapel where Bell would pray each day that he spent in residence. The watchful Mason found that "in the space of a few years" his bishop wore out no less than three copies of Lancelot Andrewes's prayerful *Precés privatae quotidianae* and turned to the life of Saint Thérèse of Lisieux.[4] Henrietta Bell appeared to be in her element. Mason would later remember her as a mature presence in this distinctive sphere: "There was a kind of natural imperiousness in her bearing which could be quite alarming to anybody who did not see below the surface and did not know what a warm and generous heart beat there."[5] Few things apparently satisfied the new bishop so much as reading poetry to guests.

For Bell the church must surely inhabit the world openly and also draw the richness of the world to itself. On Christmas Day, 1929, he broadcast something of a manifesto of his own over the BBC, and in uncompromising terms, too. "One of the most monstrous offences against religion," he urged, "is to regard Christianity as utterly unrelated to present-day life and as something eccentric and peculiar, or to regard the Church either as a hot-house or a prison. They are its worst foes who keep Christianity apart from Science, apart from Art, or apart from all manner of social and political life. They are the enemies of the Church who place a barrier between it and music, drama, poetry, sculpture, painting, or forbid any traffic with philosophy and modern thought." This gathered a formidable momentum:

> For my part, I whole-heartedly believe that the serious exercise of a man's art is itself an act of worship, and that the offering of the very best that is in him, be it poem, picture or sculpture, nobly conceived and wrought, or whatever mighty work of the inspired imagination, is

---

4. Mason, "Portrait," p. 23.
5. Lancelot Mason, "Henrietta Bell," in Foster, ed., *Bell of Chichester,* p. 173.

a song of praise and thanksgiving, or maybe a poem of intercession for God's creatures. It is for the Church, as I believe, to welcome the artist, to rejoice in his inspiration as springing from God . . . to welcome the man of science and to rejoice in his research.

The church must avow the finest in man. Bad art it should repudiate as it must bad politics. With the church, the artist and the thinker had common cause.

I believe that the Church should always be ready to blow a trumpet for Education, for Health, for Science, for Art. . . . She should also blow a trumpet for Peace and for justice, and, so stiff and unyielding should she be in her loyalty to the best, that she should not be afraid when need is, of denouncing authority in the wrong, and even opposing all her moral forces, in defence of her ideal and her trust, to the princes of the world.

John Milton had once written that he could not praise a "fugitive and cloistered virtue." "Now," Bell pronounced, "least of all on Christmas Day, can I praise a fugitive and cloistered Church."[6]

Bell the bishop enjoyed an explicit place in a formal scheme of things. This gave him that measure of self-assurance that necessarily undergirds a public presence and a public contribution. The words that he spoke would be heard; they might even yield influence. In Chichester itself Bishop Bell possessed actual authority, over appointments, movements, and decisions on the many entangled levels of parochial and diocesan life. He wrote prolifically: letters, memoranda, and sermons. A bishop is liable to receive invitations to speak at occasions. One invitation that Bell accepted declared something of his own sympathies. One Whitsunday he attended a gathering of the Independent Order of Odd Fellows, the Manchester Unity Friendly Society, in Brighton. One (deleted) section of his speech yields a revealing trace of thought. They should all, he thought,

be careful not to convert the working together of free human beings into the organization of a machine. The inner quality and richness of

6. Reproduced in Geoffrey Rowell, Kenneth Stevenson, and Rowan Williams, eds., *Love's Redeeming Work: The Anglican Quest for Holiness* (Oxford: Oxford University Press, 2001), pp. 579-80.

the lives of the mass of men and women has not been made greater and better by the progress of social organization in this country during the last century. We are becoming the servants of machinery — and unless we can stop it, the machine will get so complicated that it will destroy us and itself together.

A man is a man — not a machine, or a cog in a machine. He is not a robot but a soul, which needs the Breath of God to fill it if it is to keep alive.[7]

What kind of wisdom was this? Did it show merely the conventional apprehension of an anti-industrialist who looked back to the ideals of William Morris, or the sharp eye of a passionate critic in an age that produced Chaplin's satires on the hapless condition of a humanity caught up in Modern Times? Or did such words anticipate a future world in which the gargantuan appetites of vast bureaucracies would overtake all human values and instead create a world whose relentless pursuit of functions, statistics, and categories would stop at nothing, not even the destruction of human life itself?

Gandhi Comes to Chichester

Across the 1920s India, the "jewel in the crown" of the empire, had grown restive. Nationalist movements had gained ground across the country and mounted one challenge to British power after another. Where these were successful the movement gained confidence and momentum; where they encountered repression the movement grew in justice. Campaigns of passive resistance, civil disobedience, and noncooperation not only were effective in winning concessions but also embarrassed the show of empire. For coercive measures against peaceful men and women who sought only the freedom to govern themselves were seen across the world to be oppressive and discreditable. Politicians, diplomats, and civil servants in both Britain and India discussed time and again whether it was right to lay down a firm, unyielding line of authority or to concede in pursuit of a tolerant middle way, one that preserved the outward form of the old relationship but allowed a growing measure of self-government. There were enquiries, reports, and commissions. In Parliament the Conservative party

7. Bell Papers, vol. 345, fol. 40.

was bitterly divided, while the Labour party was ambivalent about empire altogether. In the autumn of 1931 the Indian critics were invited to London for a series of round table discussions on constitutional reform. Eighty-nine duly came. The Indian National Congress did not attend; most of its leaders were in prison.

On 11 October 1931 a modest crowd and a band of musicians by the market cross in the center of Chichester glimpsed a weekend visitor arrive in a motor car and turn deftly into Canon Lane toward the gates of the Bishop's Palace. This was Mohandas K. Gandhi, the rising prophet of the Indian independence movement, one of the newly arrived Indian delegation. To Chichester Gandhi brought his spinning wheel and — evidently — a goat. The next day he was seen walking along the towpath of the local canal. At evensong in the cathedral he was observed in a stall in the choir, to the dismay of some who thought such a position hardly appropriate for such a figure as this. The content of the long conversations that took place in the Bishop's Palace that weekend is unrecorded. But a sense of rapport hangs over the letters that emanated from the occasion. "He is obviously a good man," Bell wrote to a grouching government official, Sir Claud Schuster; ". . . I am sure he is a much better and a much bigger man than some of his adulators contemplate."[8]

Where did Bell stand in these matters? To Gandhi himself he pressed that there were many in London who wished only to be amenable and reasonable. To the men of Whitehall he urged that Gandhi was a power for good and a man of reason who must be taken seriously. Schuster found this irritating: it was difficult, he remonstrated, "to negotiate with the Orientals on an equal footing."[9] Bell replied by proposing a scheme to reduce the presence of British soldiers in India. Above all, he insisted, they must avoid a war there. Schuster relented a little. By the time their letters ended — six thousand words passed between them in October 1931 — the Permanent Secretary to the Lord Chancellor and the Bishop of Chichester were found to be respectful and sympathetic correspondents. Not that Bell had much influenced the powers and pressures that fashioned government policy, if at all. At large in Britain for a time, Gandhi, meanwhile, had achieved celebrity in the public imagination and won the hearts of northern mill-

8. Joseph Muthuraj, "An Indian Scholar Looks at Bishop George Bell," in *The Church and Humanity: The Life and Work of George Bell, 1883-1958*, ed. Andrew Chandler (Farnham: Ashgate, 2012), p. 61.

9. Muthuraj, "An Indian Scholar," p. 62.

workers whose jobs competed with the interests of impoverished Indian weavers. Bell had played his part in this, too, collaborating quietly with Gandhi's faithful Christian ally, C. F. Andrews, to introduce this persevering antagonist to a succession of church leaders who might prove sympathetic to his cause.

The round table negotiations that brought Gandhi across the oceans to Britain failed. In India itself harsher measures were introduced. The historian Gerald Studdert-Kennedy observes the arrest later of "virtually the entire group" that had come to Chichester with Gandhi that November.[10] At this juncture Bell was not drawn to ally himself with Indian nationalism. He was approachable and helpful to its sympathizers and advocates, but he refused to campaign. He did write letters. A correspondence between the Bishop of Chichester and the Secretary of State for India, Sir Samuel Hoare, came to nothing at all. Studdert-Kennedy finds that, "at the end of the day, he seems to have backed away, subdued."[11] It was not then in Asia but in Europe that Bell would come to his greatest labour and find his deepest meaning.

A Modern Diocesan Bishop

In the year of Bell's consecration, the Church of England was still caught between the activities of two parties that could barely do more than glower at each other from opposite poles. Anglo-Catholic parish priests could — and did — lead public worship into avenues quite unsanctioned by the Book of Common Prayer. Evangelicals felt like a minority in the church; they could bridle at modest accommodations and suspect heresies. All of this could turn nasty. In Birmingham, an intolerant liberal bishop, E. W. Barnes, maintained for years a state of virtual war with a number of dogged Anglo-Catholic parishes. Bell watched this with incomprehension. For his part, he saw that a bishop must serve the cause of order, not become an agent of disunity. He himself was, as he often remarked, a man under authority. In Chichester he now met dogmatic opinion and division — over ritual, for example, or church party — with polite tenacity. He had an intuitive sense of common ground, but realized that it must become some-

10. Gerald Studdert-Kennedy, *British Christians, Indian Nationalists and the Raj* (Delhi: Oxford University Press, 1991), p. 207.
11. Studdert-Kennedy, *British Christians*, p. 207.

thing more than a dilution of contrary opinions. In this dimension of his episcopacy he clearly cut a figure of authority, ordaining and instituting, tramping from west to east to confirm candidates, sitting on committees, and chairing meetings. He could be firm with clergy and even severe with anything that suggested laziness. But in many other respects he remained, unobtrusively, himself.

In 1938 Bell published *Common Order in Christ's Church*, the first of two visitation charges, an address that responded to his own questions to four hundred parochial clergy about their lives and their work across the Chichester diocese. No one who read the charge could doubt that its arguments emerged from a deep personal piety and a great sense of public responsibility. A devotion to the Book of Common Prayer lay in almost every page. Furthermore, the relationship between the local and the universal was explicitly marked: "We are watching a process of disintegration in the civilization of the West, a disintegration accompanied by a spiritual and moral upheaval. At such a time a special claim is made on the loyalty of Churchmen."[12]

Bell observed a striking decline in religious observance among the young, and sought, in a new Guild of St Richard, to offer the newly confirmed an outward mark of their commitment and something they could own for themselves. He made it a principal task to meet his clergy and to visit constantly the parishes of a sprawling diocese. Bell at large made little fuss about his privileges. Perhaps he was too secure in them? Equally, he travelled third class on the trains and never made a show of it. His secretary of many years, Mary Balmer, found him particularly tenacious in trying to pay for his ticket when no railway staff appeared available to charge him. His appeal to the loyalty of his clergy was anchored not on status or structure, but on the assurance that in their bishop the clergy of Chichester could find support, sympathy, and friendship. At the same time, he took an active responsibility for the institutions of the laity, not least for the local Bishop Otter Memorial College, which taught young women to be school teachers, visiting it at least three times a year and always being greeted there as a friend as well as an ally.

These daily duties still rested within an appeal to the creative heart and mind. Bell was adamant that from the artist and the poet the church had much to learn. His first letter in the diocesan gazette presented two photographs: one of the Chichester Roundel, a beautiful medieval de-

12. G. K. A. Bell, *Common Order in Christ's Church* (Chichester, 1938), note.

piction of the Madonna and infant Christ, which he had promptly had assessed by E. W. Tristram at the Royal College of Art ("Those who wish to see the painting may do so by calling at the Palace and asking"); and a sculpture, *The Young Mother,* by W. Reynolds-Stephen, the president of the Society of British Sculptors. He invited people from across the diocese to send in other examples so that the gazette could reproduce "beautiful modern religious works of art connected with Sussex or in Sussex churches."[13] Of music there was, contrastingly, little. Mary Balmer thought him largely untouched by music, even tone-deaf. But if this was truly so, on what did his appreciation of Albert Schweitzer and of his friend Gustav Holst rest, if it was not on their vision as musicians? If Bell, the bishop, commissioned no new work in this particular sphere, perhaps he sensed that this lay in the province of the cathedral choirmaster and organist, or that it was already well enough served? It is hard to judge.

At all events, the visitors' book that the Bells kept at the Palace showed a steady succession of artistic luminaries. Indeed, episcopacy had done nothing to dampen Bell's determination to inspire new drama. His early friendship with the dramatist Martin Browne continued to flourish. From T. S. Eliot he drew *Murder in the Cathedral* for the Canterbury Festival in 1935. It was Eliot's first play; as he later remarked, "it was to the bishop of Chichester that I owed my introduction to the theatre."[14] An exploration of the killing of Archbishop Thomas Becket by agents of King Henry II in the twelfth century, *Murder in the Cathedral* may at first appear to be only a further pageant of imaginative medievalism. But Eliot himself acknowledged the dimension of an all-too-modern pragmatism by converting his murderers at the end into self-interested public servants justifying themselves in contemporary prose.[15] Privately, at least, it is said that Eliot himself saw this work as a response to Hitler. The life of this play was striking. What began in the garden of the Bishop of Chichester would soon be performed, under the dispensation of the Rooseveltian New Deal, by the Federal Theater in New York to 40,000 people whose tickets cost, at most, 55 cents.[16]

It is extraordinary that in this busy episcopal context Bell was able

13. *Chichester Diocesan Gazette,* no. 1, p. 1.

14. Bell Papers, vol. 208, fol. 43.

15. T. S. Eliot, *Murder in the Cathedral* (London, 1935): "We beg you to give us your attention for a few moments . . ."

16. See Carl N. Degler, *Out of Our Past: The Forces That Shaped Modern America,* 3rd ed. (New York: Harper & Row, 1959), p. 424.

to research and undertake the immense, two-volume biography of Archbishop Davidson that would become his defining contribution to the historiography of the church. That he should write such a work had long ago been decided in conversations with Davidson himself. Perhaps such an achievement looked less conspicuous in its day than it would to a later one, for the public institutions of the country counted many men who could both govern and write literature, evidently without embarrassing their rival obligations or exhausting their own powers. At all events, *Randall Davidson* was a vast undertaking of 1,442 pages, perhaps the last ecclesiastical biography to apply both the approach and the ambition in scale of Boswell's *Johnson* and the august, dual-volume *Life and Letters* genre of the later nineteenth century. Humphrey Milford at the Oxford University Press proved — as Bell himself recorded — "the most patient and considerate of publishers," and the press would produce not one, but three successive editions (the second and third admitting alterations and additions).[17] Within a generation such a book was unthinkable, yet, evidently, it found an audience.

Here in *Randall Davidson* Bell is found to be very much a historian, weighing the intricacies of his sources meticulously and creating a colossal chronicle of an archbishop in office, standing stoutly at the helm of his own church and looking across to others, but equally remaining a Christian statesman who determined to be quite as much a part of the Establishment, the state, the political order, and the stage of international life. For it is a study not merely of ecclesiastical preoccupations but of a world and of an age. The gratitude of historians is perhaps not a very luminous cause to which to commit a substantial part of a life, but in this book Bell left the world of scholarship in heavy debt. Abroad it would one day come to exert at least one significant influence. A young German pastor, Eberhard Bethge, would seek to emulate the ambition, scale, and presentation of *Randall Davidson* in his own great biography of Dietrich Bonhoeffer.[18]

17. G. K. A. Bell, *Randall Davidson, Archbishop of Canterbury* (Oxford: Oxford University Press, 1935; 2nd ed., revised, 1938; 3rd ed., with a new preface, 1952).

18. As related to the audience at the Dietrich Bonhoeffer Church in Forest Hill, London, in 1993, when Bethge came to unveil a portrait of Bell executed by Hans Feibusch in his last years.

CHAPTER FIVE

The German Vortex, 1933-1937

In these Chichester years, Bell's life and work were dominated, if not quite overtaken, by a deepening apprehension that the world had grown far more dangerous. While William Temple was intently pursuing the creation of a new society at home, Bell had set his sights on the world that had somehow survived the tumult and tragedy of the Great War and yet was, within twenty years, confronting another catastrophe brought by the relentless barbarism of totalitarianism.

By now Archbishop Söderblom's great vision had inspired impressive consequences. Geneva, the home of the League of Nations, had become firmly established as the bastion of the new ecumenical movements, too. Life and Work was thoroughly reordered under a new constitution in 1930. There were study conferences on a variety of social and economic questions that were international in character and scope, above all on the great disaster of the day: unemployment. In 1932 Bell stepped firmly into the foreground of all this when he inherited the chairmanship of the central Council of Life and Work from the Bishop of Winchester, Theodore Woods. He was given two years in that office.

Economic crisis had overtaken every country, and public-spirited Christians sought answers. Surely it was the purpose of such a movement as Life and Work to frame a response? The year 1932 brought a defining moment in Basel. Here Bell found himself arguing against a young German who had become director of the movement's research center in Geneva, Hans Schönfeld. Schönfeld was an economist as well as a pastor. He believed that the mandate of Stockholm was to examine as thoroughly as possible the realities of the world's problems as they actually found them. In this, naturally, a Christian view should be borne in mind. But their first task was actually to understand. Accordingly, he wrote to Bell, they might "define the task of the Church in a concrete manner."[1]

The achievements of Schönfeld's department were prodigious, but at Basel Bell saw this tremendous accumulation of material and statistics and felt that Christian theology had been not so much left behind as left out altogether. He found he could not sign the report of the conference. It was important and valuable; but it was a paper by economists, even if they were Christian economists. "I am quite sure," he pressed, "that if the Churches are to issue a message on an economic world crisis, the message must from start to finish be not merely economic but penetrated with religious principles and making the application of fundamental Christian truth to the whole situation incontrovertibly clear in the most impressive way."[2] They must acknowledge that economic realities required not simply a new economics but a "fundamental revolution in a spiritual and moral attitude to life." Schönfeld maintained that they must still understand what was going on first if they were to reflect and act upon it credibly. Bell compromised: he would sign the report if it were made clear that this was the work of the Basel conference, but not a statement of the Universal Council itself.

After Basel there certainly was less economic material and more theological reflection. It is difficult for a historian of politics and society not to sympathize with Schönfeld and to see the dangers of Bell's position. It is also likely that Bell recognized that the gathering and analysis of statistics was a task for which many agencies could accept responsibility. Only a movement of churches could offer a vision of Christian faith.

Between 1932 and 1934 Bell was chairman of the central Council of Life and Work and thereafter chairman of its administrative committee for a further four years. This would be one of the principal contexts in which he would confront most directly the new politics of Europe. His chairmanship coincided, crucially, with an immense change.

The Arrival of Hitler

When Adolf Hitler became Chancellor of a coalition government in Berlin on 30 January 1933, international opinion had been far from acquiescent.

---

1. See Graeme Smith, *Oxford, 1937: The Universal Christian Council for Life and Work Conference* (Frankfurt am Main: Peter Lang, 2004), p. 101.
2. Smith, *Oxford, 1937*, pp. 105-6.

National Socialism was widely judged to be a threatening new force that looked anything but peaceful. Almost every day the British newspapers carried lengthy reports — by journalists like Norman Ebert in the *Times,* or Frank Voigt in the *Manchester Guardian* — documenting new outrages committed by the Nazis against Jews, against their political critics, against pacifists. The very speed with which the National Socialists moved to take over the machinery of the state was astonishing. Exploiting a stray attempt by a Dutch communist to burn down the Reichstag on 27 February, Hitler claimed powers to govern by decree. An election on 5 March proved a far from free affair; violence on the streets was now an everyday occurrence. The popular vote gave the Nazi party more seats than any other — but still not enough to claim an overall majority. Nonetheless, one provincial German state after another was being gobbled up by the new powers. Concentration camps were being established: within only a few months foreign observers were counting as many as forty-five of them holding between 35,000 and 40,000 prisoners.[3] On 23 March the movement maneuvered and coerced into law an Enabling Act that effectively laid the foundation of a new dictatorship. Civil institutions across the country were "coordinated." It was clear that the Jews of Germany faced an explicit and mounting danger.

Many Christians in Britain observed this with acute anxiety. Some were moved to act. But a debate about the efficacy of protest had already exposed a fear that foreign interventions might actually make the situation worse. In March 1933 Archbishop Lang was advised by Sir Robert Vansittart at the Foreign Office that it very likely would. This did not convince Lang, but he accepted that bold, outright condemnation could actually achieve nothing because it would simply be dismissed as the antagonism of an enemy.[4] He saw that if a protest were to influence anything at all the protester must be taken seriously. This meant voicing a criticism in restrained and responsible language and placing it, however uncomfortably, within a sympathetic understanding of German national needs and hopes. When, on 1 April, a government-sponsored boycott of Jewish business was declared in Berlin, Lang went to the House of Lords to urge lawmakers

---

3. As noted in *The Brown Book of the Hitler Terror and the Burning of the Reichstag,* prepared by the World Committee for the Victims of Fascism, with an introduction by Lord Marley (London: Victor Gollancz, 1933), pp. 291-92.

4. See Andrew Chandler, "A Question of Fundamental Principles: The Church of England and the Jews of Germany, 1933-1937," *The Leo Baeck Institute Yearbook* 38 (1993): 225-26.

to demand that it be called off at once.[5] Some thought the intervention effective. When in June Lang spoke at a public meeting at the Queen's Hall in London, he found his entire speech printed by the *Times*. But soon he learned that the German newspapers simply printed what was vaguely positive and excluded what was specifically critical.

In Chichester, Bell, too, was beginning to struggle with this. He also knew the danger that a strong public statement might compromise the prospects of a private intervention. Much would now come to depend on a measuring of unpredictable currents, configuring as best one could the public and the private, the clear word of protest and the careful maneuver. Lang, Bell, and their allies were seeking to play a game with no very clear or consistent rules with powers that were a law only to themselves.[6] The dangers of miscalculating were horrible, for the price would be paid by someone else.

The German Churches

The passage of the Enabling Act in Germany in March 1933 showed that the leaders of the Catholic Centre party were now more ready to serve the interests of ecclesiastical diplomacy than to defend the bastion of Weimar democracy. In a new concordat, the Vatican moved to sacrifice all interests that might appear political or contentious by framing clear guarantees to protect strictly ecclesiastical and educational interests. Did this show naivety on the part of a Vatican that thought such maneuvers could actually achieve anything with such a government? Or did it show that the Vatican had no illusions about this new turn of events in Germany and was determined to set down its defenses and confront a clear danger as best it could? Whatever the case, at a crucial moment the Concordat effectively stranded many committed laypeople who worked actively in the many Catholic political, social, or youth movements. The bishops in Germany were divided and the church at large unhappy and apprehensive. This debilitating sense that nothing should now be said or done against the regime promptly spread to Catholic circles abroad.

5. See *Hansard,* Debates of the House of Lords, fifth series, vol. 87, col. 225.

6. For a lengthier discussion see Andrew Chandler, "The Church of England and National Socialist Germany, 1933-1945" (Ph.D. thesis, University of Cambridge, 1991), pp. 25-31, 82-85.

For their part, the Protestants saw the challenge in different terms. There were twenty-eight *Landeskirchen,* many Lutheran and some Reformed. Since 1918 there had existed a movement to unite them, and this now took on a powerful new form. With Hitler now in power, a *Deutsche Christen* movement campaigned for the creation of a state church united around the ideals of the new state: a "Führer principle" and an "Aryan Paragraph" to ensure a non-Jewish ministry. Hitler appointed a former army chaplain, Ludwig Müller, to be his representative in all talks for church union. Müller soon became far more than this. The *Deutsche Christen* acclaimed him as their leader — and as their candidate for the new position of *Reichsbischof* of a united church. The momentum of this tide was tremendous. But there was resistance. A Pastors' Emergency League rallied around a Berlin pastor, Martin Niemöller, insisting that measures to apply "racial" principles to the ordained ministry represented a politicization, a corruption, of the church and its faith. Within months, this minority was consolidating and forming a new movement, the Confessing Church, often known to those abroad as the Confessional Church. And between the two wings existed the majority of pastors and congregations, who did what they could to maintain the Christian faith quietly and without dispute, without reference to either party. It could soon be seen that far from achieving a model of church union, the Protestants were falling apart in all manner of new ways. Hitler himself played a careful hand, but the support of the state for the *Deutsche Christen* was obvious, and soon their critics faced threats.[7]

---

7. The historiography of the German church struggle is now immense. Particularly influential as overviews in the English-speaking world have been John S. Conway, *The Nazi Persecution of the Churches* (London: Weidenfeld & Nicholson, 1968); Ernst Christian Helmreich, *The German Churches under Hitler: Background, Struggle and Epilogue* (Detroit: Wayne State University Press, 1979); Guenter Lewy, *The Catholic Church and Nazi Germany* (London: Weidenfeld & Nicholson, 1964); and Klaus Scholder, *A Requiem for Hitler and Other Perspectives on the German Church Struggle* (London: SCM Press, 1989). Scholder's vast two-volume history of the beginnings of the struggle appeared in English as *The Churches and the Third Reich* (trans. John Bowden; London: SCM Press, 1987 and 1988), but a third contribution to this odyssey, Gerhard Besier, *Die Kirchen und das Dritten Reich: Spaltungen und Abwehrkämpfe, 1934-37* (Propyläen, 2001), has not yet found an English translator and publisher. There are many valuable monographs devoted to certain aspects of the history, Protestant and Catholic, particularly by a new generation of North American scholars.

Christian Opinion in Britain

How to interpret this tangled affair from a great distance and a safe country? In Britain Christians could read their newspapers and listen to their radio sets. The ecumenists had their own connections and could place them at the disposal of others. In March 1933 a further meeting of Life and Work took place in Rengsdorf, this time with a view to affirming some union of Christian theology and sociology. Who is to know what anxious, furtive conversations took place in the corridors, halls, and private rooms on that occasion?

A handful of British Christians decided to go to Germany to see for themselves. Bell's neighbor, the Dean of Chichester, A. S. Duncan-Jones, took off for Germany early in July 1933, striking up a conversation with Hitler's official photographer, "Putzi" Hanfstaengel, on the airplane and managing to secure a short but mesmerizing meeting with Hitler himself. The new Chancellor told him that he was a Catholic who simply desired a united Protestant church so that he could deal with religious matters in an orderly manner. Moreover, Hitler added, in the struggle against communism and materialism he thought he had the right to call upon the support of the churches. Duncan-Jones was impressed by this. But he knew that this Germany was now an altered landscape. At the Kaiser Friedrich Gedächtniskirche he found a crowded congregation gathered to hear the leader of the German Christians, Joachim Hossenfelder: "The service was one of thanksgiving — the Hallelujah Chorus, Ein feste Burg, and all that kind of thing. The Nazis were much in evidence with their flags." Yet he could identify here no real spiritual unity, even sensing a tangible perplexity. Hossenfelder seemed to him merely to shout. That evening he returned to the church to hear one of the leading voices of the opposition, Gerhard Jacobi. Again, the building was full. But now there was a palpable "unity of feeling" and a powerful sense of prayer. At the end of the sermon Jacobi reported the arrest that morning of a pastor in Dahlem, who had refused to allow Nazi flags to be hung in his church. Duncan-Jones met as many church people as he could. All of those who held an independent or critical view were frightened by what was happening. Moreover, they told him that any "public expression of sympathy with those who are undergoing oppression and persecution would by the agreement of all responsible persons to whom I spoke, be absolutely disastrous."[8]

8. See Andrew Chandler, *Brethren in Adversity: Bishop George Bell, the Church of*

As the parties divided in Germany, so their sympathizers and critics divided in Britain. The contest found its characteristic arenas in the synods of the churches — in the case of the Church of England, in the Houses of Convocation and the Church Assembly — and in the correspondence columns of the press. Soon it could be seen that a gulf had opened between the chairman of the Archbishop of Canterbury's Council on Foreign Relations, Bishop Headlam of Gloucester, and his secretary, A. J. Macdonald, on the one hand, and Bishop Bell and his dean and a voluble majority on the other. For British Christians were at large hostile to Nazism and rejoiced to think that the politics of this new dictatorship were being frustrated, in however complicated a manner, by a stouthearted Christian opposition that was prepared to take a stand when political parties, civic interests, and trade unions had evidently crumbled in submission.

Headlam did not see himself as an apologist for Hitler and the Nazi state. Nazism was not his sort of thing at all. But he felt that it was the sort of thing that many Germans liked — and, if they did, that was up to them. He was sure that liberal British critics should not go about telling other nations — or their churches — what to do. He was sure that there should not be interventions. He could see the force of a broad theology that might appear to involve a nation and its sense of destiny, and he found the theology of the Confessing Church obscurantist and alien. He even suspected that the international press employed many Jews who used their position to attack an enemy of their people. Such opinions did not win much detectable support, and they were widely condemned.

Against all this, Bell and a greater number across the churches were sure that what they observed now in Germany was a dictatorship, and that a dictatorship that made totalitarian claims was both irreconcilable with Christian faith and a danger to a free church. He thought that many Germans cared for justice, tolerance, and order just as good men and women did the world over. He was prepared to intervene on behalf of those in danger if he was encouraged to do so by those who knew more than he did and if he could see that any effective good could be served. Bell did not even engage with the notion that Jews at large in the world might orchestrate a coherent campaign against the Nazi state. He saw that the persecution of the Jews in Germany was something to be wholly deplored. Although Headlam was right to argue that the pastors of the Confessing

England and the Crisis of German Protestantism, 1933-1939 (Woodbridge: Boydell & Brewer, 1997), pp. 52-58.

Church maintained a theology quite at odds with that held by English church people, it was clear to Bell and his allies that the claims and the politics of the *Deutsche Christen* movement simply did not ring true. Müller was too obviously a political creature: it was difficult to discern that he had any theological content at all. Meanwhile, his coercive deputies were frankly sinister.[9]

For all this, in Germany itself it was Müller who swept the board. By August he was *Landesbischof* of Prussia. On 27 September he was adopted by a new national synod as *Reichsbischof* of a single state church. International Christian opinion was scandalized. His subsequent acts in office made Müller look no better in the eyes of his critics. When Hossenfelder visited Britain he came close to seeming ludicrous, even faintly bizarre, to his hosts. But there were German churchmen who made a better impression. Even from a distance a figure like Niemöller appeared to possess a charismatic integrity. German pastors who worked in London, like Julius Winterhager or the young Dietrich Bonhoeffer, were evidently honest men of genuine conviction. It was with Bonhoeffer that Bell established, almost at once, a personal rapport that could only deepen. For even if the two did not quite see the world through the same eyes, they could understand that what now united them ran far deeper than the politics of churches.

The Significance of Bell

Many British observers had struggled to understand why the German churches had not protested on behalf of the Jews. At the beginning of March 1933 the Bishop of Fulham, Basil Staunton Batty, had even flown to Berlin seeking to "stir up" the churches to intervene "on religious grounds." But he had found Christians there subdued and fearful — and the Senior Superintendent of Berlin, Max Diestel, had been surprised at the very idea that the church should become involved. This menacing of the Jews, he assured Batty, was not the work of the state but the "temporary incon-

9. For all of this see Chandler, "The Church of England and National Socialist Germany," pp. 45-72. But vigorous use of these themes may be found in Tom Lawson, *The Church of England and the Holocaust: Christianity, Memory and Nazism* (Woodbridge: Boydell & Brewer, 2006), pp. 31-54. Gordon Rupp's *I Seek My Brethren: Bishop George Bell and the German Churches* (University of East Anglia Mackintosh Lecture; London: Epworth Press, 1975) remains striking and significant, not least because of the author's personal connection with Bell after the war.

veniences of a revolution."[10] By the end of that year many British church leaders up and down the country had spoken at public protest rallies. Now and then arose evidence of resentment that it was all the harder for British Christians to intervene if their German brethren gave them nothing on which to build. Were they not showing that they made more of their own sufferings than those of others who now faced the most severe and relentless persecution? About this Bell was circumspect. Perhaps he saw too sympathetically the difficulty of their own situation and knew well enough how exposed his contacts already were. But he held the two issues together as best he could and made as much as he could of anything that related them.

Bell had now begun to intervene actively in defense of his friends. It was clear to him that those who sought to maintain the independence and integrity of the church in Germany were in peril. Meanwhile, Archbishop Lang quietly received a succession of reports and visitors at Lambeth Palace and began to accept invitations to speak publicly at protest meetings. The relationship between him and the Bishop of Chichester warmed, and already by the summer of 1933 it could be seen that the two represented a firm alliance in these matters. They began to exploit every opportunity, and every channel, in search of some effective role in the crisis.

As long as the German government sought to maintain an unembarrassed relationship with other countries, there was reason to hope that the threat of combined protests in responsible quarters could at least modify the dangers that the adversaries of the *Deutsche Christen* movement faced. It helped that the Germans evidently thought an English "Lord Bishop" far more important a public figure than many in Britain itself. Between 1933 and 1935 Lang and Bell enjoyed a sympathetic audience at the German embassy, where Leopold von Hoesch and his staff had little wish to justify what was going on in their country and offered, at best, the bland apologia that was required of them.[11] When Lang published a firm protest at the appearance of an issue of Julius Streicher's paper *Der Stürmer,* in which an old slander that Jews had practiced ritual murder had been printed in May 1934, it was Bell who had showed him the offending article.[12] The letters that passed between them on this occasion showed that they shared

10. Chandler, "The Church of England and National Socialist Germany," p. 80.

11. This area is intensively explored by Daphne Hampson in her impressive, and oft-cited, "The British Response to the German Church Struggle, 1933-1939" (D.Phil. thesis, University of Oxford, 1973), various pages.

12. See Chandler, "A Question of Fundamental Principles," pp. 239-40.

a visceral indignation. For neither man was the persecution of Jews a secondary matter.

The persecution had become a refugee crisis involving many countries across Europe and beyond. The fact that Bell was now to be found in the company of the Jewish scholar and public servant Norman Bentwich is significant. When Bentwich asked him to take up the cause of "Non-Aryan Christians" in Germany, Bell set to work with a will, interceding, corresponding, and intervening. But he also placed their tragedy firmly in the context of the persecution of Jews at large there. He pressed for words of protest in Convocation, in Church Assembly, in the press. He devised plans to settle refugees in his diocese and across Great Britain. Advised that those defined as "Non-Aryan Christians" in Germany needed urgent support, he agitated for them vigorously, organizing a succession of national campaigns. Volumes of letters in his archive testify to the hours of patient, intricate labor that he committed to individuals and to families who had made their way to Britain and safety. Repeatedly Bell urged Christians to rise to this challenge, to raise money, and to organize relief. Yet the historian observes an evident paradox: for while the churches deplored the persecution of Germany's Jews, their practical efforts for the victims seemed weak, if not feeble.[13] The language of Bell's speeches and letters soon became frustrated and even embarrassed.

An International Crisis

What became quickly known as the German church struggle was never merely a domestic affair. It engaged the efforts of embassies and public movements, politicians, journalists, and writers across Europe and North America. It was fought out in the councils of the ecumenical movements — indeed, their history was increasingly defined by these new dangers. By now, Bell was widely acknowledged as one of the founding fathers of the ecumenical movement, consorting and corresponding with men like the purposeful Dutch church leader Willem Visser 't Hooft, the French

13. The historian Adrian Hastings was struck by "the limitations, rather than the generosities, of British Christian concern over the evil effects of Nazism," even going so far as to argue, "most English Christians, clerical and lay, maintained prior to 1939 a most unjudgemental respect for their political neighbour, while they looked decently the other way from their true neighbour in his desperate need." See *A History of English Christianity, 1920-1990* (London: SCM Press, 1990), pp. 344-45.

pastors Henri-Louis Henriod and Marc Boegner, the Norwegian bishop Eivind Berggrav, the Swedish bishop Brilioth, the American Presbyterian William Adams Brown, and the Swiss pastors Adolf Keller and Alphons Koechlin. It was with Koechlin, as Peter Raina finds, that Bell had a particularly instructive, and lengthy, correspondence.[14] Almost every ecumenical assembly was now entangled in the German controversy. Should there be protests and interventions? Who should represent the German church at these meetings? In which disputing faction, after all, *was* the true German church to be found? Bell was squarely in the middle of all this, and it was to Bell that all the contending parties now looked. But his own loyalties were very quickly committed to one side, and by the summer of 1933 they had already solidified. When he looked back on the crisis in later years Visser 't Hooft argued that if the ecumenical movement came to give powerful support to the Confessing Church, this was "above all due" to the Bishop of Chichester, "for he saw clearly that if, at such a critical hour, the ecumenical church did not stand by those Christians who contended for the integrity of their faith in Germany, their movement would lose its credibility."[15]

When the annual meeting of Life and Work took place in Novi Sad, in Yugoslavia, on 9-12 September 1933, the chairman of its council had his work cut out for him. Müller had dispatched a delegation to the conference led by a new "ecumenical bishop," Dr. Heckel. At Heckel the other delegates glowered. Bishop Ammundsen lost no time in pressing that the great danger to the churches now was nationalism. Heckel, no doubt looking back over his shoulder, was also in an uncompromising mood. The vision of Stockholm was, he affirmed, obsolete. If that was so, countered an indignant Wilfrid Monod, the German church should leave the movement.

Although ecumenical diplomacy proved to be as vulnerable to criticism by contending parties as any other sort, Bell's ability to hold the conference together at such a time appeared to many observers impressive. But he did not renounce his own position for the sake of universal concord. They should record firmly their deep anxiety about the plight of German Jews and their concern that the freedom of opinion had been so severely proscribed. As chairman, he would write to the leaders of the Ger-

---

14. See Peter Raina, *Bishop George Bell: The Greatest Churchman; A Portrait in Letters* (London: Churches Together in Britain and Ireland, 2006), pp. 65-174. For the whole correspondence translated into German, see *George Bell — Alphons Koechlin: Briefwechsel, 1933-1954*, ed. Andreas Lindt (Zurich: EVZ Verlag, 1969).

15. Lindt, ed., *George Bell — Alphons Koechlin Briefwechsel*, p. 5.

man churches to explain the apprehension of the council. This was greeted warmly by all but Heckel, whose position was indeed an impossible one. In doing this, Bell had taken a great deal on his own shoulders. He was now more than ever heavily embroiled in a dangerous and destructive dispute that would see no easy end.

The leading lights of all the ecumenical movements were beginning to work closely together. An international "consultative group" included Bell himself, Archbishop Temple, Visser 't Hooft, William Adams Brown, and now two of the most vivid presences in the International Missionary Council: the Anglican layman J. H. Oldham, and the Presbyterian William Paton. In April 1934 a further conference of ecumenists took place in Paris. This proved to be still more significant than Novi Sad. This time nobody could avoid the issue that stood so clearly before them: the title of the conference was "The Church and the State of Today."[16] It was this context that saw the emergence of Oldham, in particular, as the new prophet of these international Christian conferences. Oldham now saw eagerly the vision of something still more impressive: a great enterprise of all Christians devoted to the task of understanding what the church should now say to the world. For to Oldham the question of the totalitarian state was inseparable from that of the secularism of the modern world.

The leaders of the churches at large, across Europe and in North America, orchestrated their efforts in a succession of discreet campaigns. This was not yet the declamatory politics of protest. For the first three years of the Nazi era Bell and others like him perceived that careful maneuvers, and even firm threats, might secure concessions or ameliorations. Information now mattered utterly. Bell was determined to learn as much as he could from those who participated personally in the crisis. But he also wished to show that he supported them as a friend and ally. In this he showed an astute, even creative, ability to draw on the privileges of his status and to place them at the service of those who might have had a marginal role in the drama. One such was the young pastor of the German congregation in Forest Hill, in the south of London. "What would suit me best of all," Bell once wrote to Dietrich Bonhoeffer, "would be if you could come and have breakfast with me at the Athenaeum at 9 o'clock on Thursday morning. Is that too outrageous?"[17]

Whatever might be said by those who sought to distinguish between

16. See Smith, *Oxford, 1937*, pp. 110-16.
17. Bell to Bonhoeffer, 24 February 1934, Bell Papers, vol. 42, fol. 18.

religion and politics, the context that the Nazi state created dominated all their calculations. How could there be a free church in a society in which Jews were persecuted, political opponents and pacifists incarcerated, trade unions abolished, and newspapers suppressed? Private diplomatic sorties still did not reassure. In November 1934 Bell met Hitler's foreign affairs man at large, Joachim von Ribbentrop, in the Athenaeum in London. They talked for three hours. Ribbentrop was amiable and even charming. But Bell could see that they were divided by fundamental obstacles. Hitler, Ribbentrop insisted, had saved the nation, and without the nation there could be no church at all. Müller, Bell pressed, must go. Ribbentrop could not see why. At the same time, he added that Pastor Niemöller had refused to christen his own child. Bell asked him if he had heard of a protest made by British lawyers and church leaders earlier that year against concentration camps. Ribbentrop did not seem to know of this. Instead he simply ventured that in Britain the communist threat to Germany was "entirely misunderstood." The next day Ribbentrop met Archbishop Lang, who found him to be "sincere and straightforward," but "an eager apologist for Herr Hitler and his policy."[18] It was difficult to see what such encounters were actually achieving. Should they happen at all?

Bell's reputation across the churches certainly gained from the German crisis. It was where a growing number expected to find him. "You are the real *vox ecclesiae*," remarked Bishop Brilioth admiringly, in February 1934.[19] Chichester had become the heart of the support for the opposition. Duncan-Jones was now an implacable critic of the Nazi state, working with his bishop to prepare motions for the upper and lower houses of convocation. When bishops sought advice on German questions, it was not to Headlam of Gloucester but to Chichester that they turned. Bell spent numberless hours reading reports from Germany and discussing the situation with ecumenical contacts. May 1934 found Bell, Lang, and the ecumenist J. H. Oldham busily at work on a new public protest at the coercion of confessing pastors.

Indeed, the crisis had intensified. At the end of that month the Confessing movement met at Barmen to issue a declaration of principles that soon resounded abroad. But the much-derided Müller pressed on implacably, in the dubious company of a theological manager of sorts named Heinrich Oberheid and two lawyers, the president of the Prussian supreme

18. Chandler, *Brethren in Adversity,* p. 93.
19. Hastings, *A History of English Christianity,* p. 342.

church council, Friedrich Werner, and another Prussian, August Jäger, who struck many as malevolent. When he met Hitler on 18 July Müller could report that twenty-two out of the twenty-eight *Landeskirchen* were a part of the new *Reichskirche*.

Life and Work: The Council and Its Chairman Come to Fanö

On 9 August a second national synod took place in Berlin at which Müller acquired still greater power for himself and required a new oath of allegiance from all pastors and church officials. He also threatened to prosecute any pastor of the opposition who passed on information to international organizations. This was the situation that faced the ecumenists of Life and Work when they arrived at the little town of Fanö in Italy on 24 August. It fell to Bell to chair the meeting and to find some way through the German morass. He knew that both the "official" German church and the dissenting Confessing Church sought to be represented — and it was an indication of his own sympathies that he believed that the latter must be present if the former was. This was the view of his colleagues on the council, too. With Bonhoeffer's encouragement he sent an invitation to Karl Koch, who had chaired the Barmen Synod that May and had subsequently become president of a newly convened Westphalian synod. The embattled Koch could not accept it. When Theodor Heckel in Berlin heard of Bell's initiative, he exploded. Bell remained sure that the German controversy must be discussed at Fanö, and if that were so it was only fair that both points of view should be heard there. But by now he knew well the dangers of mere provocation. He decided that whatever happened, the conference must be held *in camera*.

When Heckel and his anxious delegation appeared at the conference, he walked straight into a deluge of questions on the very first day. With all this he did his best, but soon found himself caught in the middle between his critical ecumenical colleagues and the powers of Berlin, who hovered over him menacingly and advised him in no uncertain terms over the telephone. Everybody acknowledged, with varying degrees of sympathy, that returning home would be a very different matter for Heckel and his deputies than it would be for all the others.

Yet while the conference continued, somehow, news did leak out — and into the columns of no less a newspaper than the *New York Times*. Heckel was furious again, and Bell had to acknowledge that he had been undermined. There was an attempt to remedy matters, but it was too late. An incoming airplane now brought the figure of Dr. Birnbaum, brandishing full powers to supersede Heckel and represent with more conviction the case for the state church of Germany. Bell was not prepared to concede much to this. He responded by allowing Birnbaum a bare twenty-minute spot at a public meeting and then firmly excluding him from the ongoing sessions of the council. If the members of the council had not taken much to Heckel, they were soon left to reflect how much worse was his replacement. There was some hectic overnight drafting of resolutions, expressing "grave anxiety . . . lest vital principles of Christian liberty should be endangered or compromised at the present time in the life of the German Evangelical Church." These disavowed all political motives and made all due allowances for the peculiarities of the situation and for the "sins and shortcomings" of every church they represented. Yet still the council had to affirm "their conviction that autocratic church rule, especially when imposed on the conscience in solemn oath; the use of methods of force; and the suppression of free discussion are incompatible with the true nature of the Christian Church."[20]

The hapless Heckel was still there, and he contradicted this as best he could. In particular, he resented the sympathetic attention that the Confessing Church appeared to enjoy in these quarters. But these purposeful resolutions were passed by a stout majority of the council. More than this, it proceeded to affirm Koch and Bonhoeffer as consultative members.

This was the last time that Bell chaired the council, and perhaps it marked his greatest achievement in ecumenical statecraft. For the meeting at Fanö was widely held to be a conspicuous success when so easily it could have been so noisy a disaster. As Bell himself remarked to Archbishop Lang, there had been no explosion to devastate the whole movement. Equally, the council had not taken refuge in theological platitudes, generalizations, or vagaries simply to keep the enterprise safely on the road. A stern word had been spoken to censure those who abused their power and also a clear word to stand beside those who suffered under it. But Fanö also had an important, constructive consequence. It had announced the intention to hold a new international conference to discuss at far greater length these great questions of church, state, and community. A research

20. For this, and for a thorough description of the conference from Bell's perspective, see Jasper, *George Bell*, pp. 114-20.

committee had been established to set to work. It would be chaired by
J. H. Oldham.

Not that any of this improved matters in Germany itself. Indeed,
Müller and his allies were realizing a formidable momentum. He rejected
the resolutions of the ecumenists outright. He ordered that all pastors
who were married to "non-Aryan" women should be dismissed. The two
churches of Württemberg and Bavaria were brought into line and their
bishops, Wurm and Meiser, removed. That month Müller achieved his
apotheosis: he was formally installed by a third national synod as *Reichsbischof.* For their part, the Confessing pastors were looking more and more
like a new church. A month later they gathered again, this time at Dahlem,
to form a new Council of Brethren and an executive inner council. Bell
and his allies watched every detail of the narrative intently as it unfolded
before them. By October 1934 they were ready to launch a coordinated,
public *démarche* by the heads of the Protestant churches across Europe.[21]

In truth, Müller and his creatures had overreached themselves. In
unifying the church they had provoked more anger and criticism abroad
than ever. The politicians were embarrassed. On 30 October Hitler declared that he was washing his hands of the whole business. Without his
patron the *Reichsbischof* suddenly looked vulnerable. He began to repeal
his own laws. The *Deutsche Christen,* too, began to move against him.
When Müller saw Hitler once in January 1935 and again in February, the
Reichsbischof looked far less formidable while his master seemed now to be
marking a distance between them. This was beginning to look like government by perpetual crisis. March 1935 was a dangerous month: over seven
hundred pastors in Prussia were arrested and briefly detained, while Pastor
Grossmann in Berlin was dispatched to Dachau concentration camp.

That summer the church struggle moved into a distinct new phase.
On 16 July a new Reich Ministry for Church Affairs was created under a
new man, Hans Kerrl. Kerrl saw himself and his Ministry as a conciliatory
power, and he was determined to bring the antagonists together. Perhaps
it only needed a pragmatic layman to sort out all these volatile pastors?
But by now the conflict had become too polarized, too bitter; even a well-
intentioned man who made his way down the middle of this particular
road was bound to be seen as tainted in some degree by his relationship
with either side. And Kerrl was no neutral. While he sought to offer the
blandishments of sweet reason, the Confessing pastors found him simply

---

21. See Hampson, "The British Response to the German Church Struggle," chapter 5.

a more insidious threat. They rejected all of this. When a new Church Committee under the aging figure of Wilhelm Zöllner was installed, many of the Confessing pastors rejected this, too.

The Jews of Germany after 1934

Bell was an unlikely campaigner. His was not a striking public presence; his voice was gentle and rather high. He had little feel for the provocative generalizations of rhetoric. More important to him were the intricate facts that lay behind complicated issues. In a world of propaganda and confrontation he perceived that credibility and influence grew above all out of exactitude. His words were always weighed with care, for he knew that if a price were to be paid for them, it would be paid by people other than himself. Rhetorical license was human liability. As the history of the Hitler regime unfolded before their eyes, nowhere was this more dangerously the case than in the response to the persecution of German Jews.

In September 1935 Bell visited church leaders in Germany, coinciding with the passing of the new Nuremberg Laws, which defined "Jews," "Non-Aryans," and "Aryans" and deprived the first two of their citizenship. As he traveled by train and motor car through Bavaria, he reflected bleakly on the persistence of placards and posters bearing the words "Jews not wanted," and saw copies of *Der Stürmer* exhibited in glass cases on town and village streets. It was on this trip that he found himself the guest of Rudolf Hess, "a man of about 43, very dark and with a somewhat literary and student look about him." Frau Hess, who spoke English, evidently enjoyed the visiting bishop rather more than her husband.[22] This new connection came to very little beyond a smattering of letters now and then, in which Bell pressed for advantages and Hess pretended not to notice.

When Bell turned to the autumn meeting of the Church Assembly that November, it was with a new motion protesting against anti-Jewish discrimination, affirming sympathy with its victims, and threatening widespread indignation if it did not cease. Bell found a new ally on this occasion, for the motion provoked an objection from a layman, who turned out to be the German consul in Plymouth, and this brought down upon them all an explosion by the Bishop of Durham, Herbert Hensley Henson. Henson was wholly untouched by Bell's careful nuances. Instead he transported the

22. The report may be found in Chandler, *Brethren in Adversity*, pp. 97-101.

assembly by deploring this "fiction," this hallucination of anti-Semitism, drawing from the Book of Judges to lament that they could not draw the sword and go to the help of the low against the mighty.[23]

A month after the great debate at the Church Assembly, the League of Nations High Commissioner for Refugees, James McDonald, had resigned in frustration. His public letter, published by the London *Times* on 27 December 1935, was bitter and disillusioned. For three dismal years his office had tried to coordinate its efforts with international Protestant organizations and watched the refugee crisis deepen inexorably. Inside Germany the churches were intimidated and weakened by the power of the political context; outside the country the cause of international assistance appeared undermined by indifference. On 25 April 1936 the *Times* published a letter from Archbishop Lang to inaugurate a new national appeal for German "non-Aryan" Christians, part of an international church campaign held simultaneously in the United States, Scandinavia, France, and Holland. "It is all to do with human beings," broadcast Bell, "their feelings, their misery. . . . And the mere telling of the tale, if we are to use our imagination, at once throws up picture after picture of human poverty, suffering, desolation. . . . They are outcasts from Germany. They are nobody's children."[24]

This new appeal aimed at £25,000. The bishops commended it to their dioceses in their pastoral letters. In the first month £2,365 came in. But then the momentum ebbed away. In his introduction to a new book, *The Christian Approach to the Jews,* written by Charles Singer, Bell lamented, "It is humiliating, but it is true. The plight of these so-called 'non-Aryan' Christians is grievous in the extreme. . . . But the Christian Churches in England and elsewhere have made the minutest response. There have been individual Christians who have been generous. But the Churches as a whole are silent and, it seems, unconcerned."[25] Later, Bell would attribute this silence to "ignorance as well as indifference." But unlike the German church struggle, which attracted interest daily, this doleful picture

23. *Proceedings of the Church Assembly*, vol. 16 (London, 1935), 20 November 1935, pp. 466-79. For a thorough discussion see Chandler, "The Church of England and National Socialist Germany," pp. 92-100; for Henson's contribution see Owen Chadwick, *Hensley Henson: A Study in the Friction of Church and State* (Oxford: Oxford University Press, 1983), pp. 255-57.

24. Chandler, "A Question of Fundamental Principles," p. 252.

25. Charles Singer, *The Christian Approach to the Jews* (London: Allen & Unwin, 1937), p. 8.

had offered few sharp shocks, few arresting turns in a dramatic narrative, to arrest public attention. There was no conflict, no obvious resistance to attract the pens of journalists. The story was essentially the same as before, though it now affected still greater numbers of men, women, and children who faced a steadily mounting sense of impossibility. Church weeklies like the *Church Times* would remind their readers of the issue sporadically, but had nothing new to say about it. The many small refugee committees were industrious, but too many organizations can serve to make even the greatest single need obscure. As the historian Peter Ludlow has observed, the cumulative effect was often chaotic, lacking clear character and direction. Yet, Ludlow has found that this British effort was notably more successful than those in the United States, Sweden, Norway, and Holland ("the public is no longer interested in the matter," reported the secretary there) and in France, where the churches failed to organize a committee in the first place.[26] Meanwhile, the German churches could do too little to establish a robust foundation for international relief in the country where the crisis had begun.

Then something occurred in Germany itself that seemed to alter the terms of the debate. On 28 May 1936 the Second Provisional Government of the Confessing Church endorsed an appeal to Hitler protesting against the totality of claims that the state made, challenging its ideas of blood, race, and soil and its treatment of the church press, and lamenting the anti-Christian nature of the highest party figures. It was sent to the Chancellory on 4 June; by the end of July it was widely reproduced in newspapers abroad. Bell at once made much of this. But it provoked a tragedy: three men — Friedrich Weissler, Ernst Tillich, and Werner Koch — were arrested for leaking the memorandum to the press. They promptly disappeared into the concentration camp system. Tillich and Koch were soon released, but not Weissler. Friedrich Weissler was a Jew.

Kerrl's Ministry altogether failed to cultivate the pastors of the Confessing Church. The shutting down of two of their own theological colleges by police and the confiscation of their funds in November did not end their opposition. It simply alienated and embittered them still more. Kerrl grew firmer. In December he moved against the powers held by church organizations across the country. It now looked as though a dictatorial *Reichsbischof* had simply been replaced by a civil dictator behind whose

---

26. Peter Ludlow, "The Refugee Problem in the 1930s: The Failures and Successes of Protestant Relief Programmes," *English Historical Review* 90 (1975): 590-92.

courteous committees lay the cold and hard imposition of authority. Martin Niemöller found that he had been deprived of the freedom to speak in public altogether. In such ways did Kerrl weaken the very basis of the Confessing movement. When a new synod took place at Oeynhausen on 17 February 1936, the Provisional Church Administration of the Confessing Church was seen to be divided by Kerrl and Zöllner. When it gathered again in March there were no longer representatives from Bavaria, Württemberg, Hanover, Saxony, or Mecklenburg. Indeed, they now went off to create their own Lutheran Church of Germany.

However deeply divided, what all of these embattled parties did share was an apprehension that it was not Christianity, in any form — betrayed, compromised, or undefiled — that now enjoyed the favor of the state. A new, heavily sponsored German Faith Movement had grown robust and even influential. This had dispensed with the old faith altogether and sought instead to orchestrate a mélange of Teutonic myths in new and intricate public ceremonies. It was known that leading party men were adherents. What, foreign observers asked, did this officially patronized paganism reveal about this political state and its ideas? And what now would its ambitions be in the world at large?

CHAPTER SIX

A Disintegrating Peace, 1937-1939

What was now at stake in Germany — the integrity of the Christian faith itself or the right of a minority of awkward pastors to make life impossible for everybody else? Was this a persecuted church or not? Bell held fast. This could not be merely a squabble of parties while pastors were ordered to keep silence or removed to concentration camps. The support of men he knew and trusted across the ecumenical movement was fully committed to the Confessing Church. When he visited Germany himself in January 1937 Bell found Niemöller "a man of great vividness . . . a real inspiration. He was like a man on fire, but smiling and friendly all the time; and a man of very great faith . . . we could not have had a more illuminating talk."[1]

This visit came when the tide was again turning. In January 1937 nine pastors in Lübeck were arrested. The frail and hard-pressed Zöllner tried to visit them in prison, but the police prevented him. When he tried to preach in Lübeck Cathedral the pulpit was denied to him. His Committee promptly fell apart; the leading lights resigned and only a barely significant remnant remained. Kerrl's Ministry would soon follow. In February Hitler met Kerrl not once, but twice. There must, Hitler pressed, be new elections in the church. A bleak third phase in the church struggle dawned. An interim administration now struggled to hold everything together while the Confessing Church set down its own conditions for participation and appealed directly to the state for a personal hearing at the Chancellery. To this Hitler turned a deaf ear.

1. Andrew Chandler, *Brethren in Adversity: Bishop George Bell, the Church of England and the Crisis of German Protestantism, 1933-1939* (Woodbridge: Boydell & Brewer, 1997), p. 123.

Kerrl had not gone away. He had become responsible for the administration of church finances across the country. But the drama of the German churches had now taken a still more dangerous turn. On 19 February 1937 one of the three men apprehended for leaking the 28 May 1936 memorandum, Friedrich Weissler, died in Sachsenhausen concentration camp. The German church struggle had produced a martyr, but a lonely and abandoned martyr too. Only a handful of the most courageous pastors of the Confessing Church gathered at his grave. Abroad, the rest was not silence: the *Times* published a letter of protest by a number of British church leaders. Bell encouraged this. Meanwhile he wrote to Rudolf Hess, lamenting that Weissler's wife had not been allowed to see his body and urging that special care be taken of three other pastors known to be in concentration camps.[2] As far as he could judge, this achieved nothing. Then, on 1 July 1937, Martin Niemöller was arrested. This was certainly no dispute between Christians but a clear expression of state power. Would there be a trial? It was by now a pattern of the church struggle that pastors might be detained for a time and then set free. But what should a scandalized Christian opinion abroad actually do? Might he be released if the protests were loud and sharp enough?

Oxford, 1937

Since the summits of Paris and Fanö in 1934, the genius of J. H. Oldham had come into its own. Plans were laid for a great world conference on "Church, Community, and State" in Oxford in July 1937.[3] This much-trumpeted affair, carried on under the aegis of no less than six conference presidents for two relentless weeks, was without doubt the greatest ecumenical enterprise since Stockholm. Oxford dons and townspeople alike suddenly found themselves in the company of 425 worthies from 120 churches across the globe, all now to be found busily at work and at worship in their midst, in the Sheldonian Theatre, the Town Hall, the churches of the city, and the chapels of the colleges. Oldham had succeeded in attracting not only senior clergy from across the denominations, but also a number of the most striking Christian laymen at work in the political world, like John Foster Dulles;

---

2. Bell to Hess, 15 March 1937, Bell Papers, vol. 8, fol. 409.
3. See Nils Ehrenström, "Oxford 1937," in *A History of the Ecumenical Movement, 1517-1948*, ed. Ruth Rouse and Stephen Neill (London: SPCK, 1954), pp. 587-92.

the prophet of the League of Nations, Lord Robert Cecil; and also scholars of renown, like Sir Alfred Zimmern (a local guest). There were even "one or two" discreet Roman Catholic observers, somewhere about.[4] For a conference-going Christian, Oxford that July must have been very Heaven. The list of names sums up an age of luminaries: it is still extraordinary to imagine Sergei Bulgakov present in the same hall as Reinhold Niebuhr. Bell would later recall how curious it was to see Japanese and Chinese delegates sitting side by side in respectful conclave while the newspapers for sale in the street outside announced, "Japanese planes bomb Chinese villages."[5] Those who hunted for Germans found only two, one a Methodist and the other a Baptist. For the representatives of the Evangelical Church had not come. In this great conclave of Christians from so many lands, the German church looked more conspicuously solitary, and more at odds with everybody else, than ever.

Bell himself sat on the Business Committee, chaired by the indefatigable J. R. Mott, and he was also a presence on the Church and State section. Here he promptly proposed that a message be sent to the absent German church. Archbishop Lang demurred, anxious that such a missive might expose their friends to danger. But Bell was sure of himself, insisting that "silence would be conceived as a betrayal."[6] He got his way. Every word of this letter was drafted with the greatest care. "Though your delegates are absent," it declared, "the very circumstances of their absence have created a stronger sense of fellowship than before." But here, too, was a clear word of solidarity for one party alone: "We are greatly moved by the afflictions of many pastors and laymen who have stood firm from the first in the Confessional Church for the sovereignty of Christ, and for the freedom of the Church of Christ to preach His Gospel."[7]

The two German delegates at Oxford agreed at first to take this letter. Then they decided that they could not. The Methodist, Bishop Melle, suddenly made a florid speech that bewildered everybody by expressing gratitude for the mission of Adolf Hitler, whom God had sent to save Germany from bolshevism. The letter to the German church was sent through other channels.

4. R. C. D. Jasper, *George Bell, Bishop of Chichester* (London: Oxford University Press, 1967), p. 226.

5. G. K. A. Bell, *The Kingship of Christ* (Harmondsworth: Penguin Books, 1954), pp. 31-32.

6. Jasper, *Bell*, p. 227.

7. Jasper, *Bell*, p. 275.

Bell was constantly caught up in meetings and conversations at Oxford, and he was the quiet inspiration behind the two Eucharistic services on the last day, at which all baptized delegates, including associate and youth delegates, were invited to receive communion from the hands of the Archbishop of Canterbury (at St. Mary's) and the Bishop of Chichester (at St. Aldate's). From this only the Orthodox abstained. But Bell did not stand out at Oxford. If anyone did, it was Oldham. He was the constructive genius of the affair, ubiquitous, restless, looking to a future that might yield a new World Council.[8] Archbishop Temple, meanwhile, confirmed his reputation as the most sophisticated framer of conference messages that seemed to hit the right, high note, and to suit almost everyone in general without offending anybody in particular. Within only a few days another great ecumenical conference, of the Faith and Order movement in Edinburgh, had accepted the message and set about its own business with no less a will. George and Henrietta Bell were both there, too.

The tremendous momentum achieved by the ecumenists that summer must have been deeply stirring. For Bell it was not merely an ecclesiastical enterprise, but one deeply rooted in the tumbling affairs of a world in disarray. Ronald Jasper speaks of him noting, quietly to himself: "The most important thing happening in the world today is the process of destruction of Christianity in Central Europe. It is only against this background that the World Council can be understood."[9] And he had his own questions to ask: "What are these forces? Why are they succeeding? How can the Christian Churches combat these new ideologies?"[10]

The Trial of Martin Niemöller

The arrest of Niemöller had provoked a great jostling behind the scenes. Should the international churches send a representative to his trial? Should there be a private protest — or a public one? At least two German pastors visited Bell to urge intervention. Bell himself saw that any response must be at once international and ecumenical. Allies were eager to rally to the cause. Lord Cecil of Chelwood told Bell that he had only to ask for his help;

8. For a valuable discussion of Oldham in the context of the Christian debate on the totalitarian state, see Markus Huttner, *Totalitarismus und Säkulare Religionen* (Bonn: Bouvier Verlag, 1999), pp. 279-88.

9. Jasper, *Bell*, p. 231.

10. Jasper, *Bell*, p. 232.

a woman wrote to Bell asking if she could send money to the Niemöllers; an aircraft apprentice in the Royal Air Force wanted to know more about Niemöller himself.[11]

In a diplomatic meeting in Berlin that November Lord Halifax warned firmly that what happened to German pastors made a poor impression in Britain. The German Propaganda Ministry appeared to be in no hurry to make its next move, but the case against Niemöller accumulated steadily, if silently. On 20 December a letter signed by a number of British church leaders was published in the *Times*. Bell knew of it and supported it. But he did not sign it. He was still trying to measure and interpret. A show of international admiration for a controversial German pastor who had antagonized the state did appear to compromise Niemöller in the eyes of his accusers. He was now to be tried on a number of offences under old Prussian law for abusing his proper use of the pulpit. Once he knew this, Bell thought the Christians abroad must not be seen to influence what happened in a German courtroom any more than should Nazis in Germany itself.

In February 1938 Duncan-Jones and a Congregationalist, W. G. Moore, set off for Berlin hoping to witness the trial for themselves. They were turned away. What then happened was, to many minds, extraordinary. In this totalitarian state, where men and women lived daily under constant surveillance and the unyielding menace of repression, the court cleared the defendant of offences against the state, upholding only the charge that Niemöller had abused his rights in the pulpit. He received a sentence of seven months in prison and a handful of minor fines. For such a length of time he had already been held. Now Martin Niemöller was free to leave the court. But there was no time to rejoice. Almost at once the vindicated pastor of Berlin-Dahlem was bundled off to Sachsenhausen concentration camp.[12]

For many, this clarified a great deal about where the real power in Germany actually lay — and, as if there had been any doubt, what character it possessed. Protests broke out abroad, letters were written to newspapers, intercessions could be heard on Sunday mornings in many churches. On 7 March 1938 Bell met Lang in London. A united telegram was drafted,

11. Bell Papers, vol. 10, fol. 47 (Bell to Forgie, 14 February 1938), vol. 60 (Cecil to Bell, 6 March 1938), and vol. 62 (Wakefield to Bell, 7 March 1938).

12. For an extensive treatment of this see Keith Robbins, "Martin Niemöller, the German Church Struggle, and English Opinion," *Journal of Ecclesiastical History* 21, no. 2 (April 1970): 149-70.

circulated, approved. Bell dispatched it to the editor of the *Times*, Geoffrey Dawson, for publication on 10 March. Many thousands of Christians all over the world who earnestly desired friendship with Germany could only, it declared, deplore this grave action — "And we pray God in his mercy to guard our brother and to deliver him from evil." This solemn and stately pronouncement was now signed by an international ecumenical alliance including Lang himself; Söderblom's successor as Archbishop of Uppsala, Erling Eidem; Archbishop Germanos of Thyateira; the French Pastor Marc Boegner; and William Adams Brown in New York.[13]

In April 1938 the supreme church council of Prussia decreed that pastors of the Prussian churches must now swear an oath of loyalty to Hitler. At the beginning of that month a correspondent wrote to Bell that a friend had met Frau Niemöller in Berlin; that Niemöller was in solitary confinement and under nervous strain; that if they heard that he had committed suicide they were not to believe it. Moreover, if a letter could be printed in the *Times* every three weeks it was their one hope of actually keeping him alive. But by June Bell knew that Niemöller had antagonized Hitler himself and that there could be little hope of his release. In July 1938 the anniversary of Niemöller's arrest was marked by a service of intercession at St. Martin-in-the-Fields. By August Bell was working on the creation of a new "Guild of Prayer" for all those who were in prison and all who suffered in Germany and Austria, to be based at St. Martin's (subscription 3d per week, but also with a yearly rate — or even a life fellowship: £10). This was no parochial affair: Bell thought that such a guild could enroll a million members across the world. To the priest at St. Martin's he wrote, "we do not particularly want any name of any individual to be associated with the Guild: and of all the names in England my name must be absolutely obliterated."[14] This earned a reply from the vicar's secretary that special intercessions were always said at the church, "but the Vicar feels, in common with us all, that this 'special guild' approaches too nearly to the likeness of a political effort. We may well have the German Ambassador refusing to come."[15] Nevertheless, Bell persevered. He wrote to Rudolf Hess. He wrote again to Ribbentrop. There was no reply.

By now the German pastor had become an international *cause célèbre*:

---

13. Message for publication, 10 March 1938, Bell Papers, vol. 10, fol. 63, and text of telegram, 11 March 1938, vol. 10, fol. 88.

14. Bell to McCormick, 12 August 1938, Bell Papers, vol. 10, fol. 129.

15. Letter to Bell, 16 August 1938, Bell Papers, vol. 10, fol. 133.

the most famous political prisoner of his day. Bell encouraged a deputation to Berlin from the Women's International League. Franz Hildebrandt, once a curate of Niemöller and a friend of Bonhoeffer, wrote an anonymous biography of Niemöller for the publisher Hodder and Stoughton. For this Bell provided a foreword. ("It is impossible for any Christian of any country or Church to look on unmoved. The faith for which these champions of the Church in Germany are standing is the faith of the Gospel, the faith of the Universal Church.")[16] There was even talk of a film. When, a year later, Cecil warned Bell that he had heard that positive harm to Niemöller had followed from the interventions of bishops abroad, Bell was still prepared to justify himself: "But my action for Pastor Niemoeller is very definitely desired, and warmly welcomed by Niemoeller's own personal friends, and particularly by his wife, with whom I am in constant touch."[17] Niemöller had more to fear from being forgotten by the world than he had from being remembered. Bell knew that leading Nazis deprecated international protests as counterproductive. He had been told the same by the ambassador in Berlin, Sir Neville Henderson. But he would not be led by the former and he suspected the latter of going along with the Nazi view on a variety of matters far more than he should. For his part he was sure of his ground. He would not keep silence.

The Jewish Exodus

The persecution of the Jews had intensified by purposeful degrees. Bell immersed himself in correspondence, seeking to support in whatever way he could those refugees who needed resettlement and who had begun to look to him for assistance — practical, financial, pastoral. Visitors to the Bishop's Palace found the floors of the building littered with heaps of letters, all of which, Bell insisted, must receive not a standard acknowledgment but a personal reply. He had invested in a valuable relationship with the Paulusbund, a charitable organization established by Protestant "Non-Aryans" in Germany, and also in a new office run from the Marienkirche in Berlin by its pastor, Heinrich Grüber. Meanwhile, his sister-in-law, Laura Livingstone, was soon disappearing into Germany itself for long periods

16. *Pastor Niemöller and His Creed, with a Foreword by the Bishop of Chichester* (London: Hodder & Stoughton, 1939), p. 23.

17. Bell to Cecil, 3 July 1939, Bell Papers, vol. 10, fol. 236.

to do what she could for the cause.[18] A diocesan appeal raised almost £500 to pay for the education of ten refugee children in the schools of Sussex.

A Church of England committee for "non-Aryan" Christians had been founded in London in October 1937. The "inevitable Bishop of Chichester" was its chairman, and its secretary, Helen Roberts, came from his diocese.[19] Bell at once set aside any notion that this might be another body for pious resolutions and inactivity by announcing to his allies that he had visited the Home Office and offered to guarantee as many as thirty-three "non-Aryan" pastors currently at work in parishes, Lutheran or Church of England, across the country and their families, too. In such a way he saved many lives. One of these was the exiled Franz Hildebrandt.[20] Bell's maiden speech in the House of Lords, in 1938, was made on behalf of the refugees. In a lecture to the Jewish Historical Society of England he affirmed, "the problem of the refugee is the problem also of humanity."[21] In these matters he was still deftly supported by a sympathetic Archbishop Lang.

The visceral power of these realities was not felt only vicariously in Chichester. One of those whom Bell rescued from Germany was Hans Ehrenberg, a Heidelberg philosopher who had been ordained a Lutheran pastor and had suffered imprisonment in Sachsenhausen. In 1939 he arrived in Britain, but without his wife, who had to remain behind to sort out the family's affairs before following him. Exhausted and quite lost without her, and despite the "devoted kindness" that was now shown to him by his hosts, Ehrenberg almost broke down under the strain. "The torments which I had to endure while I was staying in the episcopal palace at Chichester were," he later wrote, "worse than anything I had experienced in the concentration camp."[22]

18. See James Radcliffe, "Bishop Bell and the Victims of Nazism," in *Bell of Chichester, 1883-1958: A Prophetic Bishop,* ed. Paul Foster (University of Chichester, Otter Memorial Papers No. 17), p. 95.

19. The phrase is that of Alan Don, Archbishop Lang's chaplain at Lambeth Palace. See London, Lambeth Palace Library, the diaries of Alan C. Don, various.

20. For Hildebrandt at large see Holger Roggelin, *Franz Hildebrandt, ein lutherische Dissenter in Kirchenkampf und Exil* (Göttingen: Vandenhoeck & Ruprecht, 1999); also Amos Cresswell and Max Tow, *Dr Franz Hildebrandt: Mr Valiant for Truth* (Leominster: Gracewing, 2000).

21. George Bell, *Humanity and the Refugees* (Lucien Wolf Lecture; London: Jewish Historical Society, 1938), p. 29. The text can also be found in G. K. A. Bell, *The Church and Humanity, 1939-1946* (London: Longmans, Green & Co., 1946), p. 21.

22. Hans Ehrenburg, *Autobiography of a German Pastor* (London: SCM Press, 1943), p. 116.

By Degrees into War

The public campaign on behalf of Martin Niemöller might have showed that hopes of effective protest of any kind had worn out. But it also showed that the German church struggle had almost become lost in the new landscape of appeasement. In 1938 the great hope of most British Christians was for peace. Across the country, churches and chapels had for many years now been steadfast members of a League of Nations Union, pledging their support to an international order that preserved peace through the achievement of collective security. The pacifist movements — the Fellowship of Reconciliation and the Peace Pledge Union of Dick Sheppard — had grown prodigiously through the 1930s. The Regius Professor of Divinity at Cambridge, Charles Raven, had asked "Is war obsolete?" and argued that indeed it was.[23] But the new ideals had been broken by Mussolini's invasion of Abyssinia, and while the powers convened and protested and threatened sanctions in 1936, German forces quietly reclaimed the Rhineland. In March 1938 Austria was forcibly "reunited" with Germany, and many saw that this was not merely a revision of an old treaty but the exporting of tyranny. It also made a defense of Czechoslovakia untenable — and within six months German forces were gathering against that region, too. The year 1938 brought further refugees to Britain, among them the lawyer Gerhard Leibholz and his wife, Sabine — the twin sister of Dietrich Bonhoeffer.

The new crisis that broke over the Sudetenland that autumn brought the first horrifying glimpse of war in Europe for twenty years. Churches across Britain filled with men and women praying for deliverance. At the eleventh hour, the British prime minister, Neville Chamberlain, scuttled off to Germany in search of a settlement. When he returned home it was in triumph, with the promise of peace. The great majority of the British public greeted this as a miracle. Archbishop Lang broadcast that Munich was surely an answer to the nation's prayers. In Chichester, too, Bell believed that this settlement was just. Like the great majority of British Christians, he rejoiced at Munich and believed that the world had been saved from a terrible ordeal. But gloom overcame the Chichester deanery, where the Duncan-Jones family deplored a peace bought by a betrayal of the Czech people, who could only watch as the great powers demolished their bor-

23. Charles Raven, *Is War Obsolete? A Study of the Conflicting Aims of Religion and Citizenship* (London: Allen & Unwin, 1935).

ders and bargained away the freedom of their countrymen in defense of their own interests.

The Munich euphoria lasted barely a month. Many British church people had believed that so narrow an escape from war must inspire a conversion from the old politics that had brought them all to the brink of catastrophe. But nothing in Nazi Germany had changed after all. On the night of 9/10 November 1938, the Jews of Germany and Austria suffered their first nationwide pogrom: 1,000 synagogues were burnt; 7,000 businesses were vandalized; 30,000 men were taken away to concentration camps and left there for weeks. International opinion was horrified. Now the activities of Pastor Grüber's Buro in Berlin became frantic. Outside Germany, the doughty little refugee organizations of every country intensified their efforts to rescue this afflicted people while they could. Governments, too, made new allowances and relaxed old proscriptions. Lobbied by Quakers and Jews, the British government promptly passed a bill to relax entry requirements for those under the age of seventeen. Thousands of British men and women stepped forward to offer homes to refugees. The 1938/39 *Kindertransport* saw 10,000 young German Jewish children whisked away from their benighted parents and hurriedly settled in new and often perplexing homes in the towns and villages of a new, strange land. There was barely time to bring their parents, even if there was the will.[24]

In April 1939 Bell wrote a letter to the clergy of the Chichester diocese in response to the prime minister's call for national service. The tone was distinctly stern, even austere. "The crisis through which the nation, and indeed the whole world, is passing," he declared, "is a moral crisis. We are all involved, clergy and laity alike." They inhabited a world that was marred by a simple failure to know what was actually right: "There is no clearly acknowledged standard by which human conduct is judged . . . the failure to recognise a firm moral standard is due to a failure to grasp the Christian doctrine of life. Moreover, behind this want of principles is the deeper spiritual sickness of want of faith." It is no gentle document. The letter captures a bishop in authority, telling his clergy firmly what they should do, mobilizing volunteers for military chaplaincies, hospital chaplaincies, special duties, general service. It was a time not for depression, but for "courage and confidence, for thinking of the needs of others, and for faith in God. The

24. See Vera K. Fast, *Children's Exodus: A History of the Kindertransport* (London: I. B. Tauris, 2010); also Olga Levy Drucker, *Kindertransport* (New York: Henry Holt, 1998).

supreme tragedy of war, greater even than the loss of life and the waste and destruction which it brings, is the poisoning of human relations."[25]

Men and women who moved freely in and out of the countries of Europe now began to sense that they were traveling on borrowed time. Decisions — fateful ones — must now be made. In the spring of 1939 Bell met Bonhoeffer in Chichester. On 13 March Bonhoeffer was back again, with his friend Eberhard Bethge: "There are so many things which I should like to discuss with you."[26] A further letter reveals that Bonhoeffer was a man now caught between two possible courses of action, one defined by his work for the Confessing Church, the other of "an entirely personal character and I am not certain if I may bother you with it." Bonhoeffer could not serve a German government like this, and he could swear no military oath to fight for it. If he stood up as a pacifist he would undermine his church. In truth, he did not know where to go. He thought of missionary work, not to evade his responsibilities but to offer his work where it might be wanted and needed. To Bell, he wrote, he could "speak freely."[27] The historian may only guess at the conversations that occurred in Chichester that spring. No letters from Bell survive, though there surely must have been some, handwritten and leaving no trace behind in a secretarial file. On 13 April Bonhoeffer wrote, "I do not know what will be the outcome of it all, but it means much to me to realize that you see the great conscientious difficulties with which we are faced."[28]

June 1939 found Bonhoeffer in New York. His hosts there urged him to stay. He could not. Sailing back to Britain with his elder brother, Karl Friedrich, he paused in London and there heard of the murder in Buchenwald concentration camp of the pastor Paul Schneider. His own thoughts had long before turned to self-sacrifice and death. He sought Bell again in London, but this was a tragic, narrow miss. There is a letter of farewell, dated 22 July: "I am looking forward to my work in Germany again. What sort of personal decisions will be asked from me I do not know. But nobody knows that now."[29] Three days later he boarded a train at Victoria Station in London, bound for the Continent.

Bell had by now become sure that the danger of keeping silent

25. Chichester, Chichester Cathedral library collection, "National Service: A Letter to the Clergy of the Diocese from the Bishop of Chichester," pp. 3-4, 9-10.

26. Bonhoeffer to Bell, 13 March 1939, Bell Papers, vol. 42, fol. 65.

27. Bonhoeffer to Bell, 25 March 1939, Bell Papers, vol. 42, fols. 66-69.

28. Bonhoeffer to Bell, 13 April 1939, Bell Papers, vol. 42, fol. 64.

29. Bonhoeffer to Bell, 22 July 1939, Bell Papers, vol. 42, fol. 70.

was greater than that of intervening and protesting. Prayer, too, was a public statement. On 1 July 1939 he had marked the second anniversary of Niemöller's detention in Sachsenhausen with another service in St. Martin-in-the-Fields in central London. He was now writing regularly to Niemöller's wife, Else, and adding notes that she could pass on to her husband on the once-monthly visits that were allowed to her. It was out of both necessity and affection that the Niemöllers now spoke of the Bishop of Chichester as "Uncle George." Bishop Berggrav of Oslo told Bell that the Gestapo found his handwriting impossible to decipher — but that he must never use the word "Chichester" in anything that he wrote.[30]

Archbishop Lang desperately tried to rally international Christian opinion against a war. Those who led the churches of Europe in ecumenical conferences scrambled to frame a response to the situation as best they could. There was a hasty meeting in Geneva. There many more words were set down and placed before the world. What could it avail? This was not a world governed by archbishops or pastors. Arguably more relevant was a reminder to all churches that their obligations lay not in the indulgence of national understandings but in a greater vision of a universal church. Once again, the historian of the twentieth century sees the little boat of the ecumenical pioneers turned back by the great tide of events.

On 1 September 1939 German forces moved across the Polish border; within forty-eight hours war had broken out across Europe for the second time in a generation.

30. Jasper, *Bell*, p. 241.

CHAPTER SEVEN

The War of Faiths, 1939-1942

So widely dreaded, and for so long, war was now upon them. Like most British Christians, Bell was a convinced supporter of the prime minister, Neville Chamberlain, and he must have shared in that deep, perplexed disappointment that Chamberlain himself broadcast over the BBC on Sunday, 3 September 1939. Many first heard the news from pulpits or on returning from church. The public mood was solemn, evidently united and resolute. The king broadcast to the nation that evening; his words had been drafted by Archbishop Lang only a few days before. Two hours later Lang himself spoke over the radio. Was this a new "holy war"? Very few could now lay claim to such words as these. Should they pray for victory? Lang was sure that they should. Archbishop Temple insisted that they should pray only "Thy will be done." Even so, observed Bishop Henson, it was a cause that was "only *ours* because we know it to be *His*." But he added that there should be no patriotic "tub-thumping": "We have got beyond that phase."[1] Nazism was their enemy, not the German people. It was at this time widely held that the Germans were not at liberty to oppose the state that tyrannized them.

Bell was exceedingly busy. He promptly dashed off an article on "The Church's Function in War-time" for the *Fortnightly Review*. It was, at once, a warning and a declaration of intent, pronouncing that the church must live not as a national, but as a universal body; that it must, above all things, be true to itself. "If the Church is purely national, it will fail. If it fails in war, it will be powerless in the making of peace. If the Church does not fulfil its

---

1. See Andrew Chandler, "The Church of England and National Socialist Germany, 1933-1945" (Ph.D. thesis, University of Cambridge, 1991), pp. 176-77.

function now, how will it ever persuade mankind that it has a function?"
He continued:

> This matter of functions is vital. The State has a function, and the
> Church has a function. They are distinct. The State is the guarantor of
> order, justice and civil liberty. It acts by the power of restraint, legal
> and physical. The Church, on the other hand, is charged with a gos-
> pel of God's redeeming love. It witnesses to a Revelation in history.
> It speaks of the realities which outlast change. It aims at creating a
> community founded on love. So when all the resources of the State
> are concentrated, for example, on winning a war, the Church is not a
> part of those resources. It stands for something different from these. It
> possesses an authority independent of the State. It is bound, because
> of that authority, to proclaim the realities which outlast change. It has
> to preach the gospel of redemption.

In short, the church "is not the State's spiritual auxiliary with exactly
the same ends as the State. To give the impression that it is, is both to do
a profound disservice to the nation and to betray its own principles." But
this was not all. In the development of his argument Bell insisted, "There
can be no contracting out of the national destiny. It is the Church of men,
and there are no men save those belonging to nations. The Church has a
share in all that affects the individual nation. It rejoices in the good gifts
God gives the nation. It suffers in all the burdens which the nation must
bear." But the church must still settle "the question of right and wrong —
the moral law":

> The Church then ought to declare both in peace-time and war-time,
> that there are certain basic principles which can and should be the
> standards of both international and social order and conduct. Such
> principles are the equal dignity of all men, respect for human life, the
> acknowledgment of the solidarity for good and evil of all nations and
> races of the earth, fidelity to the plighted word, and the appreciation
> of the fact that power of any kind, political or economic, must be co-
> extensive with responsibility. The Church therefore ought to declare
> what is just. It has a right to prophesy, to analyse the issues which lie
> behind a particular conflict, and to rebuke the aggressor. . . .
> It must not hesitate, if occasion arises, to condemn the infliction
> of reprisals, or the bombing of civilian populations, by the military

forces of its own nation. It should set itself against the propaganda of lies and hatred. It should be ready to encourage a resumption of friendly relations with the enemy nation. It should set its face against any war of extermination or enslavement, and any measures directly aimed at destroying the morale of a population.

Finally, "the Church is universal. Its message is for all nations. The Church in any country fails to be the Church if it forgets that its members in one nation have a fellowship with its members in every nation."[2] This article would come to be seen as one of his most important statements. Gordon Rupp, the Methodist scholar who came to know Bell in later years, found in it "a very different doctrine of Church and State from that of the classical Anglican divines from Richard Hooker onwards; something, indeed, almost Lutheran in its leaning towards two distinct regiments."[3] How would Bell himself test such arguments in the conditions of this desperate war?

Peace Aims

At the very outset of the war little ensembles of public-minded thinkers, scholars and church people, looked to establish not merely what Britain fought against, but what it actually fought *for*. There was a good deal of elevated talk in high places. As the historian Philip Coupland has observed, "Proposals ranging from the wildly utopian to the stolidly practical, for 'new Britains' and 'new worlds,' came from all corners."[4] It is tempting to see some such labors as something quixotic and irrelevant. But they showed a determination to make a purposeful stand for creative principles when the demands of political and military power might all too heavily dominate. The need for some constructive morality was surely a real one. Men and women had to know that they were called upon to suffer and even die for something better than the Treaty of Versailles and twenty years of

---

2. "The Church's Function in Wartime," reprinted in G. K. A. Bell, *The Church and Humanity, 1939-1946* (London: Longmans, Green & Co., 1946), pp. 22-31.

3. Gordon Rupp, *I Seek My Brethren: Bishop George Bell and the German Churches* (London: Epworth, 1975), p. 18.

4. Philip M. Coupland, "Anglican Peace Aims and the Christendom Group, 1939-1945," in *God and War: The Church of England and Armed Conflict in the Twentieth Century*, ed. Stephen G. Parker and Tom Lawson (Farnham: Ashgate, 2012), p. 99.

confusion and eventual disintegration. On what grounds did Britain appeal to justice? What was it now offering to a world of menacing dictators? The Peace Aims debate raised at once the vision of Europe as a coherent, geopolitical entity, and also of Britain's place within that beleaguered continent. In this Coupland finds Bell a distinctive presence: "whilst it was true that there were other Britons — in government and outside — who also spoke for European unity, there were few that shared either Bell's record of constancy or the radicalism of his vision of a *federal* Europe."[5] Indeed, in the year that war broke out he joined a new organization, Federal Union, which was dedicated to pressing for that ideal in public life. Temple, too, became a prominent advocate. For them both, Europe was united by centuries of Christian faith, by the continuing worship of churches in every country, and by common Christian precepts observable still in the life of European institutions. Surely this represented a greater reality than the passing politics of the modern nation-state. Should they not stand squarely on such a foundation and look to a future together?

That Bell should identify himself so firmly with a new political vision of Europe brought him strikingly close to the ideals of emerging, antitotalitarian circles in those other countries that either suffered dictatorships or confronted them at close quarters. When his ecumenical ally, William Paton, returned from a meeting in Copenhagen in October 1939, he could report that federalism was a vision alive in the minds of their German friends, too. Yet neither Bell nor Temple — nor, for that matter, Winston Churchill — found it easy to locate British power in such an equation. The empire, known to them all since childhood, still bestrode the earth, defining their understanding of their nation's place, and role, in the world at large. As the war unfolded, Britain's relationship with the United States would grow more and more powerful — for Europe was soon a continent occupied by German forces and governed by client states in the pocket of Berlin, while the United States stood before the world as the arsenal of democracy and the great embodiment of freedom.

From September 1939 there was little mood for a negotiated peace. Hitler was impossible; he had broken all the pledges he had given. Early in October 1939 Temple had ruled out a parley with the Nazi state, "not because it is undemocratic, which is Germany's concern and not ours, but

5. Philip Coupland, "George Bell, the Question of Germany and the Cause of European Unity, 1939-1950," in *The Church and Humanity: The Life and Work of George Bell, 1883-1958,* ed. Andrew Chandler (Farnham: Ashgate, 2012), p. 112.

because it is utterly untrustworthy." But they might assure Germans hostile to Nazism that, should Hitler be overthrown, the British government could surely negotiate a peace "not as conquerors over a vanquished foe but as colleagues in the system of Europe."[6] Temple knew that there were still those who worked for peace abroad, and they were not fools or rascals.

The war did not at first burst out into invasions and devastation. If anything — on land, at least — a protracted pause for thought seemed to occur. In Britain there was talk of a "phoney" war. Meanwhile, most countries were either uninvolved or already neutral. There was still room for maneuvers of various, quiet kinds. There were many barely observed missions and comings and goings, by industrialists, internationalists, ecumenists, or diplomats going it alone or operating under uncertain auspices. Perhaps the neutral powers could assert themselves and bring the belligerent governments to the negotiating table? Some turned their steps, surreptitiously, toward the Vatican.

In the very thick of this was the Bishop of Oslo, Eivind Berggrav.[7] Berggrav was a practical man of stature who certainly deserved to be taken seriously by men of the world. He knew that at such a juncture in the world's affairs the church must not fall silent. Finding himself in company with a wealthy industrialist, J. H. Andresen; a famous artist and committed internationalist, Hendrik Sörensen; and the Crown Prince of Norway and his wife, Princess Sybilla, he undertook an intense and intricate campaign to end hostilities before they gained too great a momentum. Together they strained every Scandinavian nerve. In the ecumenical movements Berggrav had a network at his very fingertips. But he also saw clearly that the realm of church relations, ecumenical or otherwise, was too crammed with priests and pastors, and too weak in numbers of laity, to achieve much in the realm of actual politics. It also represented too heavily opinion in the Western democracies. Soon Berggrav was establishing a quiet but genuine reputation for this sort of business. When two German churchmen, Eugen Gerstenmaier and Hans Schönfeld, approached Archbishop Eidem in Sweden that October, they were firmly pointed in the direction of the Bishop of Oslo.

At least some of this was observed, skeptically, by the mandarins of the Foreign Office in London, who soon called such adventures the "peace-

---

6. Chandler, "The Church of England and National Socialist Germany," pp. 178, 184.

7. See, at length, Gunnar Heiene, *Eivind Berggrav: Ein Biografie* (Göttingen: Vandenhoeck & Ruprecht, 1997), pp. 89-113.

feelers game."[8] In November 1939 a cluster of Scandinavian church leaders met under the auspices of the World Alliance for Promoting International Friendship through the Churches. William Paton was also there. When Berggrav flew to London in December 1939 it was Archbishop Lang who gave him an introduction to the Foreign Secretary, Lord Halifax, though he was powerless to do more. Halifax yielded nothing at all to his guest. Berggrav stayed in Britain for a fortnight, spending some of his time with the Bells in their second episcopal home in Brighton. Then he disappeared to Germany. All of this looked dramatic, but enigmatic.

After this there were discreet efforts to hold a new meeting of the Administrative Committee of a nascent World Council of Churches, in a small hotel that Berggrav knew deep in the countryside near the town of Apeldoorn, perched on the German border, but safely in the Netherlands. No German church was represented; nor were any Orthodox present. When the busy Paton invited Archbishop Temple, Bell, and a Baptist, Henry Carter, to join him at this gathering, he warned the bishops not to draw attention to themselves — to bring only one book with them and to leave their gaiters behind. They looked, remembered Henrietta Bell later, "like the worst type of conspirators as they ate a frugal meal of scrambled egg and then went off in the dusk in a very small plane."[9]

Did the churches wish to press that there should be peace negotiations? At Apeldoorn, Temple was firm about this. There could be no peace with a Nazi state. It must go. When all opinions had been exchanged and everyone was safely home again, Temple made a statement. In this, strains of piety blended with others of a more practical character. Negotiations could surely be just if certain clear conditions were affirmed: that the independence of the Polish, Czech, and Slovak nations be guaranteed; that any general peace congress should see them represented. There must be a new Europe founded upon the principles of "justice, mercy and truth."[10] But not even Temple, a master-drafter of collective statements if ever there was one, could disguise the weakness of this. The participants themselves

8. Observed, in turn, by Peter W. Ludlow in "Scandinavia between the Great Powers: Attempts at Mediation in the First Year of the Second World War," *Särtryck ur Historisk Tidskrift* (1974): 24. But see also *"Das Andere Deutschland im Zweiten Weltkrieg": Emigration und Widerstand in internationaler Perspektiv,* ed. Lothar Kettenacker (Stuttgart: Ernst Klett Verlag, 1977), pp. 141-200.

9. R. C. D. Jasper, *George Bell, Bishop of Chichester* (London: Oxford University Press, 1967), p. 315.

10. See Margaret Sinclair, *William Paton* (London: SCM Press, 1949), pp. 234-39.

knew that fine words could do little, if anything at all. It is tempting for the historian to set such efforts to one side, for they came to nothing. This would be mistaken, not least because they provide an important context for other secret sorties that would, now and then, follow. That such things were attempted in the face of the sheer monumentality of the politics of power is nothing if not impressive, but almost at once they were utterly overtaken by the force of events.

Of this war Archbishop Lang had pronounced, "The evil things which compelled us to enter must be cast out; the ground must be cleared of them before any foundations of a tolerable peace can be laid."[11] This was the firm consensus. Anyone who summoned the temerity to speak against it must trespass on the vivid justifications by which a whole nation now understood a high resolve and purpose. But this is what Bell now did. On 13 December he ventured to the House of Lords to speak in a debate on peace mediation, proposed by the Earl of Darnley. He was no pacifist, he maintained; nor did he believe that there should be peace at any price. Hitlerism was a thing he abhorred. There were two paths now before them: a fight to the bitter end, or negotiation "as soon as negotiation can be made." They must recognize that the longer this war went on the more it would spread. A fight to the end would involve the steady physical, moral, and spiritual exhaustion of the protagonists. That could help no one — no Pole, Jew, Englishman, Frenchman, or German. Only the powers of atheism and communism could gain by it. He still maintained that negotiation might yet be possible. His well-informed continental friends, who knew "more of Germany than we can know," assured him that the war was unpopular there, that Hitler knew it, too, and that "there is a willingness to accept terms corresponding to the purpose for which the British and French nations took up arms."

Could they really negotiate with Hitler? Bell thought it possible, even necessary, for if the Allies required Hitler to disappear just when his authority was at such a height his spell would be unbroken; he would only come to know the power of a martyr. If his demise was their object, peace could do that for them better than war. War could only justify and maintain him because, in the face of enemies, it must. Peace would discredit and unseat him. "My friends from neutral countries tell me that Herr Hitler is much debated in Germany today. . . . It is a question of time. In any case,

11. *Hansard,* Debates of the House of Lords, fifth series, vol. 115, col. 95 (5 December 1939).

were peace to be negotiated, certainly there are many signs to show that other influences are more likely to be decisive about the terms of peace than Herr Hitler." If they sought guarantees, their best hope was "the material guarantee involved in the situation itself . . . a solution of frontiers and nationalities which will reduce friction to a minimum."

But to this the Foreign Secretary, Lord Halifax, replied, "The whole argument . . . rests on the premise that there is to-day reasonably possible ground for successful negotiation, and it is precisely that . . . I, with great respect, but not without some knowledge, doubt."[12]

The debate was widely reported abroad: it even made the front page of the *New York Times*. Bell noted sympathetic responses with some satisfaction. But his speech also provoked consternation from many erstwhile allies. Karl Barth wrote from Switzerland that he had first thought that such words had come not from the Bishop of Chichester but the Bishop of Gloucester: "Dear Bishop," he reproved Bell, "I think you are too much a British gentleman and thus unable to understand the phenomenon of Hitler."[13] By the time he received this Bell had made a motion in Convocation, drawing from the bishops there a vague endorsement of his hope that "the statesmen of neutral and belligerent countries will watch eagerly and constantly every opportunity to negotiate a just and durable peace." But, asked Bishop Furse of St. Albans, with whom was such a peace to be discussed?

The scholar Adrian Hastings has written that Bell in all of this "lacked clarity of judgment."[14] But, however they may be assessed by posterity, these arguments did not lack sophistication, or — come to that — clarity either. It was a question of morality to distinguish between good and evil. These interventions showed that Bell, whose record of opposition to Nazism was now a long one, was still determined to navigate an ambiguous, even doubtful, gray area, and to inhabit it as best he could with others whose judgments he trusted. For policies of states, and even principles of justice, could not be sufficient things in themselves; they must constantly be examined in the light of human costs.

In time, it would be seen that a war to the end would also involve the most dubious entanglements. For now, if such arguments looked in-

---

12. *Hansard,* Debates of the House of Lords, vol. 115, cols. 251-56 (13 December 1939). Bell's speech is reprinted in Bell, *The Church and Humanity,* pp. 32-38.

13. Barth to Bell, 28 January 1940, Bell Papers, vol. 74, fol. 12.

14. Adrian Hastings, *A History of English Christianity, 1920-1990* (London: SCM Press, 1990), p. 343.

creasingly out of place in the context of British politics, that was in part because they owed a good deal to the shadows of persistent — and secret — diplomacy of the Vatican and Geneva. What divided Bell from so many others was a firm hope that Hitler would be removed from power in Germany itself. Few in British public life thought this possible. At all events, British politics had now moved decisively away from the calculations of the Chamberlain era toward the new Churchillian consensus that only utter victory could be the national goal.

Bell's advocacy of negotiations with official Germany surely did much to tar many of his future campaigns with the brush of appeasement. Furthermore, his insistence that British policy must declare the objects for which it contended looked increasingly out of tune with the temper of 1940. The war was being lost. After Dunkirk it seemed to most pragmatic British people that the framing of peace aims looked like a very remote or hypothetical exercise indeed. Even as late as the spring of 1941 Bell persevered. On 17 April 1941 he proposed that a further attempt at a negotiated settlement be made, in a public letter to the *Times*.[15] Archbishop Lang could no longer find the point of this. He wrote to Bell that he could see "Hitler & Co." respecting, and accepting, such an idea no more now than before. "I fear," he observed, "all this means — to use the language of the day — you are an optimist and I am a realist."[16]

Christianity and World Order

Bell wrote *Christianity and World Order,* the first so-called Penguin Special to appear before a broad public, in only three months. While he remarked to his editor at Oxford University Press, Charles Williams, that it was merely a *parvum opus,* it was a work done thoroughly in earnest. The vivid cover affirmed its urgent argument clearly in bold, orange print:

> This book, while it faces the gravity of the world crisis, has a spirit of hope, based on the conviction that the teaching of Christ, believed and applied, together with the fellowship of the Universal Church, alone provides the dynamic and simple faith which can yet save Western Civilisation.

15. The *Times,* 17 April 1941, p. 5d.
16. Lang to Bell, 18 April 1941, Bell Papers, vol. 84, fol. 244.

What Bell unfolded in a little over 150 pages laid out much of the controversial paradigm that he would inhabit for the next five years of his life. It is, like the article of November 1939, a resolute declaration of intent. Here his ideas tumble out from a striking breadth of sources: Catholic (the Pope's Five Peace Points, and Christopher Dawson); Protestant (the reports of the 1937 Oxford conference on "Church, Community and State," as well as Emil Brunner and Karl Barth); the historians E. H. Carr and Arnold Toynbee; Beatrice Webb; the exiled German sociologist Peter Drucker; and the exiled Lutheran theologian and philosopher, Hans Ehrenberg. Moreover, the little book attempts a purposefully global breadth, looking to the East and turning toward Asia and Africa. Each paragraph positively crackles with life, insisting that humanity searches still for what religion alone can provide, deploring the hollow affirmations of modern secularism, and pleading the divine commission of the universal church of Christ and the community of all Christians in a world of confrontation and violence. Here it is Christianity that offers the true foundation for peace and the clear prospect of reconstruction. For while the clattering of states proclaims only the will to power, the church is divinely and uniquely the manifestation of love. Only the church, as it abides in word and act, possesses the power to achieve the unification and fulfillment of mankind.[17]

Bell sent this to his ally, Bishop Henson, who wrote an amiably caustic critique, complaining that it left him with "an amalgam of impressions — fear and admiration prevailing." Bell, he thought, had "lived too much in the heated atmosphere of committees, conferences, congresses, and the like debased outcrops of modern democracy."[18] Despite Henson's comment, Bell soon could congratulate himself on reaching a considerable audience: across three years the book sold over 80,000 copies.

What made Bell a distinctive thinker in the landscape of British debate was his sustained relationship with the experiences and ideas of those remnants of European life that could now be found struggling to find their way in exile. The twin sister of Dietrich Bonhoeffer, Sabine, was by now living in Oxford with her Christian Jewish husband, Gerhard Leibholz. Leibholz was almost at once a formidable presence in Bell's world. A Göttingen professor of international law, he was superbly placed

---

17. G. K. A. Bell, *Christianity and World Order* (Harmondsworth: Penguin Books, 1940).

18. Jasper, *Bell,* pp. 248-49.

to broaden Bell's ideas and make them into something more convincing and vigorous. Not for the first time, Bell, who was not viewed with utter seriousness by his British peers, found himself admired by a continental thinker of genuine stature. Leibholz helped Bell to conquer at least some of the superficiality that so often defines the narrow perspectives of the Englishman who looks abroad. When, like so many around him, Bell was tempted to think German militarism the consequence of Prussianism, Leibholz could expose the fallacy so comprehensively that Bell would never return to it. But this was no merely cerebral correspondence. It was an extension of the world of resistance that the remainder of the Bonhoeffer family continued to inhabit, now more dangerously than ever. Any brief scrap of information was at once passed between Chichester and Oxford.[19]

Meanwhile, in wartime it was Bell's relationship with the exiled German Jewish artist Hans Feibusch that became by far the most eloquent example of his great vision of the church and the arts. Feibusch had come to Britain as early as 1934, and from there had watched his own works paraded and traduced in the 1937 *Entartete Kunst* exhibition in Germany. For a time he scraped a living designing book jackets and posters; but, somewhere in the midst of all this, he was moving toward Christianity and toward the Bishop of Chichester, too. In 1939 he had offered to paint a mural in a church as a thanksgiving for his own deliverance from tyranny. It was Bell who found for him the church of St. Wilfrid in Brighton. The two met subsequently, on New Year's Day in 1940. The commission marked the beginning of a momentous collaboration. The bishop managed to work up a succession of commissions; and, for his part, Feibusch was content to mix his own convictions with the requirements of this new company. Bell's secretary, Mary Balmer (later Joice), once found him at work on a new painting and remarked that it was traditional to place a halo around the face of Christ. When she returned she found one very faintly in evidence there.[20] However the English work of Feibusch may now be assessed (it is frankly unfashionable), he was certainly an authentic artist of a very high class indeed, and arguably of a kind that his new host country simply

19. Published in German by Eberhard Bethge and Ronald Jasper, eds., *An der Schwelle zum Gespaltenen Europa: Der Briefwechsel zwischen George Bell und Gerhard Leibholz (1939-1951)* (Stuttgart: Kreuz Verlag, 1974). A new edition in the original English is currently being prepared for publication by Gerhard Ringshausen and the author.

20. Recounted to the author by Nicholas Rutter, to whom many thanks. Mary Balmer (Joice) died in 2006.

could not have produced itself.[21] When Feibusch's work was criticized, Bell stood firmly by him.

In seeking a "reassociation" of the artist and the church, Bishop Bell found allies not merely within the church, but also further afield, introducing and integrating men and women who were often divided from each other by their usual habits and obligations. Bell would have understood that this national church existed not simply to maintain a narrow denomination of faith and worship, but to incite and to integrate private conviction and public expression of all kinds, wherever they may be found, within its walls. For Bell, the church needed to learn from the artist, to see again the gift of its gospel and to enhance its own power of proclamation. But he was also in no doubt that such a task had acquired a new force and urgency in this age of rival ideologies. In *Christianity and World Order* he had written:

> The Church . . . ought to be a rallying ground. . . . Indeed, I would say that in times like the present all those who stand for the things that cannot be shaken should give support to one another. Believers in justice and truth, in mercy and love, in art and poetry and music, have this as common ground: that the things they believe in are indestructible. They are not the same things as the Christian religion, and we must not confound them together. But they can be truly regarded as auxiliaries to the Christian religion . . . how great then is the need that those who stand for the indestructible things should live with, work with and worship with the Christian Church![22]

In 1941 it was Bell, again, who encouraged the Bloomsbury artists Duncan Grant and Vanessa Bell to decorate the walls of the parish church of St. Michael and All Angels at Berwick, in east Sussex. The result was a set of paintings in which circling figures achieved something of the effect of the Italian Renaissance, but with twentieth-century clothes on. Here the figures of a soldier, an airman, and a sailor appear; in the opposite corner is the figure of Bishop Bell himself and, beside him, the local vicar. There were a few local protests, but Bell himself turned up to dedicate the pictures in October 1943, looking inordinately cheerful.[23]

---

21. See David Coke, ed., *Hans Feibusch: The Heat of Vision* (London, 1995).
22. Bell, *Christianity and World Order*, pp. 146-47.
23. See the guide produced by the church itself.

Internment and the Refugees

By September 1939 over 80,000 refugees from Germany, Austria, and Czechoslovakia were found to be living precariously as refugees in Britain. Most were Jews, but there were also a significant number of intellectuals and political opponents of the Nazi state. All of these now found themselves labeled as "enemy aliens," to be placed in categories of discernible loyalty to the host country. The system, almost from the first, looked shaky.

With the threat of invasion, government restrictions on refugees now resident in Britain intensified. All were cleared away from the south coast, where an attack was expected. There were fears of a lurking "fifth column"; there were calls for a mass internment of refugees, men and women, no matter in which category of loyalty they had found themselves. To this demand an uncertain government conceded, setting to work and putting some 25,000 in patrolled areas, camps certainly, but of a sort. Most were ordinary houses that had been hastily emptied and fenced off with barbed wire. In such a manner did as many as 10,000 refugees spend a perplexing year on the Isle of Man, living in requisitioned hotels and long terraces of boarding houses overlooking the sea and overlooking each other. Bell saw most of the thirty-three pastors he had guaranteed only a year before, and some of their wives, duly apprehended. One pastor with whom Bell evidently did not much bother was Fritz Wehrhan, who had been a chaplain to the German embassy and served two Lutheran parishes in the capital. The internment of the others he deplored. At Chichester the correspondence files swelled with letters of sympathy and support, testimonials, interventions, and visits to the Home Office.

On 12 June 1940 Bell ventured into the House of Lords and spoke out firmly against all of this. He repudiated altogether the basis of the policy: that internment was demanded by national security and justice. It was a speech that provoked a faintly incredulous reply from Lord Marchwood: "most of your Lordships must have listened to the right reverend Prelate with amazement." Did the bishop realize that they were actually at war?[24] But Bell knew that Archbishop Lang supported him; a letter to the Home Secretary from Lambeth Palace was dispatched directly. By the beginning of August 1940 Bell had visited a number of camps on the Isle of Man and another, Huyton, also in the northwest of the country. On 6 August he was

---

24. See Charmian Brinson, "'Please Tell the Bishop of Chichester': George Bell and the Internment Crisis of 1940," in Chandler, ed., *The Church and Humanity*, p. 82.

back in Parliament to press his case still more firmly. He did appreciate, he observed, the courtesy shown to him by the officials there who were trying to administer, as kindly as they could, a difficult regulation. To them he would send his sympathy and goodwill. But the impression that these places gave was a painful one. A visitor to Huyton was greeted by "a high palisade of barbed wire with a passage, also of barbed wire, guarded by soldiers. . . . Beyond this palisade," he went on, "I saw crowds of men, useful men, able men, distinguished-looking men, walking aimlessly about, with absolutely nothing to do, in a restricted place. These men are shut off from their families, which they feel very keenly. They are shut off from the world." Now Bell counted some of these to be his friends. He knew them to be friends of this country, too, not enemies. The "great majority" were refuges from Nazism. Many of them Hitler would see executed at once if he could; many others he would not even view as human beings at all. The government, Bell insisted, must surely see that "all the difference in the world" stood between "aliens of enemy nationality" — some of whom, but not many, were Nazis — and these refugees. It was a distinction owned by international law.

Moreover, this arbitrary policy did not make practical sense. Bell knew that as many as 150 men and women now found in the Central Promenade camp in Douglas had once been imprisoned in German concentration camps. The writer "Sebastian Haffner," whose work had been commended by the Ministry of Information, was now to be found interned uselessly on the Isle of Man, as was the author of a textbook used by the Air Ministry to instruct classes of British airmen, as well as a number of experts on machine guns and tanks. When the nation confronted an hour of need, what possible point could there be in locking away a great number of "doctors, professors, scientists, inventors, chemists, industrialists, manufacturers, humanists — all wanting to work for Britain, freedom and justice"?[25]

In the bishop many of the interned now saw a patron. The needy letters tumbled in. Archbishop Lang wrote to Bell, "I cannot tell you how grateful I am for all the noble work you are doing. . . . I should feel that the Church had been wanting in an obvious duty if you had not been able with your exceptional knowledge and your indefatigable zeal to take it up."[26] In September, when the invasion scare was at its height, there were further

---

25. The speech may be found in Bell, *The Church and Humanity*, pp. 38-47.
26. Brinson, " 'Please Tell the Bishop of Chichester,' " p. 85.

visits. Bell collaborated thickly with the Dean of Liverpool, F. W. Dwelly, and struck up a kindly and supportive rapport with a young, hard-pressed, and increasingly isolated Methodist minister of Port Erin, J. Benson Harrison, who now found Rushen internment camp on his doorstep. The governor of Rushen, Dame Joanna Cruickshank, warned Harrison that the Bishop of Chichester was "a highly dangerous man."[27]

It was in this landscape of internment camps and hostels that many now encountered the figure of the Bishop of Chichester for the first time. A young Berlin Jew, Ulrich Simon, had come to England as a refugee and experienced the perplexities and privations of one flung onto foreign shores by persecution abroad. In 1941 Simon found himself living in a community of other disenfranchised souls in the Sussex village of Nuthurst. This was Micklepage, an aggregation of unhappy, wary, disorientated men and women, all of them German, most of them Jewish, now interned by an anxious British government as "friendly enemy aliens." Simon, who would one day become a priest of the Church of England and a distinguished voice of protest against the ravages of his age (and the accommodations with which Christianity met them), recalled how

> Bishop Bell was given a triumphant entry, but his personality had nothing of the charismatic leader. Never has there been a more normal human being. What made him remarkable was the absence of eccentricity, let alone ecstasy. . . . He made peace in the community just by his presence.[28]

By the time of this visit, observers could see that the internment policy was running out of steam. Growing numbers were being released — among them all but one of Bell's pastors. When Bell made a third speech in the House of Lords, on 17 December 1941, it was to press that those locked away in the camps set up in Canada and Australia now be released as quickly as those in British camps. Was this a victory? Of a kind, it certainly was. But did it show that attitudes in the committee rooms and corridors of government had yielded a deeper acknowledgment of Germans who might repudiate Nazism and even seek to labor against it? This was a question to

27. Charmian Brinson, "The Anglican Bishop, the Methodist Minister and the Women of Rushen: George Bell, J. Benson Harrison and Their Work for Women Internees," *Humanitas: The Journal of the George Bell Institute* 7, no. 2 (April 2006): 123.

28. Ulrich Simon, *Sitting in Judgement, 1913-1963: An Interpretation of History* (London: SCM Press, 1978), pp. 85-86.

be tried not only in Britain, but in British policy toward those who lived in Germany itself.

Cardinal Hinsley and the Sword of the Spirit

Colored by the experience of war, the ecumenical mood in Britain also grew more determined. Bell himself favored the prospering of friendships more than the grinding away of systems — and there could be no doubt that the cause of friendship between Protestants and Roman Catholics had been advanced, not least between the Bishop of Chichester and the Archbishop of Westminster, Cardinal Hinsley. Hinsley had been purpose-fully dispatched to London by Pope Pius XI in 1935. At that time he was known hardly at all in Britain: most of his career had been spent teaching ordinands in Rome and traveling across Africa, first as the pope's Apostolic Visitor and then as Apostolic Delegate. But his coming to Westminster had produced a bracing change. For Hinsley brought a quite new mind and approach. The old defensive, and even suspicious, introversion was set aside. Hinsley cared more for people, as he met them in the conditions of everyday life, than he did for vast, redundant campaigns in cathedral-building. He also knew how to value and cultivate the gifts of the laity. He was the first Archbishop of Westminster to meet often, and work closely, with the Archbishop of Canterbury, even exploring now and then possibil-ities for joint actions. Indeed, Lang enjoyed Hinsley enough to recommend that he become a member of the Athenaeum Club, and this is where they often met.

Hinsley looked closely at questions of politics, economics, and so-ciety, cared passionately for justice, and was as deeply caught up in the contradictions of his age as any other public-minded moralist. He hated tyranny, be it from the Left or the Right. In this he was sure that he spoke the mind of the Catholic Church across the world. When war came, it found Hinsley a patriot. When France fell, he told the prime minister that they would be better off without it. Churchill prized this. When Hinsley invited Bell to stay with him in October 1941, Bell found it "a wonderful experience of charity, devotion and wisdom," and he observed how "the murder and destruction of war horrified him." Hinsley agreed wholly with Bell that justice arose from natural law and that Christianity was the foundation of civilization. He believed urgently in the cooperation of Christians in a world of conflict and tyranny. "It was clear," Bell found, ". . . that the Cardinal had a strong belief in personal relationships, and in the coming together, as friends, of like-minded men and women who, whatever their differences, were animated by the same Spirit. When I left Hare Street the next morning I felt a richer man, richer spiritually as well as richer in wisdom."[29]

Bell took a ready part in the innovations of the "Sword of the Spirit" movement, by which Protestants and Catholics began the task of thinking and working together in pursuit of religious freedom. This burst of creative confidence was powerfully felt across the churches. Undeterred by a heavy bombing raid over Westminster, a great meeting took place over two days at the Stoll Theatre in London in May 1942, a first session devoted to the discussion of "A Christian International Order," chaired by Cardinal Hinsley, and a second to "A Christian Order for Britain," chaired by Archbishop Lang. Bell was immersed in this. His speeches of this period show that he was drawing ideas and inspiration as freely from the Vatican as he was from anywhere else. At the close of the Stoll Theatre gathering, Bell simply turned to Hinsley and asked if he would be prepared to lead them all in saying the Lord's Prayer. That it actually happened marked a quiet revolution, but an authentic one in ecumenical relations. Suddenly, almost anything appeared possible.

Hinsley, Lang, and Bell had agreed that there must be regular consultation and collaboration from now onward, "a plan of action which will win the peace when the din of battle is ended."[30] There was a brief flourish of committees, and Bell was seen to be the main architect of a Joint Statement on 28 May 1942. But the glorious moment was already slipping into the equivocations and distinctions of division. Hinsley did what he could from his house in Hare Street, but his room for maneuver was, in truth, not very great. Meanwhile, Lambeth Palace had been bombed; when Bell visited Archbishop Lang there late in July he found him in dire straits, sleeping in the cellar and eating where he could, often at his club. Suddenly he looked elderly, and vulnerable. The Sword of the Spirit was, he remarked, effectively a Roman Catholic enterprise; the initiative lay there and there it could only remain. The movement certainly did mark an advance, but it also acknowledged that nothing more than a solemn kind of parallelism in the activities of the different traditions could, for now, be manifested.

On 26 October 1941 Bell preached on "The Basis of Christian Co-operation" at Cambridge. "There is," he affirmed, "an age-long conflict,

---

29. George Bell, tribute, in *Blackfriars* 24, no. 278 (May 1943): 165-68.
30. Jasper, *Bell*, p. 250.

as all of us know, between evil and good. It is always raging, and its bat-
tleground is found in every nation and in every human heart. But there
are moments in history when this conflict assumes a special intensity, and
the Forces of Darkness hurl themselves with a more deadly vehemence
than ever against the Forces of Light. It is in just such a moment that we
are called to live to-day." The advent of the totalitarian state had made the
conflict of ages still "more manifestly one between Christianity and anti-
Christ. Nowhere has the nature of this conflict been more acutely realised
than in Germany itself." It was as vital that Christians work together now
as it was for the Allied powers to do so. The factor of faith was vital; the fall
of France had shown that it was the difference between victory and defeat.
The churches were weakened by their divisions, but they must unite on the
ground of the great principles that they shared. It was "love, not doctrine,
nor order," which bound Christians to one another. How, then, should
they proceed together?

> First, the collaboration should be not just an occasional demonstra-
> tion, but a reality everywhere. It is people who collaborate, and people
> in a particular place. Therefore, let us begin wherever people of a co-
> operative spirit are to be found; and not spend our effort on organisa-
> tion at the centre. . . . Far more important is the encouragement and
> extension of local Christian fellowship, local united meetings, local
> united councils and united study, and the coming together in faith,
> hope and charity, of Christians of the different Churches, in towns
> and villages, as friends.

Such a movement, Bell insisted, "should be predominantly lay. It
is in the civil order, and in the actualities of daily life, that the Christian's
decisions are made." Moreover, "Faith is expressed in part through prayer.
All can say 'Our Father' together; and, where prayer in common is not
possible, all may pray, as individuals, for one another; and so everywhere
praying, ardent souls may bind together our torn and struggling humanity
with invisible, but effective, chains of love."[31]

For those who looked for ecumenism in doctrine and structure, this
was perhaps something of a disappointment, even an evasion. For those
who found the essentials of ecumenism in other things, it was fundamental
— and within the power that they held in their own hands, here and now.

31. Bell, *The Church and Humanity*, pp. 219-31.

CHAPTER EIGHT

Resistance in Germany and the Politics of War, 1942-1945

War brought austerities. Bell lost his chauffeur to the Royal Air Force and had to ask Henrietta to drive him to places untouched by the railway. Most of the domestic staff disappeared. Bell had no idea how to wash up and put away: he did it only once and it proved almost impossible to locate anything afterwards. Life at the palace in 1942 was, Mary Joice observed, "spartan."[1] Meals and afternoon tea were regular fixtures in the day, but the bishop was evidently indifferent to what he ate. After worship in the chapel and a breakfast combined with the opening of letters, he worked through the morning. After lunch and, if Henrietta managed to persuade him to it, a brief walk around the garden, he returned to his study and often was not seen again until midnight, or later. At some point the Bells took up residence in Brighton, which was a far more convenient location from which to lead the diocese, much of which found Chichester distant.

The German People and the Nazi State

In September 1939 it was widely held in Britain that this was Hitler's war and not freely that of the German people. Of them Archbishop Lang had said in the House of Lords, "We believe that many, perhaps most of them, are as opposed to the war as we are, but they cannot speak their minds. . . . Our feelings towards them, surely, are rather of sympathy than of en-

---

1. Mary Joice, "George Bell at Work," in *Bell of Chichester, 1883-1958: A Prophetic Bishop,* ed. Paul Foster (University of Chichester, Otter Memorial Papers No. 17), p. 33.

mity."[2] Perhaps the German people might win the war for them? The Royal Air Force bombed them with leaflets. Yet there was no revolution in Germany, and the German people appeared to do all they could to win Hitler's war for him.

Already in November 1939 Archbishop Lang had observed with friends that public opinion against the German people at large was rising. Once the borders of Europe had closed, little was heard of churches in Germany, only snippets or snatches yielded by intermediaries through neutral countries. Virtually no mention of them throughout the whole war occurs in the reports of the Archbishop of Canterbury's Council on Foreign Relations. What did come to the attention of British church leaders brought no encouragement. When Bishop Marahrens of Hanover was reported as saying, "Our German people is fighting for the country of our fathers in order that German blood may return to German blood," this went straight off to Lambeth Palace and provoked utter incomprehension.[3] When the Norwegian Bishop Berggrav, casting about for peace, had visited London on 29 January 1940, and Archbishop Lang had asked him what were the attitudes of "ordinary decent Germans" toward Hitler, Berggrav was not reassuring.[4] On 4 March 1940 Bell had convened a modest meeting of allies under the auspices of Lionel Curtis, the *eminence grise* of the new Royal Institute of International Affairs and friend of the young German lawyer, Helmuth James von Moltke, at Chatham House. Try as they might, none of them could discern any way of reaching church people in Germany. Even if messages got through they would only be dismissed as propaganda sent from an enemy power. When it was heard that Martin Niemöller had offered his services as a former U-Boat captain to the state that had imprisoned him, the public mind was still more bitterly disillusioned.

When France had fallen, this mood intensified and grew bitter. Public hostility against Germany soon found its prophet in a retired diplomat, Lord Vansittart. A series of lectures first broadcast over the BBC Overseas Programme was published as a book, bearing the admonitory title *Black Record*. First published in January 1941, it had already been reprinted six times by the end of February. Vansittart asserted that Nazism, and the war that it had brought, was no accident in German history. It was an ex-

2. *Hansard*, Debates of the House of Lords, fifth series, vol. 114, col. 921 (1 September 1939).

3. Bell to Alan C. Don, 5 October 1939, Bell Papers, vol. 83, fol. 188.

4. "Germany in Time of War," memorandum by Archbishop Lang, Lang Papers, 29 January 1940, vol. 84, fols. 152-54.

pression of German character as history itself had revealed it. Tacitus had observed it. Charlemagne had fought a new war every year; Frederick Barbarossa had fought one war for thirty years; Frederick the Great was always fighting somebody. The three wars of Bismarck were but a preparation for the Great War of the Kaiser in 1914; the defeat of 1918 had simply been a temporary reverse and 1939 a taking up of the thread. Prussianism begat militarism; militarism begat Nazism. Hitler was "the natural and continuous product of a breed which from the dawn of history has been predatory and bellicose." Not every German was like this, but good Germans were usually found to be too few and far between — and they never turned up when they were needed: "The German is often a moral creature; the Germans never; and it is the Germans who count." They were not beyond redemption, but it could only be wrought by "the most thorough spiritual cure in history."[5]

Bell saw that this was dangerous to almost everything that he believed in. Now he was often to be seen in the House of Lords, and frequently to be heard there, too. No longer would a letter to the *Times* suffice, or a motion in Convocation. Parliament became a crucial arena for him. Here, too, he repeatedly crossed swords with Vansittart, who continued to press that National Socialism was the expression of the German character and that any distinction between the Nazis and the Germans was simple foolishness. Vansittart carried many with him, and the Bishop of Chichester did not always appear to prevail. After he chaired a difficult meeting in a troubled parish, a woman shouted at him, "Get back to Germany where you belong!"[6] But soon all of this was to receive a sudden jolt into a new and far more urgent reality.

"To Sigtuna . . ."

The legacies of the Stockholm conference of 1925 were many and varied: a rich stock of vivid ideals but, far more than this, a great, inhabited realm where even a brief, unobtrusive conversation, almost lost to the crowded memory, might years later suddenly flare into unexpected life. It was as

5. Sir Robert Vansittart, *Black Record: Germans Past and Present* (London: Hamish Hamilton, 1941), various references, chapters 1-7.

6. To which Bell responded, "I will not be interrupted." Remembered by Bernard Vick in 1998, in Foster, ed., *Bell of Chichester, 1883-1958*, p. 72. The remembrance offers no date.

long ago as 1929 that Bell had met the young German pastor Hans Schön-feld, then busily at work at the International Christian Social Institute in Geneva. With the coming of war Schönfeld and his family had stayed in neutral Switzerland, although visits to Germany continued, now and then, in no very safe conditions. In wartime, as in peacetime, Schönfeld had sought somehow to maintain connections not only between Confessing pastors and the international church, but also with others who had not committed their loyalties so firmly to Niemöller and his allies. This had brought him into a number of relationships that did not quite satisfy those who saw issues of justice in clear, partisan terms. In particular, Schönfeld was made dubious by his long association with his paymaster, Theodor Heckel, at the foreign department of the state church. To be sure, Schön-feld's position had been quite different from that occupied by Dietrich Bonhoeffer, with whom Bell had, almost at once, found such a marvel-ous intimacy. But now the two German pastors and the English bishop were about to converge dramatically. In May 1942 the three men faced each other in two momentous encounters in a little ecumenical institute in neutral Sweden.

For this great moment the scholar inherits three principal sources: the intricate personal journal that Bell kept, day by day, of the visit, along with the assorted papers that he brought home in his case; an article that he subsequently published in the *Contemporary Review* just after the war, in October 1945; and a public lecture that he gave in Göttingen many years later, in 1957. The first show a man laboring to bring to something unex-pected and extraordinary a steady sense of responsible action; the second two fuse a recollection of details, which may be more or less exact, with interpretations that had begun to settle within a scheme of justification, a need still to convince the ambivalent. As the last of the three, the Göttin-gen lecture might appear the weakest in its claims, and yet it is difficult to discern the workings of Bell's memory and the extent to which preparation for an important occasion concentrated the mind in a new intensity. By then he had also gained new material.

It was the British government that brought Bell to Sweden in May 1942. Previously constrained, links between Britain and Sweden had re-laxed by a fraction. The Ministry of Information perceived that contacts between those responsible for the cultural institutions of the two countries might prove beneficial. In consequence, the eager young director of the National Gallery in London, Sir Kenneth Clark, soon flew to Stockholm for conversations with his Swedish equivalents. Why not foster an ecumenical venture, too? Bell, as Jasper writes, was the "obvious" candidate.[7] On 13 May he took off from Hendon for the Swedish capital, where he bumped into his old friend, T. S. Eliot, coming the other way. This was no brief tour: across three weeks one meeting followed another. The British Minister there, Victor Mallet, was struck that his new guest could preach to a congregation of over a thousand on a bank holiday while turning up as a guest of honor at a Rotary Club luncheon to be received by "the Crown Prince, the Commander-in-Chief of the Air Force, and some of the leading business men in the capital."[8] Such activities were exactly what had been called for by the sponsoring powers. As Bell would later remark, nothing here suggested any great drama to come. But suddenly, on the night of 26 May, the script was utterly cast aside in a room in the Student Movement House in Stockholm. Here, to his amazement (it was his own word), Bell found Hans Schönfeld, fresh from Geneva, urgent, agitated, "clearly suffering under great strain."[9] Schönfeld was there on no ecumenical tour of duty. He had come only to see Bell; he had come because he had to tell him that there existed inside Germany a movement of Christians, officers, trade unionists, working men, and civil servants dedicated to opposing the Hitler state: "There was, he said, a growing movement of opposition to Hitler, and men were on the look out for a chance to attack him." In these circles there were ambitions, too — not only for a just peace but for a new, federal Europe. But would the Allied powers make peace with a Germany that was no longer governed by Hitler? Bell must have been rooted to the spot by this. The two men agreed to meet again. In the meantime, Bell reported what he had heard to Mallet, whose response was alert, even sympathetic, but circumspect.[10]

On 29 May Bell and Schönfeld met again, and now Bell learned that the churches of Germany, Evangelical and Catholic, showed firm evidence of opposition to the Nazi state. Schönfeld talked of a General Superintendent Blau in Posen, of Bishop Wurm, and of Hanns Lilje. Furthermore, there was "a block of Christians belonging to both confessions who were speaking strongly of three human rights — the right of freedom, the right of the rule of law, and the right to live a Christian life." This movement of

7. R. C. D. Jasper, *George Bell: Bishop of Chichester* (London: Oxford University Press, 1967), p. 266.

8. Jasper, *Bell,* p. 267.

9. Here I have drawn from Bell's Göttingen lecture. See G. K. A. Bell, "The Church and the Resistance Movement," *The Bridge,* November 1957, pp. 3-17, here p. 5.

10. Bell, "The Church and the Resistance Movement," pp. 5-6.

opposition was led by ideals that closely resembled Bell's own: "All those opposed to Hitler . . . were agreed about the necessity of a Christian basis of life and government, and very many were looking to the Church leaders for help and encouragement."

Bell wanted this set down in writing. He even boldly asked for names — and he got them: men formerly of the German general staff, Colonel General Beck and Colonel General Hammerstein; the once-mayor of Leipzig, Carl Goerdeler; the trade unionists Wilhelm Leuschner and Jacob Kaiser. Schönfeld, Bell remembered later, "emphasized the importance of Beck and Goerdeler. A rising led by them should be taken very seriously."[11] Fearful that none of this would be viewed seriously, Bell asked his visitor to set all of it down in writing. Schönfeld undertook to do so. This second meeting, Bell later recalled, lasted about an hour.

Bell must surely have sensed that his travel journal had now acquired something far greater than an ordinary significance. This visit had become, deeply, a matter of history. The page for Sunday, 31 May, begins with two words: "To Sigtuna." For in Sigtuna lay another church foundation, the Nordic Ecumenical Institute, run by Harry Johansson. There was lunch; there was tea; there was suddenly another guest: for the first time since the tumultuous spring of 1939 Bell, "astonished" a second time, found Dietrich Bonhoeffer standing before him. The historian who is almost too familiar with the story must surely pause to acknowledge the emotional impact of this encounter.

The conversation flowed, first with the hosts present but then in private. Bonhoeffer knew nothing whatever about Schönfeld's visit, as Schönfeld knew nothing at all about the mission of Bonhoeffer.[12] When Schönfeld again appeared, something very like a summit conference began, with the ecumenical Swedes joining in, too. Schönfeld began to imagine how the powers might come to terms and end this war. He saw that Germany's position, militarily and territorially, was strong. But then Bonhoeffer interrupted. For him such calculations were not enough to satisfy a Christian conscience: "we should not be worthy of such a solution. Our action must be such as the world will understand as an act of repentance." Bell vigorously endorsed this and held on to it. Moreover, Bonhoeffer was sure that

11. Bell, "The Church and the Resistance Movement," p. 8.
12. For a close examination of this it is still important to consult Eberhard Bethge, *Dietrich Bonhoeffer: Theologian, Christian, Contemporary* (London: William Collins, 1970), pp. 662-64.

nothing short of the occupation of Berlin would do. Schönfeld accepted this, but hoped that the Allies would come "not as conquerors but to assist the German army against reactionary or hostile forces."[13]

As Schönfeld and Bonhoeffer had come as emissaries, it was with the intention of turning Bell into one, too. This news must be taken to the British government. "The resistance movement's aim, I was told again, was the elimination of Hitler, and the setting up of a new *bona fide* German Government which renounced aggression, and was based on principles utterly opposed to National Socialism."[14] But it must be actively encouraged if it was to gain ground. Above all, if it appeared that the Allies would simply treat such a government in quite the same way as it would a Nazi state, for what object could such a movement be said to contend? The resisters must be credible in the eyes of doubters if they were to stand the least chance of success. The two pastors would need to know the view of the government in London. If there were to be further discussions they could think of a further German, Adam von Trott, who might be well suited to take it all on. Trott, they knew, was a friend of the son of the British politician Sir Stafford Cripps.

Bell could see that this would be to ask a great deal of politicians in London. He anticipated, at best, "reserve" and saw "the probability of the Foreign Office taking the view that the whole situation was too uncertain to justify any action on its part." But still they must try, and in Sweden and Switzerland their ecumenical connections could provide the channels they needed. Only a day later Bell was told that such a use of Sigtuna must be ruled out as "inconsistent with Sweden's political neutrality."[15] Very well, they were left with Geneva and the redoubtable Willem Visser 't Hooft.

On 1 June the three men met once more. Letters to family and friends were passed on, in particular for Gerhard and Sabine Leibholz in Oxford. It was Schönfeld who gave to Bell a "short message of greetings" from another compatriot, Helmuth James von Moltke, to Lionel Curtis. By the end of the day Bell had a thorough statement from Schönfeld and a letter of gratitude, too: "I cannot express what this fellowship you have shown to us means for us and our fellow Christians who were with us in their thoughts and prayers."[16] From Bonhoeffer there was a further letter: "It still seems

---

13. Bell, "The Church and the Resistance Movement," p. 8.
14. Bell, "The Church and the Resistance Movement," p. 9.
15. Bell, "The Church and the Resistance Movement," p. 9.
16. Schönfeld to Bell, n.d., Bell Papers, vol. 42, fol. 250.

to me like a dream to have seen you, to have spoken to you, to have heard your voice. . . . The impressions of these days were so overwhelming that I cannot express them in words."[17]

Bell was to fly back to Britain on 2 June, but flights between the two countries were grounded by stormy weather. Another week had passed before, eventually, he was able to set off home, no doubt clutching his case firmly in his hands.

The Response of Whitehall

Bell now found himself pitched into the labyrinthine world of international politics, and politics of the highest and most dangerous kind. This visit to Sweden was a crucial moment in his own history, a point around which so much in his life, work, and self-understanding would come to revolve. In so many ways it would define him.

On his return to Britain he set about lobbying the government to offer some recognition, and some encouragement, to those Germans who sought the removal of the Hitler regime and the achievement of peace in Europe. A visit to Whitehall took place on 18 June. He was asked to write fully to the Foreign Secretary, Anthony Eden; this letter went off at once. Eden was surprised to receive such material from such a source. In private, he spoke of the Bishop of Chichester sarcastically and suspected him of pacifism. Bell might well have suspected already that such seed was not being cast on promising soil. What did the gurus of the Foreign Office make of this? The dominant character of their notes was skeptical, but they agreed that Eden should see Bell, as long as he observed "the great importance of secrecy in matters of this kind." Alexander Cadogan, their supreme voice, asked, "What would be interesting would be to see what any group of this kind can *do.*" He repeated that total defeat and disarmament was "probably the only condition" of negotiations. In short, the political culture that would soon formulate a policy of "unconditional surrender" was to these Whitehall minds already a reality.[18]

On 30 June Eden saw Bell for the first time. Bell handed to him

---

17. Bonhoeffer to Bell, 1 June 1942, Bell Papers, vol. 42, fol. 72.

18. Foreign Office Protocol, 18-23 June 1942, to be found in Jorgen Glenthoj, Ulrich Klabitz, and Wolf Krötke, eds., *Dietrich Bonhoeffer Werke*, vol. 16: *Konspiration und Haft, 1940-1945* (Gütersloh: Christian Kaiser Verlag, 1996), pp. 321-23.

Schönfeld's statement. The questions were firmly stated. Could the Allies offer both private and public assurance that they would negotiate a settlement with a new German state that renounced aggression, that governed by law and social justice, that sought to rule by Christian principles, that undertook to work with other nations in a new European Federation, that would "restitute" and restore the Jewish populations of Europe and seek with other governments a "comprehensive solution" of the "problem," and that would seek to cooperate with Russia? Eden appeared to Bell "much interested." But he suspected this enterprise. Were these two German pastors being used, even without their knowledge, by other, more sinister forces? There had been "peace-feelers" before, in Turkey and in Madrid. He also saw that the British government must not even begin to venture into negotiations with the enemy without declaring itself openly to the Soviet and American governments. Bell pressed that his contacts would need a reply. Eden promised to think about it.

In truth, Eden was frankly doubtful. He saw the higher political plane clearly and knew that it must not be compromised. He was also surrounded by men in whom a weary skepticism blended with a waspish cynicism, for the mandarins of the Foreign Office felt that they had heard rumblings about such things before — and grumbled that nothing had ever come of them. For them this was simply another round in the "peace-feelers game." Bell had now offered them firm evidence, not least a number of recognizable names. It made no difference. Some of these names had been known before. What had they ever done? There was too little here to distract experienced men of hard policy. One remarked acidly, "The Bishop of Chichester and his like have learnt nothing from two German wars and are now busily, in all innocence, trying to lay the foundations of a third."[19]

Bell did not lie low while the discussions took place in the offices and corridors of the Foreign Office. He saw Sir Stafford Cripps, who spoke warmly of Adam von Trott and recalled a memorandum from Trott that he had received in May from Visser 't Hooft. Cripps was struck by this new material from Schönfeld and offered to take it up with Eden himself. Of this conversation, and others like it, the men in Whitehall heard. Far from improving Bell's prospects, the impression of him quietly lobbying in the background counted against him. The confidential remarks made by the Foreign Office men became quietly, dangerously, sarcastic. On 17 July Eden

---

19. Foreign Office Protocol, 1 July–2 August 1942, *Dietrich Bonhoeffer Werke*, vol. 16, pp. 330-33.

sent Bell his verdict on the whole matter: "without casting any reflection on the *bona fides* of your informants, I am satisfied that it would not be in the national interest for any reply whatever to be sent to them. I realise that this decision may cause you some disappointment, but in view of the delicacy of the issues involved I feel that I must ask you to accept it, and I am sure that you will understand."[20]

Bell did not understand, and he did not acquiesce. He wrote again. He bowed to the decision, as he must: "But I do greatly hope that it may be possible for you in the near future to make it plain in an emphatic and public way that the British government (and the Allies) have no desire to enslave a Germany which has rid itself of Hitler and Himmler and their accomplices." Recalling a speech of Churchill in May 1940, he pressed, "If there are men in Germany also ready to wage war against the monstrous tyranny of the Nazis from within, is it right to discourage or ignore them? Can we afford to reject their aid in achieving our end?"[21]

Eden did not want to perpetuate this. At least a fraction of him must have felt that he was too busy with the conduct of the war to argue with a bishop who was hardly known to him, an idealist no doubt, but an amateur who was caught almost accidentally in very deep waters indeed. One of the mandarins at the Foreign Office, Geoffrey Harrison, had heard that the Bishop of Chichester was now "talking very freely" about his Sigtuna meeting. In this he was behaving like another church leader, the Dutch Visser 't Hooft, who had given "gratuitous and widespread advertisement in this country to this alleged anti-Nazi organisation." It was now the "considered view of the Foreign Office" that it was "inconceivable" that the German secret service could allow all these secret emissaries to travel about without knowing what they were up to: "If they are allowed to go abroad it is because the German authorities are satisfied that they can do no harm to Germany but may be able to do harm to us." Harrison wanted to see people like the bishop reined in. The Foreign Office should be consulted before the Passport Control Department allowed either the Bishop of Chichester out of the country or Visser 't Hooft in.[22]

Eden dutifully replied to Bell that in a speech that May he had already declared that only when a German resistance had "taken active steps" to

20. Eden to Bell, 17 July 1942, Bell Papers, vol. 42, fol. 272.
21. Bell to Eden, 25 July 1942, Bell Papers, vol. 42, fol. 275.
22. Minute by G. W. Harrison, "Germany: Bishop of Chichester," 21 July 1942, *Dietrich Bonhoeffer Werke*, vol. 16, pp. 333-35.

overthrow the regime would anyone actually believe in them. Beyond this he did not think it wise to advance. He acknowledged that resistance must be a dangerous business, but movements of resistance against Nazism could actually be seen at work across occupied Europe. Where were they matched in Germany itself? "We do not intend to deny to Germany a place in the future Europe, but . . . the longer the German people tolerate the Nazi regime the greater becomes their responsibility for the crimes which that regime is committing in their name."[23]

Eden must have thought this sufficient. It was not. Bell wrote again. He saw clearly that the Germans must "do their part." But the occupied nations had been promised deliverance and Germany had "not exactly been promised that." His contacts were fully aware of "the grave character of the responsibility" borne by the German people for what was happening. But the hopes and principles set down in his documents "ought to be powerful factors in making the opposition declare itself more and more plainly."[24] There was now little to be lost. Bell visited the American ambassador, J. G. Winant: "I again emphasized the reality and significance of the German Opposition." Winant he found friendly. He undertook to pass this on to the State Department in Washington.[25] But the rest was silence.

It was finally on 23 July that Bell dispatched a telegram to Visser 't Hooft in Geneva: "Interest undoubted, but deeply regret no reply possible."[26]

One Vital Month: March 1943

Whatever room for maneuver had existed for men like Bell or Bonhoeffer in the summer of 1942 was soon severely eroded by the high politics of the great powers. In January 1943 the Casablanca conference pronounced the Allies' demand for the unconditional surrender of Germany. The military historian Basil Liddell Hart, with whom Bell corresponded upon questions of obliteration bombing, deplored this as "the most stupid and untimely step that could have been taken."[27] Bell himself did not doubt that Nazi propaganda would exploit such a declaration to the full, and in this he was

23. Eden to Bell, 4 August 1942, Bell Papers, vol. 42, fol. 278.
24. Bell to Eden, 17 August 1942, Bell Papers, vol. 42, fol. 279.
25. Bell to Winant, 1 August 1942, Bell Papers, vol. 42, fol. 292.
26. Bell to Visser 't Hooft, 23 July 1942, Bell Papers, vol. 42, fol. 273.
27. Liddell Hart to Bell, 12 February 1943, Bell Papers, vol. 38, fol. 87.

right. But two statements by Stalin, in which their eastern ally affirmed Russia's intention to destroy not Germany but only Nazism, now yielded the foundation for a new intervention. Bell would seek to draw some strain of encouragement for the resisting Germans, not from confidential meetings and private correspondence, but by exploiting his public position and its privileges and by moving for a public statement in the House of Lords. If the British government now looked to its alliance with the Soviet Union to define its attitude to this "other" Germany, then he would do the same.

Bell now employed Stalin's own words as a peg on which to hang a new parliamentary motion, "Germany and the Hitlerite State." His speech was nothing if not thoroughly prepared. He was assisted by another friend of Adam von Trott, Wilfrid Israel, who met him at the Grosvenor Hotel and the Athenaeum, and W. W. Schutz of the German department of the Ministry of Information. Bell also took the step of writing to other peers — Cecil, Noel-Buxton, and Addison — to ask for their support in the debate. Meanwhile, the government fidgeted and did its best to throw obstacles in his path. The motion, as Eberhard Bethge has observed, was set down for one date, then another, and then another. All of this shows the Bishop of Chichester more and more to be a figure at work in a distinct subculture of committed friends and allies, some of them refugees, some of them scholars, some of them church people — a minority struggling for some kind of purchase on the attentions and mechanisms of the state. But it was a state that had dug a moat around itself and pulled up its drawbridge.

The year 1942 ended. Now the prevarications of the Foreign Office at last fell silent. On 10 March 1943 Bell finally had his day in the House of Lords. "My question," he began, "is very simple: Do His Majesty's Government make the same distinction as Premier Stalin makes between the Hitler State and the German people in their prosecution of the war and their view of our war aims?" "The present war," he declared, "is not a war of nation against nation. It is a revolutionary war, it is a war of faiths in which the nations themselves are divided." To be sure, he did not acquit "the Germans as a whole of some guilt of accepting the Nazi régime," but he did not hold them especially responsible for its arrival. Their nation had fallen into the hands of criminals. Nazism had not arisen from the German people; it had been imposed upon them by "certain powerful anti-democratic forces, partly in military and partly in industrial circles, who betrayed their own country for their selfish ends." Certainly it was nothing like the logical outcome of their history: What if anything before even remotely resembled it? "It is a simple matter of fact that Germany was the first country in Europe to be occupied by the Nazis." And Germans had resisted them. Vast numbers, said Bell, had refused to bow the knee to Baal. Upon the outbreak of war there had been mass arrests, and hundreds of thousands carried off to concentration camps. Early that year the *Times* had reported the arrests of more thousands during the previous three months. Hundreds since had been executed. This unhappy Germany was beyond doubt a fact, and one that the Nazis themselves allowed for: Hitler so feared an uprising at home that he maintained almost a million S.A. and S.S. soldiers there.

The concentration camps had not claimed all the dissenters. An opposition, "very subtle and determined," remained at large, listening to the wireless, passing on rumors and complaints, making illegal prints, holding secret meetings, sabotaging munitions and industrial factories. It was all recorded by the Nazis themselves, whose newspapers published "numberless executions week by week." If they asked for more from the German people they should remember that "spies and assassins are everywhere with their machine guns and revolvers." But "most effective and world resounding" had been the resistance of the Christian churches. Before the war, claimed Bell, "they were not afraid to denounce the Nazi Government, not simply for interference with religious exercises, but for their denial of freedom, for their rejection of the rights of man, of the individual and the family, for their idolatry of race and for their contempt of the law." This opposition of the churches, Protestant and Roman Catholic, remained the "most conspicuous and steadfast" now. It arose in the sermons of Bishops Wurm and Bornewasser, of Cardinal Faulhaber and Bishop von Preysing, in the Fulda Declaration, and especially in the words of Bishop von Galen that had been carried across Germany by a fleet of motor dispatch riders.

Nazi propaganda preached that however real the distinction between Nazi and German may be, the Allied governments did not themselves subscribe to it, instead judging all Germans enemies alike. In such circumstances Germans must rally behind Hitler, who posed as the only barrier between them all and disaster. Bell affirmed that such cynical manipulation must be contradicted: acquiescent silence could only play into its hands. They must leave the German people in no doubt that a renunciation of Nazism — its conquests and ambitions, its anti-Jewish laws and crimes, and all it stood for — would ensure not their destruction, but their return to a "proper place in the family of nations": "Remove Hitler and you will be free." The resistance of the dissenting Germans should not be exaggerated, but "no wise statesman" would disregard it: "They have a great faith in the possibility, once given help from outside, of very vigorous action."[28]

No later historian could find this speech invulnerable to criticism. Drawing together a variety of stray episodes, only glimpsed from a great distance, and making of them a robust foundation for argument was no easy task. But this was not merely a description of the state of Germany offered for its own sake; it served a purpose. Bell perceived how the resistance needed encouragement. He saw clearly that Britain must provide it. But he still had to reckon with his old adversary Vansittart, who was there in the House of Lords to cross him. Of resistant Germans Vansittart declared, "I have spent a time looking for them with a microscope, from the practical point of view, and I have invariably found a full stop. . . . The Germans have fought us like one man and seventy million tigers." He had listened for voices of protest against Nazi inhumanities, and heard none: "Hardly a German soul bothers — not even the women." The truth, he concluded, was that no line could be drawn between Germany and the Hitlerite state, for they were one and the same: "There is really no such place as Hitlerite Germany. Hitlerite Germany be hanged!"[29]

Bell had looked to allies in the House of Lords. Archbishop Temple had intended to speak in support of this motion. But now, occupied elsewhere late into the afternoon, Temple received warning that the House was "rather restive" after his contribution to an earlier debate on an important contribution to the history of British social welfare, the Beveridge Report, for which he had arrived only in time for his speech and departed almost at once after it. A second brief appearance, he judged, might do more harm than good. But the old relationship with Temple's predecessor, Archbishop Lang, was still warm. Now ennobled as Lang of Lambeth, he at once rose to repudiate Vansittart, almost tripping over another peer, Lord Ponsonby, who was eager to do the same. Vansittart, Lang remarked with gentle condescension, had begun well, but soon transgressed to his old ways: "He said he was astonished at his own moderation. He must be alone in that astonishment." Yet Lang was unsure that Bell's bold and thorough distinction between German and Nazi could be so absolute. It could not be denied that, for the last century "since Germany's Prussianization," the

---

28. *Hansard,* Debates of the House of Lords, fifth series, vol. 126, cols. 536-45 (10 March 1943). Or see G. K. A. Bell, *The Church and Humanity, 1939-1946* (London: Longmans, Green & Co., 1946), pp. 95-109.

29. Debates of the House of Lords, vol. 126, cols. 549-56.

"overwhelming mass of German opinion" had betrayed "a readiness to be regimented" by a succession of self-assertive and aggressive governments. But, he added, few knew more about the German people than the Bishop of Chichester, and Lang, too, knew of Germans hostile to Nazism. He agreed that they must dispel the notion that was, he thought, prevalent in Germany, that this was a war for national existence in which defeat must mean destruction. He too hoped that the government would endorse the distinction that Stalin himself affirmed, and offer hope to those Germans who were untainted by Nazism and strove against the Hitler regime.[30]

This motion drew from the Lord Chancellor, Viscount Simon, assurances that the government did seek, "in every way," to encourage the German opposition to Nazism; that the hope of the German people lay not in Hitler, but in their abandonment of his "monstrous claims and crimes"; that Germany would have a place in the future Europe. Bell, concluding, stressed these things once again, lest there be any doubt of them. The task he had set himself surely looked to have been accomplished.[31] "My dear George," Lang wrote to him afterwards, ". . . I think your material for argument & your earnestness had a great effect on their decorous Lordships."[32]

Heinrich Fraenkel, whose wireless talks to Germany had so encouraged Bell, was enthusiastic. Now, he said, he had much to broadcast. Schutz had cabled news of the debate to Zurich and Stockholm. Bell himself investigated with the Ministry of Information possibilities of sending a number of copies of the House of Lords debates published in *Hansard* to Sweden. Only the eminent ecumenist, Professor Siegmund-Schultze, exiled in Zurich since the early years of the Hitler regime, was uncertain of its value, remarking that Germans may think the British government intent only upon German disunity. This was acute. Shortly afterward the Royal Air Force dropped thousands of leaflets reporting the debate over Germany itself.[33]

In 1942 Anthony Eden had assumed that if any act of resistance against Nazism were to occur in Germany itself the British government would come to know of it. This was a fallacy. The belligerent powers now existed in quite different, barely connected worlds. Yet in the very month in which Bell made his speech in the House of Lords, two attempts were

30. Debates of the House of Lords, vol. 126, cols. 556-61.
31. Debates of the House of Lords, vol. 126, cols. 573-81.
32. Lang to Bell, 12 March 1943, Bell Papers, vol. 5, fol. 180.
33. For these letters from Fraenkel and Siegmund-Schultze see the Bell Papers, vol. 5, fols. 180-208.

made to assassinate Hitler, first in an airplane over Russia, using explosives dropped in arbitrary fashion by British bombers, and then in Berlin itself.

It was only days later, on 5 April 1943, that Dietrich Bonhoeffer was arrested at his parents' home in Charlottenburg, Berlin. Of this, too, Bell had no inkling.

At Large in a World at War

To look now for the characteristic George Bell of these years is something best done within the covers of one slender book that he published when the war was over: *The Church and Humanity, 1939-1946*. It remains perhaps the single indispensable exposition of the arguments by which Bell still most claims our attention, offering many of the speeches that he made on behalf of refugees; against obliteration bombing; in the cause of those Germans who resisted Hitler; in the name of a Europe wracked by the experience of war, dislocation, and famine. Humanity, Bell insisted, was made in the image of God, and no humanity that disowned God could hope for justice, let alone completeness. Christians had been cast on the defensive by the fierce aggression of new ideologies, and they must resist them. More than this, the crisis of the age called upon the church's power to offer a critical, creative vision of its own faith and works. For the world burns before us and must be saved by men and women of faith who have the courage to stride into the midst of the drama, strive with every sinew to redeem it, and bear the price they must surely pay for this, courageously and faithfully. This is the world of Dietrich Bonhoeffer and of Martin Niemöller, but of countless others, too, whose names will never be known to history. The rightful place of a Christian, and an English Christian too, is to inhabit such a world and such a time, not at a safe distance, but beside them. "The Church," Bell pronounced in March 1943, "has still a special duty to be a watchman for humanity, and to plead the cause of the suffering, whether Jew or Gentile."[34]

It is a vivid world, still. That a Christian bishop could effectively work on behalf of a political conspiracy that would involve the death of the head of a European state remains a striking fact. Bell had now immersed himself not in the peculiarities of the British landscape, within which he looked increasingly solitary, but in that wider realm of European

34. Bell, *The Church and Humanity*, p. 117.

resistance against Nazism, one in which Bishop Berggrav continued to profess the cause of religious freedom, even while enduring house arrest by German occupying forces; in which his fellow ecumenist Visser 't Hooft offered hospitality and encouragement to agents from various resistance movements in Geneva; in which Archbishop Saliege in France and Archbishop de Jong in the Netherlands protested publicly against the deportations of Jews to the death camps of the east; in which Bell's old friend Velimirovic, now bishop of Zica, was subjected first to house arrest and then to a short period in Dachau concentration camp in Germany. In this context ecumenism had acquired a still more urgent force. Moreover, the very character of Christian piety at large was stirring into something altogether more intense, profound, and eloquent. Men and women came to know the meanings of love and hatred as they had never done before; many who once had hardly considered religion now prayed in the face of peril, grief, and death.

What now of the German churches? Earlier, in the summer of 1942, a little conference of British and exiled German theologians had taken place in Cambridge, intent on excavating the Barmen Declaration. A paper was given by a refugee pastor, H. H. Kramm, now adopted by the Congregationalist Mansfield College in Oxford, and another by an English Anglican, the principal of the Queen's College in Birmingham, J. O. C. Cobham. When Bell was asked to write a foreword to these contributions in a series published by *Theology,* he remembered how the declaration had first broken upon them all "like a thunderbolt," even if the British churches had hardly known how to interpret it. He continued:

> I am bound to add, with some sense of humiliation, that we were all looking at the attacks on Christianity in Germany in far too external a way. We were too much like critics in the stalls, watching a play. We were too little alive to the agonizing fact that we ourselves were deeply affected. . . . More than that, not only was our neighbour's wall ablaze, but, in a more subtle and not less dangerous way, our own wall was ablaze too![35]

Bell sought to represent the tumultuous realities of the Continent to those who might otherwise scarcely have known what was going on

---

35. "The Significance of the Barmen Declaration for the Oecumenical Church, with a Foreword by the Bishop of Chichester," *Theology Occasional Papers,* new series, no. 5.

there. It was in Sweden in May 1942 that one of his old ecumenical allies, the bishop of Strängnäss in Sweden, Gustaf Aulén, had passed on to him a selection of wartime numbers of the Norwegian church journal *Kirke og Kultur*. Now, in 1943, this precious trove became the core of a new book, which also comprised a collection of pastoral and public letters issued against the German occupation by the Norwegian Church. This enterprise, soon quite forgotten or overlooked, showed Bell at his most intently collaborative, setting to work with the Church of England's emerging Scandinavian church expert, Herbert Waddams, and a little ensemble of sympathetic British friends and Norwegian exiles who were now to be found in London. "The purpose of this book," wrote Bell, "is to bring English-speaking readers into contact with Bishop Berggrav, now a prisoner of the Nazis in a small forest cabin outside Oslo. He is the life and soul of the struggle of the Norwegian Church against Nazi violence and godlessness." Berggrav was, he added, "one of the greatest contemporary Churchmen, whom I am proud to call my friend." It is not difficult to see why Berggrav should matter so greatly to Bell. In his introduction he was able to write of a man whose qualities were obviously the very things he most prized: a Christian who possessed a true prophetic force; a bishop who was rooted in the historical and contemporary landscape of his own people, in a great vision of the universal church, in the search for peace and righteousness: "He takes his own line, is independent, and is never afraid to speak out if he thinks a thing is right."[36]

The context of this war did not deflect Bell from his commitment to the realm of the arts. Indeed, it deepened. When he had been invited to write a short, richly illustrated book on *The English Church* in 1942, the enterprise had offered him a happy distraction from weighty matters, and an opportunity to produce something attractive in both literary and visual terms.[37] In 1943 a gathering dedicated to "the Church and the Artist" brought Edward Maufe, Martin d'Arcy, Dorothy Sayers, Henry Moore, T. S. Eliot, and Hans Feibusch through the front door of the Bishop's Palace. Even if this did more to signal a new intent to blend religious faith and artistic creation than actually to achieve anything immediate and tangible, the very fact of such a meeting of minds set down a striking mark.

36. G. K. A. Bell and H. M. Waddams, eds., *With God in the Darkness, and Other Papers Illustrating the Norwegian Church Conflict, by Eivind Berggrav* (London: Hodder & Stoughton, 1943), pp. v-vi, 6.

37. G. K. A. Bell, *The English Church* (London: William Collins, 1942).

The Jews of Occupied Europe

Mass deportations of German Jews to eastern Europe had begun in October 1941. In December the systematic killing of Jews in mobile gas chambers began at Chelmno. In Britain some such facts found their way into the *Jewish Chronicle,* but even after the Polish occupation of 1939-1940, the newspapers at large appeared wary of what might be simple "atrocity" propaganda. In 1942 the *Times* contained only sporadic reports of ghettos and deportations, yet in that year camps with permanent gas chambers were built at Belzec, Sobibor, Treblinka, and Majdanek in Poland, and Birkenau, beside the Auschwitz concentration camp, in Upper Silesia. On 3 July 1942, the month in which deportations from the Netherlands and occupied France began, the *Church Times* reported,

> It is asserted that one million Jews, representing one-sixteenth of the entire population of Jewry throughout the world, have been massacred in countries controlled by the Axis since the outbreak of war. Most of the victims have perished in Poland, some by mass execution and others as a result of being herded into hideously overcrowded ghettos.[38]

But this was a stray report, and British newspapers, secular or religious, still said little.

There was one conspicuous public meeting, even so. In October 1942 a public protest took place at the Royal Albert Hall, led by Archbishop Temple, the Moderator of the Free Church Council, and that principled internationalist and advocate of the League of Nations, Viscount Cecil. A new body that Bell actively supported, the Council of Christians and Jews, began to lobby the government for a statement of some kind. Then, in December 1942, the narrative of protest suddenly grew intense. At this time Temple and Bell were in constant touch. It was Temple who took the public lead. On 5 December 1942 the *Times* published a letter in which Bell expressed "our burning indignation at this atrocity, to which the records of barbarous ages scarcely supply a parallel." The government must surely offer sanctuary to all who could escape; those who were guilty must be held to account when the war ended — they must announce it.[39] On 9 December the Archbishop of York, Cyril Foster Garbett, went to the

---

38. *Church Times,* 3 July 1942, p. 371b.
39. The *Times,* 5 December 1942, p. 5c.

House of Lords to deplore "the deliberate and cold-blooded massacre of a nation. It is horrible to think that these things are now happening."[40] On 16 December Temple led a deputation, representing all the churches and this time including a representative of Cardinal Hinsley, through the door of the Foreign Office.

Eden's Under-Secretary of State, Richard Law, began to feel under pressure. To his visitors he appeared sympathetic; to his superiors he insisted that he had given nothing away. On 17 December 1942 the government issued a public declaration in the House of Lords that the Allied governments would pursue justice on behalf of the victims when victory gave them power to do so. Bell did not stand in the foreground here: it was better that Archbishop Temple should claim it. Meanwhile, he was not sure how best to judge the apparent silence of German church leaders, which was increasingly criticized by other church people in Britain, Temple among them. When, in February 1943, the Church of England Committee for Non-Aryan Christians discussed the plight of the European Jews, Bell himself noted to Temple, "the question was asked whether, somehow or other, the conscience of German churchmen in Germany itself could not be aroused on the basis of facts presented to them, of which it is very likely they are ignorant."[41] There was an attempt to dispatch a memorandum to Archbishop Eidem in Sweden; and even though a copy was also sent through the Swedish embassy in London, no reply was made.

Temple had now grown restive at the evident weakness of British policy. On 23 March 1943 he went to the House of Lords to urge that all possible aid be given by the Allied governments to those who could escape this massacre:

> My chief protest is against procrastination of any kind. . . . It took five weeks from December 17 for our Government to approach the United States, and then six weeks for the Government of the United States to reply, and when they did reply they suggested a meeting of representatives of the Governments for preliminary explorations. The Jews are being slaughtered at the rate of tens of thousands a day on many days.

40. *Hansard,* Debates of the House of Lords, fifth series, vol. 125, cols. 486-87 (9 December 1942).

41. See Andrew Chandler, "The Church of England and National Socialist Germany, 1933-1945" (Ph.D. thesis, University of Cambridge, 1991), p. 208.

He concluded, "We at this moment have upon us a tremendous responsibility. We stand at the bar of history, of humanity and of God."[42] When in April 1943 the British and American governments met in Bermuda to explore their response to the crisis, the upshot seemed to their critics indistinct, if not altogether dismal. Those who had looked for a vigorous, urgent policy did not fall silent now. By 3 May the beleaguered Law complained to Eden, "We are subjected to extreme pressure from an alliance of Jewish organisations and Archbishops."[43]

On 28 July it was Bell's turn to take up the cudgels in Parliament. In response to a motion of Lord Davies, he lamented that the Allied governments had shown "a deterioration of determination to grapple with the problem." "Again," he pressed, "we have to stress the issue of immediate action." The official statement of the Bermuda conference on the refugees had not even mentioned the Jews by name. Yet of all those who had been victimized by Nazi persecution across Europe, "none . . . have been singled out by the Nazis for mass murder because of their race, as the Jews have been." The machinery for inter-governmental intervention existed and needed only to be applied. They must appeal to neutral countries and exploit the opportunities offered by their colonies. What of their own resources? "It is impossible to believe that out of 20,000,000 tons of Allied shipping, four or five small steamers of 20,000 tons could not be got to transport refugees to Palestine." He concluded, "It is in face of this systematic mass murder, especially in the last twelve months, that I and so many others plead with the Government to act in a new way. With the appeal of the stricken people ringing in our ears we should be false to our tradition if we failed to do everything we can."[44]

Controversy: The Bombing of Germany

In "The Function of the Church in Wartime" Bell had demanded that political and military policy be tested by the fire of Christian understanding and criticized if it were found wanting: "The Church therefore ought to declare what is just. It has a right to prophesy." It was now that Bell acquired a far

42. *Hansard*, Debates of the House of Lords, fifth series, vol. 126, cols. 811-21 (23 March 1943).

43. See Bernard Wasserstein, *Britain and the Jews of Europe, 1939-1945* (Oxford: Oxford University Press, 1979), pp. 201-2.

44. *Hansard*, Debates of the House of Lords, fifth series, vol. 126, cols. 846-50 (28 July 1943).

greater reputation for provocation and controversy. For by now the Bishop of Chichester had also raised hackles in official quarters by speaking against the development of "area" bombing against German cities.

A bishop venturing into political waters is inevitably vulnerable to the criticism that he is an amateur in a field in which professionalism governs all questions, great and small. The organization of a society in wartime naturally intensifies this kind of protectionism. What, after all, did the bishop of a church actually know about the practical business of conducting a national foreign policy and devising a military strategy? To this there was an obvious rejoinder: What, then, do politicians and generals know about morality? And yet, if a war must be legitimate, where did these notions of legitimacy come from? In Britain between 1939 and 1945 it was common currency that they must derive from the Christian faith. With that, a bishop like Bell found his legitimacy. Even politicians who rankled at episcopal interventions, like Lord Vansittart, acknowledged that the church had a responsibility to offer a view of some kind.

Bell had already publicly questioned Allied bombing strategy early in the war. He saw that a technique of "area" bombing had been applied by the Royal Air Force almost from the beginning. A letter of protest had been published in the *Times* on 17 April 1941 ("If Europe is civilised at all, what can excuse the bombing of towns by night and the harrassing of non-combatants who work by day and cannot sleep when night comes?").[45] Later, when Bell attempted to launch another resolution in the Upper House of the Convocation of Canterbury, this time on bombing strategy itself, he had exasperated even his friends and was effectively suppressed after being shouted down from the floor.[46] He wrote to Edwin Lutyens that he feared for the architecture of Germany. (Lutyens simply forwarded this to the Chief of Air Staff, Sir Charles Portal, who returned a mollifying reply.) He wrote to the *Chichester Observer*. In his own diocese some sensed ambivalence. There were two fighter bases near Chichester; did the bishop visit them as he should? When Chichester Cathedral put on a Battle of Britain service for the Royal Air Force in September 1943, the dean, A. S. Duncan-Jones, apologetically wrote to his bishop that it would be better if he did not attend.[47]

---

45. The *Times*, 17 April 1941, p. 5d.
46. Andrew Chandler, "The Church of England and the Obliteration Bombing of Germany in the Second World War," *English Historical Review* 108 (October 1993): 930-31.
47. Chandler, "Obliteration Bombing," p. 937.

None of this appeared to deflect Bell. Indeed, he had yet to reach a climax. By the summer of 1943, as a series of devastating raids was unleashed over Hamburg, he had fixed his own sights on a further motion in the House of Lords.

In this question, as in others, Bell knew that if he were to be influential he must be credible in the minds of rational men who looked for proof, not rhetoric. Credibility of this kind was founded squarely upon the marshaling of information. One of the fascinations of his campaign against obliteration bombing is to view his own correspondence on the matter as it accumulated parallel to that of the Air Ministry, which knew that he was preparing for a speech and sought to anticipate his arguments. In this steady task Bell found one constant ally, the military historian Basil Liddell Hart. Liddell Hart was hardly in the front line of this war; he had retired from the army with the rank of captain in 1927 and for ten years had worked as the military correspondent of the *Daily Telegraph*. But his reputation as a military historian was unique, in part because he was viewed as one of the handful of analysts who had predicted that a second war with Germany would be quite unlike the first, that it would prove to be a war of mobility and tanks and technology. That such a figure (incidentally, the son of a Methodist minister) should also resist the bombing of German cities gave the Bishop of Chichester exactly the kind of authoritative validation that he needed. It also offered him the opportunity for guidance of an authoritative kind. He probably barely sensed that the government viewed Liddell Hart, too, as something of a loose cannon. At all events, as the bishop and the critic quietly prepared in their studies, so did the officials of the Air Ministry in their offices.

Eventually, the scene was set for a motion on the bombing policy of the British government on 9 February 1944. Finding his old friend sitting pensively on the Bishops' Bench beforehand, Lord Woolton now approached Bell quietly with the words,

> George, there isn't a soul in this House who doesn't wish you wouldn't make the speech you are going to make. . . . You must know that. But I also want to tell you that there isn't a soul who doesn't know that the only reason why you make it, is because you believe it is your duty to make it as a Christian priest.[48]

48. See Woolton's recollections in 1958 in the Bell Papers, vol. 367, fols. 325-26.

In the eyes of many, what followed would define Bell's public career more than any other occasion. It was, arguably, a great speech that has remained important in the minds of those who seek words of principle and protest in the world of the twentieth century.[49] Perhaps above all it was a plea for honesty, for using the right word to describe precisely what actually happened rather than the disingenuous word that allowed obfuscation, deceit, or false comfort.

Bell began with due care: the question of this bombing strategy was "beset with difficulties" and must make members of the government itself anxious, as well as "large numbers of people who are as resolute champions of the Allied cause as any member of your Lordships' House." That went for Bell himself, too: "If long-sustained and public opposition to Hitler and the Nazis since 1933 is any credential, I would humbly claim to be one of the most convinced and consistent anti-Nazis in Great Britain." In the challenge that he now set down he made no criticism of British airmen, who, facing "tremendous danger, with supreme courage and skill, carry out the simple duty of obeying their superiors' orders."

That a distinction in principle should be drawn between "attacks on military and industrial objectives and attacks on objectives which do not possess that character" was generally admitted:

> At the outbreak of the war, in response to an appeal by President Roosevelt, the Governments of the United Kingdom and France issued a joint declaration of their intention to conduct hostilities with a firm desire to spare the civilian population and to preserve in every way possible those monuments of human achievement which are treasured in all civilised countries. At the same time explicit instructions were issued to the Commanders of the Armed Forces prohibiting the bombardment, whether from the air or from the sea or by artillery on land, of any except strictly military objectives in the narrowest sense of the word. Both sides accepted this agreement.

To be sure the governments of Britain and France had added the proviso that they "reserve the right to take all such action as they may consider appropriate." Moreover, on 10 May 1940, "the Government publicly

---

49. For example, it may be found alongside the likes of Gandhi, John F. Kennedy, and Martin Luther King in Brian MacArthur, *The Penguin Book of Twentieth Century Speeches* (London: Penguin Books, 1993).

proclaimed their intention to exercise this right in the event of bombing by the enemy of civilian populations. But the point which I wish to establish at this moment is that in entering the war there was no doubt in the Government's mind that the distinction between military and non-military objectives was real."

The principle that lay at the root of that distinction had also been accepted as a point of international law. In 1922 the Washington Conference on Limitation of Armaments had appointed a Commission of Jurists to frame a code of rules about aerial warfare. Article 22 set down the view that "Aerial bombardment for the purpose of terrorizing the civilian population, of destroying or damaging private property not of military character, or of injuring non-combatants is prohibited," while Article 24 affirmed, "Aerial bombardment is legitimate only when directed at a military objective — that is to say, an objective of which the destruction or injury would constitute a distinct military advantage to the belligerent." Meanwhile, they could turn to the Hague Regulations of 1907. Bell warned, "it is common experience in the history of warfare that not only wars but actions taken in war as military necessities are often supported at the time by a class of arguments which, after the war is over, people find are arguments to which they never should have listened."

Bell acknowledged that the *Luftwaffe* had bombed Belgrade, Warsaw, Rotterdam, London, Portsmouth, Coventry, Canterbury, "and many other places of military, industrial and cultural importance." But Hitler was a barbarian: "There is no decent person on the Allied side who is likely to suggest that we should make him our pattern, or attempt to be competitors in that market." Furthermore,

> It is clear enough that large-scale bombing of enemy towns was begun by the Nazis. I am not arguing that point at all. The question with which I am concerned is this. Do the Government understand the full force of what area bombardment is doing and is destroying now? Are they alive not only to the vastness of the material damage, much of which is irreparable, but also to the harvest they are laying up for the future relationships of the peoples of Europe as well as to its moral implications?

The second objection was practical: "I fully realise that in attacks on centres of war industry and transport the killing of civilians when it is the result of bona-fide military activity is inevitable. But there must be a fair balance between the means employed and the purpose achieved. To obliterate a whole town because certain portions contain military and industrial establishments is to reject the balance." The realities of this policy could be seen in Hamburg, a city that certainly contained many legitimate targets, but was also "the most democratic town in Germany where the anti-Nazi opposition was strongest." Now the city had witnessed "unutterable destruction and devastation." At least 34,000 people had died. "Never before in the history of air warfare was an attack of such weight and persistence carried out against a single industrial concentration. Practically all the buildings, cultural, military, residential, industrial, religious including the famous University Library with its 800,000 volumes, of which three-quarters have perished — were razed to the ground." They might then turn to Berlin:

> The offices of the Government, the military, industrial, war-making establishments in Berlin are a fair target. Injuries to civilians are inevitable, but up to date half Berlin has been destroyed, area by area, the residential and the industrial portions alike. Through the dropping of thousands of tons of bombs, including fire-phosphorus bombs, of extraordinary power, men and women have been lost, overwhelmed in the colossal tornado of smoke, blast and flame. It is said that 74,000 persons have been killed and that 3,000,000 are already homeless. The policy is obliteration, openly acknowledged. That is not a justifiable act of war. Again, Berlin is one of the great centres of art collections in the world. It has a large collection of Oriental and classical sculpture. It has one of the best picture galleries in Europe, comparable to the National Gallery. It has a gallery of modern art better than the Tate, a museum of ethnology without parallel in this country, one of the biggest and best-organised libraries — State and university, containing two and a half million books — in the world. . . . It is possible to replace flats and houses by mass production. It is not possible so quickly to rebuild libraries or galleries or churches or museums. It is not very easy to re-house those works of art which have been spared. Those works of art and those libraries will be wanted for the re-education of the Germans after the war. I wonder whether your Lordships realise the loss involved in that.

Such bombing could only be called indiscriminate. The rhetoric that justified such a policy was indiscriminate, too. Air-Marshal Sir Arthur Harris had said, "We are going to scourge the Third Reich from end to end."

What would be caught up in this great offensive? Furthermore, "To justify methods inhuman in themselves by arguments of expediency smacks of the Nazi philosophy that Might is Right." The conclusion was unequivocal:

> Why is there this inability to reckon with the moral and spiritual facts? Why is there this forgetfulness of the ideals by which our cause is inspired? How can the War Cabinet fail to see that this progressive devastation of cities is threatening the roots of civilisation? How can they be blind to the harvest of even fiercer warring and desolation, even in this country, to which the present destruction will inevitably lead when the members of the War Cabinet have long passed to their rest? How can they fail to realise that this is not the way to curb military aggression and end war?[50]

To this Lord Cranborne made a thorough reply. These distinctions were hard to draw. Berlin was, in effect, one great armaments factory. The other cities that had been bombed were all involved in manufacturing for war. They must acknowledge, above all, that "war is a horrible thing." Lord Fitzalan of Derwent, a leading Roman Catholic, replied that he was "an out-and-out bomber." But he did not want Rome to be bombed.[51] Only two other peers spoke; the rest kept their silence. It is not clear whether Bell left the chamber feeling that a heroic stand had been made or something of a damp squib had occurred. Very possibly he felt an immense relief simply that it had been done.

How should the scholar view this occasion? It did not speak simply of a clash between the old powers of church and state, but revealed something more diffuse and fragmented, quite as the construction of the state itself allowed. For the establishment of the Church of England was founded on the argument that the state was Christian and its officers worked as Christian laity. This logic may have looked rather threadbare by the middle of the twentieth century, but it still represented something significant in the fabric of public authority. Bell might well insist on the distinctness of the functions of church and state, but he knew that many of those who led the political life of the nation were Christians as committed as any priest or bishop. Bell's own political friendships were not as extensive as those of

---

50. *Hansard,* Debates of the House of Lords, fifth series, vol. 130, cols. 739-41 (9 February 1944).

51. Debates of the House of Lords, vol. 130, cols. 741ff.

Archbishop Lang, and evidently he made little effort to cultivate a constituency in the House of Lords itself. But he had friends there. In the House of Commons he knew well the Labour politician Sir Stafford Cripps, who was a devout, even austere, Anglican and one prepared to make much public sense of his faith. In 1944 Cripps was running the Ministry of Aircraft Production, responsible for the manufacture of all the bombers that attacked the cities of Germany each night. It was often said by Archibald Sinclair at the Air Ministry that British policy had not changed in essentials during the war. It was simply that it was being pursued with more aircraft. It was this task that Cripps oversaw. In German matters Cripps was often an ally of the Bishop of Chichester, but he was not one now.

It was not only in Britain that this intervention provoked concern that Bell had compromised himself in the paradigm of church and state. In occupied Norway Bishop Berggrav was at first baffled to read a report of this speech. Years later he would recall: "During the war I read in some Finnish paper a report of his speech. . . . I was really shocked, because to us in Norway, this was not good politics. At the same time I felt that he was right, but had the impression that this would block his further way in the church."[52]

Beyond Westminster, Bell was criticized — inevitably — for undermining the war effort. He reported to a friend that he had not expected to receive "such a torrent of commentary and indignation in the press as it has elicited." His secretary found herself trying to intercept angry telephone callers. Yet Bell did win a cluster of committed allies and sympathizers from all kinds of different quarters, political, military, and ecclesiastical. His postbag — or what remains of it, for it is perfectly possible that the most vituperative assaults were destroyed by his protective secretary — reveals a diverse picture, but one largely in his favor. A young priest wrote to him, "It is heartening indeed to know that at last the voice of sanity and Christian charity has been lifted in high places and the surrender of principle to expediency challenged by a representative of the English Church." He went on:

> It may interest you to know that after listening to the 9 p.m. News I went with a Padres Brains Trust into a local factory to answer the religious questions of workers during the break on the night shift in their canteen. One worker expressed his amazement that a Bishop of

52. See Berggrav's recollections of 1958 in the Bell Papers, vol. 367, fol. 327.

all people! should raise his voice against the government on such an issue. . . . His expression of strong support for you my Lord received murmuring assent from all parts of the canteen. I add in my own visitations in this district that I am constantly hearing expressions of disgust and horror at our bombing policy.

Another vicar, in London, wrote, "I have evidence, though most of it is highly confidential, that a number of the R.A.F. boys are seriously perturbed by what they have to do." A Royal Air Force sergeant in Staffordshire remarked:

It has been distressing to note the increasing ruthlessness of our attitude to this devastating form of warfare & the development of a frame of mind which can dismiss the maiming and slaughter of thousands of human beings in a single night as "grim necessity." One wonders if the age of reason is over; if those virtues of mercy & forbearance which have dignified the human race are not rapidly becoming things of the past.

A major wrote from the United Services Club in London, "Many young airmen who have to carry out these bombing raids feel deeply that they are being asked to do more than is required by military necessity and they are most unhappy about it." A retired Royal Navy Commander wrote that he had been waiting to see when the church would "stand up for the principles of Christianity in this matter," and now one member had at last done so. A journalist reported, "You may be interested to know that, in company with four other hard-bitten newspapermen, I was discussing what you had said and, at the end of a somewhat heated debate, 'Fleet Street's view' was 4-1 in your favour!" A mother who had lost her son, a violinist in peacetime who had become an aircraft navigator in war, thanked Bell and deplored "this sickening business of retaliation."[53] But across the armed services views could be harsh. When transport was requested for a visit by the Bishop of Chichester to a local Royal Air Force station an officer retorted bitterly, "Let the bugger bike."[54]

53. For these letters, and more, see the Bell Papers, vol. 70, fols. 22ff.

54. Giles Watson, "In a Filial and Obedient Spirit: George Bell and the Anglican Response to Crisis, 1937-1949," *Humanitas: The Journal of the George Bell Institute* 1, no. 1 (September 1999): 5, a striking article by a gifted scholar.

Crises polarize opinion; divisions are inevitable, and they grow rigid as parties become antagonists. They can also isolate, as the individual who holds to a firm view may well find his allies slipping into the discreet background. Yet, at the same time, he might find himself in new and even surprising company and be much the richer for it. Bell did not provoke the admiration of many bishops. The new archbishop of Canterbury, William Temple, was of quite a different view and said so often enough.[55] Only one bishop, Hone of Wakefield, wrote with his warm support and showed that he had read the debate thoroughly. But others within the church and without now turned to the Bishop of Chichester to say and do the things that others had, in their eyes, left unsaid and undone. Some found themselves thinking of a bishop with respect and interest when otherwise they might hardly have considered such a figure a part of their moral universe at all. This surely represented a public influence of a kind.

Even in a democracy, moral individualism has its costs, and this speech cost Bell a good deal. Yet it also has its gains. Bell will have known this, and known how to value it. As for a military policy that had a powerful political significance and involved a vast commitment of resources and an immense loss of Allied lives, Bell was surely too realistic to think that a quiet speech by a solitary bishop in Parliament could change anything of such great substance. It did not.

The Vision of Europe

It was in the midst of the austerities of occupation and the dangers of resistance that European federalists in many countries continued to hope. Bell was of this company. In March 1943 he published an article entitled "The Church and the Future of Europe" in which he affirmed, "I believe in the essential unity of Europe," for it was in centuries of Christian faith that he found it alive and he saw that these ages had not died. Many Christians in Germany had witnessed against the new barbarism of Hitler and his party state. Now they heard protests from church people in the occupied countries, in Holland, in France and Belgium, in Greece and Yugoslavia. The church remained the "teacher of justice" and the proclaimer of the moral law in the affairs of men; it was still "the watchman for humanity." It was the church that professed the very things by which a new Europe must seek

55. See Chandler, "Obliteration Bombing," pp. 932-37.

to live, a gospel of redemption, reconciliation, and forgiveness. When this war at last was over let the leaders of all the churches congregate at once in some neutral city, embodying the universal church before any peace conference of politicians could assemble: "Let theirs be the first voice sounding a universal note." By "a crusade of conversion" would the souls of millions be filled "with the hunger for justice and the spirit of love."[56]

There was a good deal of Söderblom in all this. But had such rhetoric lost a clear sense that the churches, too, had often been as brutally compromised by this age of totalitarianism and war as had so many other powers? In the last months of the war Bell had confronted the disintegration of the Continent squarely but insisted that Europe still possessed a genuine unity in four common spiritual traditions: humanism, science, law and government, and Christian faith. Of these it was the last that still seemed to him the greatest. He judged that the churches had in all countries labored against Nazism. Now they must take their place with trade unions and "all men of goodwill" in the task of reconstruction.[57]

The Destruction of the German Resistance

In 1944 Bell could not know that in Germany the circles of resistance were gathering their forces as best they could for a final decisive enterprise against the Nazi state. When news began to break of the attempted coup of 20 July 1944 the situation seemed to many in Britain almost incomprehensible. Churchill, in the House of Commons, was dismissive. There was little reason for those who knew nothing of its background to be otherwise. Germany had waged war across Europe; its crimes were vast and without number. Now it was losing the war on every front; the generals who had directed its course so earnestly were turning upon their leader and on each other. But as they began to emerge in newspaper reports, Bell recognized the names that Bonhoeffer and Schönfeld had given him two years before. This was the same resistance, and it had failed. Busy beneath the surface for years, its leading lights were now hopelessly exposed to retribution. News of the fate of its participants followed surely enough. Gerhard Leibholz was a friend of Berthold von Stauffenberg and had worked with him.

56. Reprinted in Bell, *The Church and Humanity*, pp. 110-22.
57. Speech of 19 December 1944, reprinted in Bell, *The Church and Humanity*, pp. 158-64.

The *Times* reported that Claus von Stauffenberg had been shot by a firing squad. His fellow conspirator Ludwig Beck was dead. Lists of suspects were soon being published, and they named Dietrich Bonhoeffer and his brother, Klaus. On 17 August Bell wrote to Leibholz, "I am terribly stricken to read in the *Daily Telegraph* that Goerdeler has been arrested. Your wife and Dietrich are constantly in my thoughts."[58]

On 11 September Leibholz wrote to Bell that Adam von Trott, and others, had been executed: "You know it was Adam von Trott who always gave Dietrich the possibility of going abroad and also of meeting you in Sweden."[59] To Bell it came as a "sad confirmation": "I am writing to Sir Stafford Cripps and to Lionel Curtis, to be sure they know. I agree with you on the miserable playing down of the significance of the Hitler plot. It is tragic to think what might have been prevented had the Foreign Office only believed what they were told, and acted on it in 1942."[60]

Four Deaths and the Passing of an Age

If the Bishop of Chichester is in these years of war often glimpsed as a solitary, even alienated figure, a conspicuous individualist isolated by his principled interventions in a world of pragmatists, the truth was that he was still in his element in vigorous company. He surely knew that solitude, however righteous, will change nothing in a world of men, powers, and politics. Indeed, he was truly fortunate in his contemporaries, and although many of his greatest influences were international, he remained in robust, good company at home. He will have known that his effectiveness as a man in public life depended on this.

The character and temper of British Christianity in these war years had grown markedly ecumenical. The Sword of the Spirit was no stray salvo of idealism. A British Council of Churches was inaugurated at a great service in St. Paul's Cathedral in 1942, a significant achievement and an enduring one. Those who cared most deeply for such a vision had by now come to look to a number of significant presences in their midst for decisive leadership and creative progress. Bell had come to cherish a sense that his views of many things, not least the place of Christianity in the narrative

---

58. Bell to Leibholz, 17 August 1944, Bell Papers, vol. 40, fol. 258.
59. Leibholz to Bell, 11 September 1944, Bell Papers, vol. 40, fol. 265.
60. Bell to Leibholz, 14 September 1944, Bell Papers, vol. 40, fol. 267.

of Europe, were shared by Cardinal Hinsley at Westminster. The Roman Catholic David Mathew recognized that "the quality that most appealed to the Cardinal was reckless and self-sacrificing moral goodness, and it was this that led to his always deepening affection for the Bishop of Chichester."[61] But Hinsley, so prodigious in spirit and purpose, had now grown frail, almost blind, nearly deaf. On 17 March 1943 he died at Buntingford, having left directions that he should buried after a low requiem mass and with as little pomp and expense as possible. As far as many English Roman Catholics could see, with his passing the ecumenical clock simply stopped dead in its tracks.[62]

Many of Bell's wartime activities had been shared with a second, dynamic force, the inveterate Presbyterian missionary William Paton. Paton's background lay in the International Missionary Council, but he had returned to Britain in 1936 and there had grown exceedingly busy, not least in laboring to save the ecumenical movements from too Eurocentric a view of the world at large. Paton was a convinced internationalist who had published a bold polemic, *World Community,* in 1939. Once a pacifist, like so many Paton changed his mind in 1940. Since the furtive negotiations of the first autumn and winter of the war, Bell had come to collaborate closely with him against internment, but he must have also relished the sheer range of experience, in India and in China, and the breadth of creative thought, which the restless Paton brought to their labors. He knew Visser 't Hooft and Eivind Berggrav well, and his acquaintance had an American dimension that Bell, so much the European, never quite sought or achieved. In 1941 Paton had produced another book, *The Church and the New Order,* a discussion of peace aims that acquired a wide international readership and attracted the critical attention of Dietrich Bonhoeffer in Berlin. By 1942 he had become immersed in the creation of the World Council of Churches. It was Paton who proved to be the essential author of a new document in July 1943, "A Christian Basis for Reconstruction," which showed the extent to which the discussion of peace aims in Britain was now colored by the parallel explorations of church people in the United States. With such work Bell was utterly in sympathy, not least in its

---

61. David Mathew, *Catholicism in England: Portrait of a Minority, Its Culture and Tradition* (London: Eyre & Spottiswoode, 1948), p. 262.

62. A characteristically shrewd assessment of Hinsley in the round is offered by Michael Walsh, in *The Westminster Cardinals: The Past and the Future* (London: Continuum, 2008), pp. 111-34.

insistence that this was not merely a conflict of nations, but of faiths.[63] But this paper would be Paton's last contribution: within days he was dead. He had worn himself out at forty-seven.

Bell's great friend of forty years, William Temple, had succeeded Archbishop Lang at Canterbury only in 1942. British Christianity in wartime had found immense confidence in the vitality of Archbishop Temple. His popularity, both within the church and without, was extraordinary: resented by the political right, he was soon proclaimed by journalists as "the people's archbishop." His Penguin Special, *Christianity and Social Order,* was published in 1942, the very year in which he came to Canterbury. It outsold Bell's earlier volume in that series and inspired a still greater enthusiasm across the churches for vigorous, progressive political thought. As the tide of the war turned, idealists even glimpsed the promise of a new, social state. By then the friendship of Temple and Bell had grown ripe. They were not allies in every matter, and in the controversy over obliteration bombing they were at odds. But in their insistence that Christianity was not merely a religion of the individual and heaven, but a faith that demanded that individuals must take their place in the world, not as bystanders but as participants, they were wholly united. Bell was in no doubt about the great stature of the new occupant of Lambeth Palace. He found him "pre-eminently a prophet, that is 'one who speaks for God as the inspired revealer or interpreter of His will.' "[64]

But the archbishopric of Canterbury had found Temple an ill man, afflicted by attacks of gout. When in the autumn of 1944 he turned up to speak to the gathered clergy of the Canterbury diocese, he was carried into the meeting in a chair. It was suddenly, on 26 October 1944, that he died. He was sixty-three. This disaster even provoked a Christian as sober as Lang to question his own faith. It also created a vacancy. The oligarchs of church and state began to chatter again. It was heard that Temple himself had seen Geoffrey Fisher, the Bishop of London, as his successor, and not George Bell of Chichester. It was muttered that Churchill would never appoint to Canterbury the bishop who had spoken against the bombing of German cities. Somewhere in this tangle Fisher did indeed become Archbishop of Canterbury. This appointment has provoked debate ever since. Very likely the roots of the decision lay not merely in Bell's political con-

---

63. Margaret Sinclair, *William Paton* (London: SCM Press, 1949), p. 243.

64. G. K. A. Bell, "Memoir," in *William Temple and His Message,* ed. A. E. Baker (Harmondsworth: Penguin Books, 1946), p. 43.

troversialism in wartime, but also in his ongoing commitment to issues that were not so much domestic as universal. Arguably, Fisher's appointment foreshadowed a growing tendency in the church to concentrate primarily on its own affairs and to organize its structures more efficiently. Like everything else in British society, the Church of England needed to be modernized. Fisher was the man for the job. At Chichester, Bell himself was subdued. There could be no doubt that he sensed that he had been set aside. Nor was he offered the now vacant see of London. Though he said nothing that was not dutiful and proper, those who knew him most intimately found him to be wounded. Chichester would be no stepping stone to a higher station. It would be his bastion for the remainder of his career. His own name would become attached to it, finally and indelibly.

A fourth, defining death was at first unknown. In April a little collection of political prisoners, including a British secret agent, a Russian Air Force officer, and a German general were driven by their guards across the diminishing face of the Third Reich. It was curious company in which to find a German pastor, but one had joined them at the concentration camp at Buchenwald on 7 February. By April they had reached Schönberg. Here, on 8 April, the pastor was abruptly separated from the other prisoners. As he was about to leave he turned to the British agent and said a few words. The next day he was hanged at Flossenbürg with the former head of German counter-intelligence, Admiral Canaris, and his erstwhile collaborator, Colonel Hans Oster.

On 30 May 1945 Adolf Freudenberg, a German pastor now based in Geneva, sent a brief telegram to another exile, Julius Rieger, in London: "Just received sad news that Dietrich Bonhoeffer and his [brother] Klaus have been murdered in concentration camp Clossburg near Neustadt about 15 April." The Leibholz family must be informed.[65] How the news reached Bell in Chichester is not clear. A letter of 23 July, from Sabine Leibholz to Bell, said, "I feel I must thank you for all you have been to Dietrich during all these years. I know how much your friendship and the fellowship of your Church meant to him during the long time of his struggle and trial." She enclosed a small photograph of her twin.[66] On 27 July a memorial service for both brothers took place at Holy Trinity Church, Kingsway, London. Bonhoeffer had, Bell believed, died as a hostage. It was a death for Germany and for Europe: "As one of a noble company of martyrs of

---

65. Quoted in Eberhard Bethge, *Dietrich Bonhoeffer: Theologian, Christian, Contemporary* (New York: William Collins, 1970), p. 833.

66. Sabine Leibholz to Bell, 23 July 1945, Bell Papers, vol. 40, fols. 303-4.

differing traditions, he represents both the resistance of the believing soul, in the name of God, to the assault of evil, and also the moral and political revolt of the human conscience against injustice and cruelty."[67] Two days later a further letter from Oxford brought news of the deaths of two brothers-in-law, Rudiger Schleicher and Hans von Dohnanyi.

Determined now to show the world that this German resistance against Nazism had possessed integrity, Bell busied himself with an article, "The Background to the Hitler Plot," for the *Contemporary Review*, while Leibholz advised quietly and firmly in the background. In this he laid before the public a thorough description of his last encounter with Bonhoeffer and Schönfeld in Sigtuna.[68] Soon such efforts were giving Bonhoeffer a growing reputation. Bell wrote of him to another journal, *Time and Tide*. The Bishop of Rochester, Christopher Chavasse, wrote to Bell to ask about "that great German pastor who was your friend" for a series he was writing on "Present day heroes of the Cross."[69] But the story of Bonhoeffer's death would not be known to Bell for many years yet. When hostilities had ceased, the captured British agent to whom Bonhoeffer had briefly turned as he was finally taken away returned to Britain. He was struck by a sense of public hatred "of all things German" and hardly knew whether or not to write to the Bishop of Chichester.[70] On 17 September 1946 he sent a letter with a recollection of Bonhoeffer's last hours to the Bishop's Palace. In the archive this letter stands alone. There is no copy of a reply. Evidently Bell did not see this letter, by Captain Sigismund Payne Best, at all. He was in Norway. His secretary acknowledged it, but nothing followed from the bishop himself.

In the long interval, Eberhard Bethge had begun to collate, organize, and publish the literary remains of Bonhoeffer in Germany, and now he found a new and growing audience. The Bishop of Chichester made his own presence felt when what became, in English, *The Cost of Discipleship* was published in Britain in 1948. In his foreword he wrote:

"When Christ calls a man," says Dietrich Bonhoeffer, "he bids him come and die." There are different kinds of dying, it is true; but the essence of discipleship is contained in those words. . . . Dietrich him-

---

67. The full text may be found in the Bell Papers, vol. 42, fols. 78-83.
68. The article was reprinted in Bell, *The Church and Humanity*, pp. 165-76.
69. Bishop of Rochester to Bell, 11 December 1945, Bell Papers, vol. 42, fol. 110.
70. Payne Best to Bell, 17 September 1946, Bell Papers, vol. 42, fol. 122.

self was a martyr many times before he died. He was one of the first as well as one of the bravest witnesses against idolatry. He understood what he chose, when he chose resistance.[71]

In 1950 a striking wartime memoir, *The Venlo Incident,* was published in London.[72] Bell eventually came across the book and in it found mention made of the last days of Dietrich Bonhoeffer. On 21 September 1953 he wrote to Payne Best at the address of his publishers, Hutchinson and Company, in London. Now he had clearly returned to his correspondence files and retrieved Payne Best's letter of 1946. Had there, he now asked, been a "particular, precise" message to him from Bonhoeffer, or simply "a message of general remembrance and affection"?[73] Only two days later Payne Best replied. There had indeed been a message from Bonhoeffer, "certainly the last words he spoke to a friend before his execution":

> It was a moment of fearful urgency with the S.D. thug at the door calling to him to hurry when Bonhoeffer, taking me aside and speaking with intense earnestness, gave me his last message to you, twice repeating it in the same words and asking me not to fail to give it to you. I remember that the thought flashed through my mind, that perhaps the message was a prearranged code which only you would understand.[74]

Then, on 13 October, Payne Best wrote another letter, for now "halfforgotten things have sprung back to life":

> As nearly as I can remember, Dietrich's actual words were: — "Will you give this message from me to the Bishop of Chichester, tell him that for me this is the end, but also the beginning — with him I believe in the principle of our universal Christian brotherhood which rises above all national hatreds and that our victory is certain — tell him too, that I have never forgotten his words at our last meeting."[75]

---

71. Foreword by Bell in Dietrich Bonhoeffer, *The Cost of Discipleship* (London: SCM Press, 1948).

72. Sigismund Payne Best, *The Venlo Incident* (London: Hutchinson, 1950).

73. Bell to Payne Best, 21 September 1953, Bell Papers, vol. 42, fol. 150.

74. Payne Best to Bell, 23 September 1953, Bell Papers, vol. 42, fol. 151.

75. Payne Best to Bell, 13 October 1953, Bell Papers, vol. 42, fol. 154b.

CHAPTER NINE

The New World Disorder, 1945-1948

With the explosion of two atomic bombs over Hiroshima and Nagasaki everything, it seemed, had suddenly changed, utterly. Evidently Bell, like so many others, took some time to come to terms with this, but on 14 August 1945 he voiced his own protest in a letter in the *Times*. If this was a legitimate act of war, what could not be? In the following months he played a loyal part in a new report produced by the young British Council of Churches, entitled *The Era of Atomic Power*. It was published in May 1946. Some found the document equivocal. When it prompted a further statement from the Church of England, *The Church and the Atom,* the Church Assembly found the Bishop of Chichester a firm critic of anything that conceded, however rationally, to a new international morality that made the possession of nuclear weapons possible. This dangerous new reality would not go away. Indeed, Bell would turn to it again and again.

The Ruins of Europe

The intense disappointment over Canterbury must have done much to hasten Bell's understanding that it was in that other realm of church life, the international ecumenical movement, that he held a fixed place and was much honored. His reputation among Christians in many countries had grown luminous. Now old friends and allies in many countries were at last free from confinements and obstacles, and to London and to Chichester there were constant visitors. To Chichester came Bishop Fjellbu from Norway and Professor Alivisatos from Greece. Bishop Berggrav lost little time in traveling to Britain, where he found Bell very much at home in the House of Lords. Bell took him to call on Churchill, and left the two men alone, sitting quietly outside the office of the now ousted prime minister — rather like a servant, thought Berggrav — while they talked together. When Berggrav at last managed to draw Bell into the conversation he found Churchill "very benevolent" to the bishop who had so antagonized him during the war.[1] For Churchill's mellow generosity could be as marvelous as his colossal obduracy.

It is difficult to trace much continuity between the early ideals of the wartime Peace Aims movement and the confined, thwarted vision that now broke across this bleak, post-war landscape. But the word "reconstruction" was heard everywhere. International agencies were already stirring to meet what was already an almost immeasurable challenge, in resettling refugees, rebuilding towns and cities, and reorganizing civil institutions and governments. In this the place of religion was acknowledged by political powers in the West as well as by churches. Ecumenists everywhere were exceedingly busy. In Geneva the powers of Adolf Keller's Central European Bureau of Inter-Church Aid were much enhanced under the aegis of the coming World Council of Churches. This now served and coordinated a number of national church bodies, which, in their turn, sought to organize relief.

Bell had seen and heard for himself how dire was the need for assistance, for peace had shattered almost every border. Countless refugees and displaced men, women, and children were now caught in flight, seeking family members, searching for past possessions, hoping to find new homes. Almost at once Bell set off for the Continent, eager to see everything for himself and to do whatever he could. Already in 1944 he had been busily at work with a new Committee for Christian Reconstruction in Europe. In March 1945 he was in Paris. He was also asked by the Church Assembly to chair a commission to recommend how best the Church of England might support such work. The raising of money was vital. The national committee promptly decided that it must raise £1 million. Bell's commission proposed that the Church Assembly contribute £250,000 to that campaign, each diocese in turn giving a share of that sum. Casting a sidelong glance to a new, and bleak, book published earlier that year by the writer Leslie Paul, Bell remarked to the people of Chichester, "We do not need to hear much more of the *annihilation* of man. We do need news

---

1. Berggrav to Henrietta Bell, 9 October 1958, Bell Papers, vol. 367, fol. 22.

of the *redemption* of man."[2] A more formidable Committee for Christian Reconstruction followed, and it proved a thoroughly ecumenical affair. Bell chaired it jointly with the Baptist M. E. Aubrey. "If you are a Christian," pronounced Bell, "you must not only be your brother's keeper in the sense of refusing to commit the sin of murder which Cain committed; you must save your brother; you must do everything possible to meet all his needs."[3]

Returning: Germany in 1945

Bell had long viewed the future of Germany as the crucial question that must define and determine the future of Europe. With the coming of peace he was at once restless to go there himself. This was no easy task: the terms of occupation were disputatious, and Germany was now a country divided into military zones. To visit the country demanded the cooperation of the Allied powers, something that was all too fragile and liable to disintegrate at any time. Those who sat on top of all of this had more than enough on their hands without looking after a stray, touring bishop. Meanwhile, in Geneva Visser 't Hooft was warning that German church leaders were quarrelling with each other.

The churches of Germany were still essentially regional and still divided by the arguments of the church struggle. Above all they were weak and disorientated. The ranks of the Confessing Church had been depleted by the sufferings of war: 1,858 pastors had died in the armed forces.[4] Some of their *Deutsche Christen* adversaries whose names had once become notorious abroad had also perished. Ludwig Müller had committed suicide in July 1945; his deputy in 1933, August Jäger, had been publicly executed in Poland for war crimes. Others, like Joachim Hossenfelder and Friedrich Werner, were still in evidence and quietly tracing a careful line toward respectable, and unrepentant, retirement. In Hannover Bishop Marahrens

2. R. C. D. Jasper, *George Bell, Bishop of Chichester* (London: Oxford University Press, 1967), p. 289.

3. "If Thine Enemy Hunger," a broadcast of 3 March 1946, to be found in G. K. A. Bell, *The Church and Humanity, 1939-1946* (London: Longmans, Green & Co., 1946), p. 247. Here Bell was talking of famine in Germany, but also of famine in India.

4. Gordon Rupp, here turning to Eberhard Bethge. See Gordon Rupp, *I Seek My Brethren: Bishop George Bell and the German Churches* (London: Epworth Press, 1975), p. 20.

had managed to become a controversy in himself.[5] Unity would demand a great deal of pulling together. Could German church people achieve this without the encouragement of the wider Christian church?

Some of those now at work in administering the occupation at the Allied Control Commission saw that a visit from the Bishop of Chichester might prove to be a very good thing. The place of religion in the work of reconstruction and de-Nazification was acknowledged. Furthermore, church people themselves pleaded for this. A conference of German church leaders at Treysa late in the summer of 1945 proved a dispiriting spectacle. It showed that a still vigorous Bishop Wurm commanded enough respect to oversee a gathering of clergy, and it also revealed that, for all their privations, the pastors of the Confessing Church now stood firmly in the foreground. But the statements made at Treysa did little but inch toward an acknowledgment of responsibility for the crimes of Nazism. The pastors also resolved to begin again the work of uniting Evangelical Christians in Germany. It was significant that Evangelical relief work was now trusted to Eugen Gerstenmaier, a man who had been heavily involved in active resistance against the Hitler regime. Wurm had boldly pronounced that Treysa inaugurated a new chapter of German church history. But appearances could be deceptive. About the record of the church under Nazism there was no universal agreement. Many were deeply resentful of criticism. What, after all, had they actually done wrong? They had neither commissioned nor participated in crimes.

It is difficult to know quite what Bell expected to encounter when, on 17 October 1945, he took off for Germany, bringing with him a scholarly Methodist minister, Gordon Rupp, who was fluent in German. The next day he turned up in Stuttgart, one of a weighty delegation representing the emerging World Council of Churches, expressly to meet the new Council of the German Evangelical Church. The atmosphere was distinctly uneasy. Bell's diary notes each man in turn and describes his traits succinctly. He found Wurm ("kindly, quiet, shrewd") in the chair, and Niemöller ("in good health. Slight") as vice-president. Meiser ("businesslike") was there, too. Bell also noted a young pastor, Eberhard Bethge ("excellent").[6] Hans Asmussen told Bell that in prison he had read the complete works of Shakespeare seven times.

5. For a detailed study, see Gerhard Besier, *"Selbstreinigung" unter britischer Besatzungherrschaft: Die Evangelisch-Lutherisch Landeskirche Hannovers und ihr Landesbischof Marahrens, 1945-1947* (Göttingen: Vandenhoeck & Ruprecht, 1986).

6. Travel diary, Bell Papers, vol. 45, fol. 12.

It was widely judged that Bell's presence at this meeting proved essential. Such an occasion was, he knew, historic. "It is," he said to them all as they stood before him, "with an extraordinary sense of happiness that I find myself face to face with the clergy of the German Evangelical Church."[7] (An earlier draft of these words spoke not of "clergy," but of "leaders.") He came as a bishop of his church; as a bearer of greetings from the churches of his own country, of the Archbishop of Canterbury, of many friends who had come to Britain as exiles, "friends of yours and mine"; and, above all, as "a brother in Christ, and as an old friend of the Confessional Church." For years now they had followed, with great admiration, the witness of those Christians who had stood up against the crimes of the Nazi state, "and against the regime itself" — and here Bell purposefully added, "the brave, utterly dedicated, most gifted and ardent soul Dietrich Bonhoeffer." In such suffering the ecumenical church, too, had suffered. From such sacrifice had the whole church learned. What they all shared was the knowledge that, above all, "War is a terrible scourge for all who take part — terrible in its hatred, terrible in its devastation, and its slavery. No humane person could fail to be stirred to the depths by the cruelties done to Jews, to displaced persons . . . in their millions." Now they must turn to the future. In this new World Council of Churches Bell saw clearly "a matter of life and death today," manifesting the incarnation of their one Incarnate Lord in the "the social, national and international affairs of men."[8]

Conferences of church leaders who are searching for ecclesiastical unity in a world of divisions are not above hiding behind merely pious invocations that offend nobody by saying nothing. But at Stuttgart the mood was austere: there was nowhere to hide, and few rhetorical fig leaves were on offer. "War guilt" stood squarely at the top of the agenda, and a still only recently freed Martin Niemöller had been smoldering too long in a concentration camp to be equivocal. Bell noted Niemöller's words carefully: "Instead of this yammering about defeat, we should all go on our knees and thank Almighty God that the war ended the way it did. Had there been a German victory, we should none of us be here to-day. There would have been no Christianity in Germany." Bell wrote down the words of what became known as the Stuttgart Declaration eagerly. He knew them to be fundamental, at least in his world.[9] Quite what

7. Bell Papers, vol. 45, fol. 311.
8. Bell Papers, vol. 45, fols. 311-14.
9. Bell Papers, vol. 45, fol. 337.

other German pastors made of them was, perhaps, something for which he could only hope.

In his formal report of this visit Bell placed the meetings of these church leaders at the beginning of the text. But their discussions and resolutions still take up only two pages in a document of nine pages, and the weight of the report concerns the plight of Germany itself. For several years Bell had read accounts of the destruction of German cities by bombing missions. Now he was there himself. "It is," he wrote,

> unbelievable unless you see it with your own eyes. . . . Here and there within a town there are sections which have escaped total destruction; but generally speaking the whole fabric of the towns has collapsed. . . . Berlin is like an inferno in ruins. . . . It is extremely difficult to find out where the great bulk of the population live . . . an enormous number of people must live in cellars and holes and corners of all sorts. . . . The Germans have been, they know, overwhelmingly defeated, and the vastness of the catastrophe stuns or half-stuns them.

There was an "acute" need for new leadership. "De-Nazification" meant different things in different occupied zones: the Americans were arbitrary, the French and British more discriminating. It appeared obvious to Bell that to deny public responsibilities to men and women who had been merely members of the Nazi party, or to those who had any connection with it, represented "real injustice." On these terms who would be left to teach the schoolchildren? Large numbers of political prisoners had been detained without charge or trial and denied visitors. Food supplies were stretched; where people were weakened by hunger, epidemics were widely feared. The country was full of refugees: men, women, and children expelled from the East, "homeless, penniless, outcast . . . a piteous spectacle." Hundred upon hundred passed haphazardly through two shelters, one a barracks and the other a prison. Bell observed them, "crowded every-where . . . utterly destitute, and in many cases sick, with wounds and sores on their legs — relics of humanity."[10]

In Berlin Bell went off in search of Bonhoeffer's mother and father. Paula Bonhoeffer gave him her son's copy of the *Imitatio Christi* and he accepted it quietly, bending down to kiss her forehead. Trailing behind,

10. "Bishop of Chichester's Visit to Germany, October 18-30, 1945," Bell Papers, vol. 45, fols. 336-44.

Gordon Rupp observed the bishop later walking through a *Lehrter Bahnhof* now crammed with refugees, with no German words to console, simply smiling at those whose eyes he met and patting the heads of the children as he went. He then preached to "a vast, overflowing congregation of pale, bitter people" in the *Marienkirche*, from which Pastor Grüber had once organized the emigration of "Non-Aryan" Christians before the war. Soviet soldiers patrolled the outside of the building as they worshiped.[11]

Bell admired the efficiency and spirit that he found at work in the British zone. But he perceived that the German people still did not know what their conquerors actually intended to do. Bell was, frankly, nervous: "There are great spiritual possibilities in the German people: but there are great dangers. A wrong move now might drive them into the worst kind of militarism." His conclusion was somber:

> The future of Europe really depends on a liberal and democratic policy being shown to the Germans now, and a sense of hope and encouragement and worth-whileness of effort for the future being given. But depression, dismemberment, destruction of industrial and other resources is in my opinion bound to lead sooner or later to another world war. The choice before Germany and Europe is between militarism and peaceful democracy, or, to put it on another plane, between nihilism and Christianity.[12]

The Allied powers held the future of this broken Germany in their hands. It was in such a fragile and dangerous context that Bell placed the new task of post-war reconstruction, the unfolding trials at Nuremberg, and the role of the church in Germany. It was for the other churches to offer all Christians in Germany every encouragement and actual support. For the consequences of failure now must surely be beyond their imagining.

Bell and the Question of War Crimes

The historian Charmian Brinson has shown that during the Second World War Bell interceded not only for those he considered unjustly interned but

---

11. Rupp, *I Seek My Brethren,* pp. 27-28.
12. "Bishop of Chichester's Visit to Germany, October 18-30, 1945," Bell Papers, vol. 45, fol. 344.

also on behalf of at least two stray women who supported Oswald Mosley, the leader of the British Union of Fascists. He found merely that they had "a rather deluded form of patriotism." One of them, Lucy Heath Pearson, had been released at the end of 1940. "I think," she later wrote to Bell, "you are the only Bishop — whether Anglican or RC — who has concerned himself with us."[13] The story is striking and significant. It also colors a far more powerful narrative in Bell's political interventions after the war. For between 1945 and 1950 time and again he would question a succession of trials for war crimes in occupied Germany. The historian Tom Lawson has lambasted Bell for what he regards as "a monumental error of judgement. He found himself arguing that individuals responsible for atrocities should be allowed to go free, unencumbered by guilt but without penance, for the sake of the future, and in doing so he effectively denied their victims the dignity of justice."[14] Why, then, did this happen?

During the war Bell appeared sure that justice must be served by "properly appointed tribunals." But as early as September 1942 he was privately anxious about how a credible process and judgment might be delivered. Some objections were obvious: How could this be anything other than the questionable "justice" meted out by victors? What of the war crimes committed by Allies? As there existed no international basis for a court of law, the legal process could only derive from the Allied powers themselves. The League of Nations still existed, but only in name; the United Nations Organization was still only an aspiration. And by what actual laws could the defendants be arraigned? They did not yet exist. If they were framed later, how could it be right to apply them retrospectively? What was set down as a crime after the war would not have existed as one during the conflict itself.

When he had spoken in a debate in the House of Lords in February 1943, Bell was clearly concerned that the punishment of atrocities in wartime might extend to so great a number that it would deny that a German criminal elite that commissioned such things could be distinguished from ordinary Germans who were utterly intimidated and haplessly caught up in its designs. So many Germans did not want this war; so many wanted

13. Charmian Brinson, " 'Please Tell the Bishop of Chichester": George Bell and the Internment Crisis of 1940," in *The Church and Humanity: The Life and Work of George Bell, 1883-1958,* ed. Andrew Chandler (Farnham: Ashgate, 2012), p. 86.

14. Tom Lawson, "Bishop Bell and the Trial of German War Criminals: A Moral History," in Chandler, ed., *The Church and Humanity,* p. 131; see, too, Tom Lawson, *The Church of England and the Holocaust* (Woodbridge: Boydell, 2006), pp. 139-66.

no part in atrocities at all. To spread too wide a net would show that trials for war crimes might become part not of the administration of justice but of a war against the whole German people.[15] And what would all of this do for the cause of reconciliation? A sustained campaign of prosecutions on no very firm legal basis might alienate Germany and undermine the cause of reconciliation in all Europe. Surely, nothing must be allowed to endanger that. They had reason to fear all too deeply that a failure to reconcile the nations would lead to further war and destruction. Instead of building a future together, both victor and vanquished might end up locked in a divisive and destructive past.

In the new peace Bell was equivocal about the process of de-Nazification that the occupying powers now sought to apply, often chaotically, across German society. Did membership of the Nazi party, however nominal, really show a schoolteacher or a civil servant to be wholly compromised? Where to draw the line? When the International Military Tribunal was established Bell did not remonstrate. He saw Hitler's "co-assassins" in the dock and was sure that it was right to put them there. Nuremberg would show how criminal the Nazi era had been and draw a firm line under it. Then they must turn to build a new Europe where such things could not happen again. Yet the indictments and the trials continued under royal warrant. The prosecutors turned from those who had commissioned crimes to those who had been their instruments.

Bell intervened on a number of occasions. One trial was of Eberhard von Mackensen, who had been complicit in a reprisal murder of 335 Italian civilians, personally commissioned by Hitler on 24 March 1944. Mackensen denied the charges. Bell accepted his denial. He would intervene again on behalf of anther general, Erich von Manstein, who enjoyed the support of Bishop Wurm in Württemberg. Lawson has argued that the case showed the Bishop of Chichester to be clinging to a simplistic myth that German generals remained honorable. His view of history was itself "skewed." He even suggests that Bell felt "a sense of community" with these generals.[16] Some, like Konstantin von Neurath, foreign minister in the early years of the Third Reich and in wartime responsible for overseeing anti-Jewish laws in Bohemia and Moravia, were known to be practicing Christians. When the former *Gauleiter* of East Prussia and leader of the Nazi government in German-occupied Ukraine, Erich Koch, was put on trial, Bell learned that

15. Bell, *The Church and Humanity*, pp. 86-94.
16. Lawson, "German War Criminals," p. 138.

he, too, was a committed Christian. But in 1942 Koch had commissioned the murder of Ukrainian Jews. In the House of Lords Bell opposed Koch's extradition to the Soviet Union. As evidence for the prosecution against Koch accumulated, Bell desisted. In all this Lawson has found that Bell was not even "primarily" concerned with the actual guilt of those on trial — and yet who had known, and deplored, more than he?[17] Furthermore, in working as Bell did, was it not the case that he kept company with at least a few dubious figures who still lurked in the corridors of British authority?

It is important to see how Bell's German sources were leading him in all this. It is also important to recognize that Bell confined himself to only a modest number of careful interventions. Meanwhile, the judgments at Nuremberg were not above throwing up some striking anomalies. A number of these figures, like the diplomat Ernst von Weiszäcker, who appeared in the dock as the decade drew to an end, had inhabited a complicated, compromised gray area of Nazi policy, often on no very clear terms. But if Bell had argued that a politician like Vansittart disclosed a vested interest in showing all Germans to be tainted by Nazism, was he himself guilty of turning a blind eye and a deaf ear to credible accusations of guilt simply to maintain his own argument that Nazis and Germans could be distinguished? It is doubtful. In seeking a viable view that was at once Christian in principle, credible in law, and constructive in pragmatic understanding, Bell was often in danger of being as much at sea as any other foreign observer at that time, and not a few of the lawyers, too. No participant in these debates perceived, argued, and judged what they saw in the terms that have come to satisfy the requirements of later Holocaust scholars. We struggle still to find a secure way to interpret the shades of guilt and innocence by which so many who made their way through the history of the Third Reich lived and worked and had their being.

The World Council of Churches Comes of Age: 1946

The World Council of Churches was still, as its letterhead of these years declared, "in the process of formation." Bell was immersed in this: it was more and more the context in which the world found him. The great, crowning moment of all these hopes and labors came in Geneva, that bastion of internationalism, in February 1946. The eager participants who now assembled

17. Lawson, "German War Criminals," pp. 143-46.

there had emerged from years of war and danger — almost blinking into the new daylight of a world in which international peace, however compromised by the new confrontations of the Cold War, was an established fact. Visser 't Hooft would later remember the great act of worship in St. Peter's Cathedral that bound them together: "The vast church was overcrowded. The organ filled the great space with joyful sound. A long and colourful procession filed up the nave slowly. Men who had wondered whether they would ever see each other again walked side by side."[18] And here, in this service, was a foreshadowing of future methods: a careful division of tasks and sharing of burdens. The New Testament lesson was read in Greek by Archbishop Germanos, the prayers of intercession by Archbishop Fisher and Bell's Swiss friend, Alphons Koechlin. There was not one sermon, but three: by Chester Miao from China (in English), the Norwegian Bishop Berggrav (in German), and the German Martin Niemöller (in French).[19] In his sermon, Berggrav looked back on years of silence enforced by the divisions and privations of war and found that

> we have lived together more closely during these five years than we did when we could communicate with the outside world. We have prayed together much more, we have listened together much more to God's word, our hearts have been alongside one another. . . . Christ has said to us during the war: "My Christians, you are one."[20]

Many abroad wanted Bell, not Archbishop Fisher, to chair the first meeting of the full provisional committee of the World Council, when it gathered in Geneva. Both men must have known this. But there were more substantial things now before them. What kind of edifice should ecumenical Christians actually build on such a foundation? Christians often apprehend the exceptionalism of church life and insist that it is at any time something quite distinct from everything else going on. However this may be, the birth of the World Council was recognizable to a far wider body of opinion as an expression of a broad reconstruction of European society, which touched churches because they were a part of a civil order in need of renewal. It was an example of that purposeful internationalism that would also found the United Nations Organization and create new interna-

18. W. A. Visser 't Hooft, *Memoirs* (London: SCM Press, 1973), p. 196.
19. Visser 't Hooft, *Memoirs*, p. 196.
20. Visser 't Hooft, *Memoirs*, p. 195.

tional instruments for economic revival. This made many exciting things possible, not least patronage. The World Council needed investors, and they did not come in the form of archbishops and superintendents. They came from the ranks of an idealistic laity. Much of what was constructed was now owed to the American philanthropist John D. Rockefeller, whom Bell and Visser 't Hooft visited in New York. Rockefeller gave over $1 million to the new organization, half of which created the Ecumenical Study Centre at Bossey[21] and the other half of which was given to the cause of church aid and reconstruction in Europe. A decade later, and much to Bell's satisfaction, Rockefeller would make a further donation of $260,000 for international study.[22]

The Olaus Petri Lectures, 1946

Many Christians in Britain might well have sensed that the ecumenical vision had come of age. Archbishop Fisher was reinvigorating domestic debates with an invitation to other traditions to adopt episcopacy and unite. The Anglican Church was looking to the future. A new Lambeth Conference was around the corner.

When Bell was invited to give a series of lectures at the University of Uppsala in October 1946, he seized this opportunity with both hands, disappeared into his library, and committed himself to a mountain of reading and a concentrated spell of intense, constructive thought. He would draw from the words of the divines of the seventeenth century and from the assorted schemes and adventures of later generations a distinctive, coherent claim for an Anglican "genius." For this was a church both Catholic and Reformed, and one uniquely placed to integrate traditions that claimed simply to be one thing or the other.

When these lectures were published as *Christian Unity: The Anglican Position*, Bell himself prefaced the lectures with the observation that this was, so far as he was aware, the first attempt at such a "conspectus." Ronald Jasper agreed, finding them "a successful attempt to break new ground."[23]

---

21. For an eloquent survey of the history of Bossey see Hans-Ruedi Weber, *A Laboratory for Ecumenical Life: The Story of Bossey, 1946-1996* (Geneva: World Council of Churches, 1996). But Weber's earlier book, *The Courage to Live: A Biography of Suzanne de Diétrich* (Geneva: World Council of Churches, 1995), is equally to be admired.

22. See Jasper, *Bell*, p. 319.

23. Jasper, *Bell*, p. 346.

The lectures were, as Bell himself owned, largely defined by a "simple" narration of ecumenical encounters, between Anglicans, Protestants, Roman Catholics, and Orthodox. But for the Church of England the lectures were prepared to advance confident claims: it was a church that possessed a certain distinctive "wisdom." Such qualities had yielded an ecumenical vision throughout its history, and now in an age of ecumenical movements and hopes it was "peculiarly fitted" to look both one way, to the Protestants, and the other, to the Catholics, offering its *via media* to all the churches. Though it was a modest church in size, its place was a fundamental one. It had shown itself to be a church of scholarship, humanity, and reason.

The Anglican Church was, solidly, an episcopal church, but one that viewed bishops as a matter not of doctrine but of church order. Bell was at pains to demonstrate that the divines of its decisive, early age had been at one in pronouncing that "although episcopacy was indeed of divine or apostolic institution, it was not a commandment which admitted of no exception, and true churches could and did exist without it."[24] But episcopacy was still a reason to hope for union, not merely an obstacle standing in its way:

> It is hard to see how a common, non-episcopal ministry for a re-united church could be other than a new creation, fashioned indeed from Scriptural and historical elements, but remaining the product of negotiation and the circumstances of a particular time . . . only the Episcopate can secure and make real the relation of the ministry to the entire Church.[25]

It was quite wrong to argue that ministers ordained in another tradition should re-ordained. Their ministry was wholly credible as it was. But a consecration by a bishop would give such ministers a new relation to the apostolic ministry, a new authority, and a new place in the whole.

Bell maintained the view adopted by the 1938 report of the Church of England on Doctrine: "we are much nearer to the truth, and, as I believe, to the genius of Anglicanism if we think of the Christian body not as consisting of a single true Church or group of churches, with a number of 'schismatic' bodies gathered about it; but as a whole, which is in a state

---

24. G. K. A. Bell, *Christian Unity: The Anglican Position; Olaus Petri Lectures at Uppsala University, 1946* (London: Hodder & Stoughton, 1948), p. 23.

25. Bell, *Christian Unity*, p. 178.

of division, or 'schism.'" They must not overlook the very real measure of union that Christians had already found with each other. If the churches could not but negotiate still over structures and positions, they must, above all, own that these things of "outward organization" were not, at the last, fundamental:

> There is no longer such a thing as a temporal Christendom: nor is it likely that there will be again. What we must seek is a Christendom of souls — that is to say, living human beings, spiritually united, and working in a spiritual way upon the people and things of this world. We who believe in Christ can be united in Christ; and, as such a spiritual unity, we can be His agent for the achievement of the universal unity of men.[26]

---

26. Bell, *Christian Unity*, p. 189.

CHAPTER TEN

Ecumenical High Tide, 1948-1954

Chichester and Its Cathedral in 1948

The vast questions that now overtook the whole world may well have seemed to leave a quiet English cathedral city wholly undisturbed. Yet somehow the Bishop of Chichester managed to hold these quite different worlds together. In truth, in its way post-war Chichester offered much to do. What we know about Bell in these years is that his patterns, and hours, of work appeared to his intimates relentless and unsparing. Roy Porter, his domestic chaplain in the later 1940s, once recalled a Bell who "really was at work all day. I always remember after I had been here a couple of months, I said to him, 'I know you can do this, but I really can't. I really must have a day off!' He was very kind and said yes, but it never really happened!" Porter also recalled how Bell "could not abide shifty, deceitful people. Some of the clergy tried to pull wool over his eyes over things, and that really irritated him. He very rarely lost his temper, but when he did it was memorable."[1]

Reconstruction was not only a European imperative. In Britain a new Labour government had swept into power with a mission to nationalize all the major industries, achieve a new, universal system of National Insurance, and create a National Health Service in which every man, woman, and child could be treated without facing the threat of doctors' bills. The mood for change was contagious. Even the Church of England caught

---

1. An interview published in the *Chichester Observer* on 4 March 2004 and reproduced in Phil Hewitt, *Chichester Remembered* (Chichester: Philimore, 2004), pp. 157-58. My thanks to my father for this reference.

it. Archbishop Fisher, bluff, pragmatic, constructive, now came into his own. He saw clearly that this was a new society of mass migration, housing estates, and welfare politics. The ancient church could not afford to rest content with its old patterns. There must be new churches built and new priests ordained for new congregations. Meanwhile, every diocese in this post-war society faced the need to reform itself. The cathedral church of Chichester, too, had reason to scrutinize its affairs. Indeed, the bishop would soon do so for himself.

According to a remark made later to a future cathedral librarian, Mary Hobbs, it was in November 1947 that Bell found his dinner at the Athenaeum interrupted by another member of that club, who showed him a Sotheby's catalogue listing a large number of volumes offered up for sale by the Dean and Chapter of Chichester Cathedral. "Ah, Bishop," came the provocative remark, "I see you are selling your books!" Bell himself was utterly oblivious of the whole business. Dinner came to an abrupt end. In Chichester he demanded an explanation. Dean Duncan-Jones was not merely unrepentant. He was hostile. This was the business of the Administrative Chapter, not the bishop. The books were simply unsuitable for the use of the cathedral itself, and they could hardly preserve them. It was no service to the books themselves if they fell apart under a leaking roof. An agitated correspondence was soon accumulating while Bell chased about, trying as best he could to buy stray volumes back. But for most, it was too late.[2]

What began with books soon spread to a host of other issues. The upshot was a visitation charge, an episcopal report, reviewing the entire function of the cathedral; it was published in 1948. Bell found the cathedral facing hard times by retrenching. It was not only that treasures were being sold. A third residentiary canonry had been suspended. Where would it end? Was it not better to work instead for new ways of increasing income? "The more you can make the Cathedral the concern of every churchman in the diocese, the sooner will your difficulties disappear, and the greater will be your reward."[3] For all of this, Duncan-Jones, his old ally in so many international causes, found it exceedingly hard to forgive Bell. Yet the 1948 visitation charge is acknowledged now to be a masterpiece of its kind, and

2. See Mary Hobbs, "Book Crisis at Barchester," *The Book Collector* 44, no. 1 (Spring 1993).

3. G. K. A. Bell, "The Function of Chichester Cathedral" (Diocese of Chichester, 1948), pp. 29-30.

no scholar of the life and work of an English cathedral in the twentieth century can disregard it.

The Church of South India

Though he had so often proven essentially a European in his commitments, Bell remained sharply observant of the life of the church in India, and in these affairs he would intervene again. On 27 September 1947 a great service had taken place in St. George's Church in Madras to mark the creation of a new, united Church of South India. The culmination of many labors over long years, the new church needed friends and allies abroad. At once it confronted a waspish army of High Church critics across the Anglican Communion who feared that, in uniting the ministry of priests ordained by bishops with that of ministers ordained in other traditions, the apostolic succession had been compromised. These debates found Bell, like Archbishop Fisher, intently fixed upon the creation of viable churches capable of living in their own worlds as well as in the wider body of the church. Both men also knew how to value the ecumenical richness on which the participants readily drew.

At the 1948 Lambeth Conference Bell was given the task of chairing a committee concerned to voice "the Unity of the Church." With this came a report on the Church of South India itself, which proposed that the conference "rejoices and gives thanks to God" for what had been accomplished there; the critics rose against such words. When voting took place it could be seen that the bishops were split almost in half between those who "rejoiced" and those who did not. The word itself was abandoned. The new church was not admitted into the Anglican Communion.

This controversy did not rest with ecclesial principles alone. The Church of South India depended heavily upon money provided by missionary societies — and the Society for the Propagation of the Gospel was in character a High Church body opposed to the terms of the union. All of this Bell found "very depressing."[4] He saw the young church quickened by a vigorous and committed vision of mission. This was surely fundamental.

---

4. Joseph Muthuraj, "An Indian Scholar Looks at Bishop George Bell," in *The Church and Humanity: The Life and Work of George Bell, 1883-1958*, ed. Andrew Chandler (Farnham: Ashgate, 2012), p. 70. But see, too, Bengt Sundkler, *The Church of South India: The Movement towards Union, 1900-1947* (London: Lutterworth Press, 1954).

At the same time, he knew that his secretary, Mary Balmer, was firmly on the side of the critics — so he asked his chaplain instead to type all the letters that addressed the issue.

Bell would visit India in 1949. He found himself above all moved by "the devotion of this brave and growing Church." He was still speaking on behalf of it in Convocation in 1955. By then its critics were a spent force, a declining, carping minority. They should not, Bell remarked irenically, expect a Church of South India to look exactly like their own. What mattered was whether it bore the "important features" of the "primitive Catholic Church." Archbishop Fisher — and the passage of time itself — would be responsible for sorting much of this out, but many Christians in India knew that in Bell they had a firm advocate and friend. Half a century after his death, his name would still be honored there.

The WCC and the First General Assembly: 1948

Bell was elected Moderator of the Central Committee of the new World Council of Churches at its first assembly in Amsterdam in August-September 1948. By now the ecumenists had established firmly that their essential currency was the *word*, mounting up in correspondence, conversations, declarations, lectures, sermons, pronouncements of all kinds. It is hardly surprising that the ecumenical movement would soon be known, not in narrative histories rich in incident and personality, but in an evolving canon of reports and pronouncements published rather dutifully in a succession of anthologies.[5] After Amsterdam the bluffly pragmatic Archbishop of Canterbury, Geoffrey Fisher, remarked "that the total number of words spoken at the Assembly must be something like the numbers which indicate the distance between the earth and the farthest stars."[6] Was this praise? Fisher was not much of a man of words. He preferred to get things done, particularly things that would be valued by practical people.

The rhetoric of post-war ecumenism was superbly confident. It was not hedged about by equivocations and doubts, or the need to throw a wary eye toward another faith or constituency. These men and women

---

5. See, for example, G. K. A. Bell, *Documents on Christian Unity* (Oxford: Oxford University Press, 1924, 1930, 1948, 1958).

6. W. A. Visser 't Hooft, ed., *The First Assembly of the World Council of Churches* (London: SCM Press, 1949), p. 7.

talked of the church as though they really did have a vision of what it was. There was apparently little question as to what must be done, and little doubt that it could be achieved. It was possible to identify "common beliefs and common problems."[7] It was uplifting to explore "God's design," to speak of "truth," to point the way to "renewal."[8] World mission was still a robust dimension of ecumenical understanding. Most church leaders in Western countries maintained that Christianity provided the historical foundation and continuing character of their particular societies without thinking such a view anything other than obvious.

Bell was wary of corporate machinery. But he was now, as before, deeply absorbed in it. It is difficult to know how he found himself reflecting on the new mechanics of international ecumenism. For the WCC certainly was a construction. Creating a working constitution was by no means any more straightforward here than it would be in the world of secular politics. There had to be a definition of functions, a division of interests, a drawing of lines. This was inevitably a taxing business, and careful symmetries created on paper rarely correspond neatly with the untidiness of human experience. But there was confidence in forms, too. This was, after all, a *council.*[9] To the founding fathers a council was a formidable thing. A stable organization needed to be defined by departments — at first, it was Reconstruction and Youth and the creation of a commission on International Affairs. There was a Central Committee (of ninety, meeting annually), which appointed an Executive Committee (of twelve, meeting twice-yearly). Periodic General Assemblies would become not only rallies of a kind but also decision-making bodies visibly anchored in the support of the constituents who had sent delegates. The Central and Executive Committees became crucial, seeking to steer the movement in between the assemblies, discussing, devising, engineering, responding to the world at large. It was assumed that the natural vehicle for self-expression and progress was the conference.

7. Visser 't Hooft, *First Assembly,* Report of Section 1, p. 53.

8. See all the volumes prepared for the Amsterdam and Evanston General Assemblies: *Man's Disorder and God's Design: The Amsterdam Assembly Series,* 5 vols. (London, 1949), and Henry Ehrenström, Nils Ehrenström, and Henry Dusen, eds., *Six Ecumenical Surveys: Preparatory Material for the Second Assembly of the World Council of Churches, Northwestern University, Evanston, Illinois* (London: SCM Press, 1954).

9. According to Visser 't Hooft, it was the American Samuel McCrea Cavert who ventured the term. See *The Genesis and Formation of the World Council of Churches* (Geneva: World Council of Churches, 1982), p. 87.

When the first meeting of the Central Committee took place in Bell's own Chichester, in July 1949, the bishop saw to it that local civic authorities played their part as hosts. Apparently the visitors were surprised to find themselves in such company at all.[10] That was revealing. Meanwhile, Visser 't Hooft was proud of the interest Queen Wilhelmina took in the new Council; she became, in a fashion, not only a steadfast friend of the movement but an ally, too. Inevitably, showing that ecumenism claimed a place in the public forum also threw up dangers. President Eisenhower appeared at Evanston and proved characteristically gracious. But some were left to wonder if this all came too close to placing the Council firmly in the hands of American power in the context of the Cold War. More happily, when the Secretary General of the United Nations, Dag Hammarskjöld, made a speech, it showed a clear sharing of interests. Hammarskjöld had known the Söderblom family, and Visser 't Hooft regarded him as "in a sense a member of the family."[11] Indeed, the WCC of Bell and Visser 't Hooft and the United Nations of Hammarskjöld had much in common, for both affirmed the ideals of an ethical internationalism.

In 1948 there was some agitation over the idea of a single president of the Council. But how could one person embody such a vast enterprise as this? The upshot was another collective entity, a *presiduum* of six, with a further (honorary) president — John R. Mott — to boot. This debate threw up a further dilemma: Should there be a representation simply of confessions or of physical geography? This virtually created two rival schools of thought.[12] The controversy exposed a difference between the internationalism of Söderblom, which still mattered to a man like Visser 't Hooft, and an ecumenism defined by ecclesiastical premises. Inevitably, the dimensions of history, confession, and geography intertwined.

The "younger" churches of the southern hemisphere were prickly about the dominance of the old churches of the North. A hectic attempt to secure a visible presence for Chinese Christianity produced a fair amount of last-minute comedy.[13] The Central Committee became a roving committee, showing a presence in certain places in order to achieve visibility there and to demonstrate that Indians were as important to the movement

---

10. R. C. D. Jasper, *George Bell, Bishop of Chichester* (London: Oxford University Press, 1967), p. 325.

11. Visser 't Hooft, *Memoirs*, p. 251.

12. As acknowledged by W. A. Visser 't Hooft, *Memoirs* (London: SCM Press, 1973), pp. 61-62.

13. As recounted wryly by Visser 't Hooft in his *Memoirs*, p. 212.

as Germans or Americans. Bell labored as dutifully in this landscape as anybody else.

For all these efforts, the WCC had no relationship with the Roman Catholic Church and very little indeed with the Orthodox world. What could be done about this? In a new book, his 1954 Penguin Special, *The Kingship of Christ,* Bell wrote bleakly of the "refusal" of Rome.[14] Quite simply, the Vatican found the whole enterprise flawed by faulty ecclesiology. The persevering labors of the Secretariat for Promoting Christian Unity would begin only in 1960, after Bell's death, under Pope John XXIII, and soon after would find their place within the new context created by Vatican II.[15] No official Catholic observers were present at Amsterdam or Evanston, but five official observers would go to New Delhi in 1961.

To many ecumenists the greatest challenge lay squarely to the East. An engagement with Orthodoxy was crucial if the new Council were to establish in reality the claims it ventured on paper. Long, even surreptitious, efforts to connect with the remaining leaders of the Russian Orthodox Church inside the Soviet Union had come to nothing beyond a succession of oddities and confusions — and now eastern Europe and much of central Europe, too, lay in the Soviet orbit. The Hungarian church was at first lost to the ecumenical cause and only slid back into view by degrees and on heavy terms. The new World Council was determined not to concede even to such realities as these. It wanted the Russian Church on board. What it got, in New Delhi in 1961, certainly appeared an impressive step forward — but it would bring profound liabilities, too. Official Orthodoxy was Soviet Orthodoxy.

Europe and the Schuman Plan, 1950

During the war Bell had spoken in the House of Lords of Europe as a "problem."[16] Afterward he had resisted as best he could the division of Germany, observing in the House of Lords in June 1947, "If Germany is

---

14. See G. K. A. Bell, *The Kingship of Christ* (Harmondsworth: Penguin Books, 1954), chapter 7.

15. For a good taste of the new thinking, its opportunities, and its limits, see Augustin Cardinal Bea, *The Unity of Christians,* ed. Bernard Leeming, S.J. (London, 1963).

16. March 1943. Highlighted by Philip Coupland in his article, "George Bell, the Question of Germany and the Cause of European Unity, 1939-1950," in Chandler, ed., *The Church and Humanity,* p. 152.

divided, Europe will be divided . . . there must be no iron screen, either in imagination or reality. . . . Let Europe be envisaged as a whole."[17] More strikingly, in October that year he had presented a motion to the Convocation of Canterbury that called for the "progressive establishment of a United States of Europe with a common foreign, military and economic policy."[18] But no speeches to Parliaments, secular or ecclesiastical, could alter the immense power of division in the new Europe. This was now, inescapably and rigidly, a Europe of Eastern dictatorships and Western democracies. When, early in 1948, the British government had pressed that there be a "Western Union" comprising the democracies, Bell found the initiative vague and urged something clearer: "It is time for definition and action, unless we are all to be drowned. So there must be a common economic plan in which all shall join; there must be some sort of common political structure and there must be a real military alliance."[19]

It was in capitals other than London that bold and persevering efforts were now being made to achieve something of enduring value. A courageous participant in resistance against German occupation, Robert Schuman, had by now moved into the foreground of French political life, from which he now ventured a firm plan that would make impossible a future war between European nations and build one economic market, beginning with the iron and steel industries. Schuman was convinced that one nation-state should not be the highest power to judge the good of the many. Instead, he looked to a supranational authority. In Britain Lord Pakenham welcomed this as "a sublime example of Christian statesmanship."[20] Bell, too, knew how to prize this. He made sure that he was in Parliament when the Schuman Plan was debated by the House of Lords on 28 June 1950.

This plan, he acknowledged, was a great initiative. Yet the response of the British government had been a cool one. Why? They had only to look at Korea to see that the world was volatile, while in Europe France faced crisis; West Germany was still finding its feet; Italy, Greece, and Belgium were insecure. Britain alone was "stable, intact, firm and soundly democratic." These qualities must be offered to the new European movement. Indeed,

17. *Hansard,* Debates of the House of Lords, fifth series, vol. 148, cols. 525-29 (11 June 1947).

18. See Coupland, "The Question of Germany," pp. 124-25.

19. Coupland, "The Question of Germany," p. 126. The full speech may be found in *Hansard,* Debates of the House of Lords, fifth series, vol. 154, cols. 346-52 (3 March 1948).

20. As quoted by Bell, Debates of the House of Lords, vol. 167, col. 1163 (28 June 1950).

Bell went so far as to pronounce, "Britain is the natural centre for European thought." To those who judged that its responsibilities lay not with Europe but with its empire and its relationship with the United States, Bell affirmed that these were the very strengths that it should now bring into European life. The country should seek to play its part in this new and hopeful current, and do so from the very beginning. The preservation of national sovereignty was "not itself a Christian principle. The partial fusion of sovereignty is in accordance with Christian principles, if it is in the pursuit of noble ends and justice and peace. . . . I hope with all my heart that His Majesty's Government may still see their way to full participation in the discussions to which M. Schuman has called all free nations."[21] These were surely conspicuous words. But British politicians would remain lastingly ambivalent about the ideal of European union, as the leaders of individual churches remained ambivalent about movements of Christian union. Many of the speeches that were heard in Parliament in the summer of 1950 could, with a few editorial adjustments, have served there just as well half a century later.

Nuclear Politics and the Challenge of Communism

The force of the Cold War now dominated the calculations of the ecumenists.[22] Caught hopelessly in this relentless deepening of the gulf fixed between East and West, the churches were simply not free to establish their own independent narratives. It was a landscape wholly defined by confrontation and dictatorship and haunted by the dreadful prognostications of an age of nuclear weapons. From this there would be no escape. The Finnish historian of ecumenism Jaakko Rusama has shown how significant a role Bell played in turning the advent of the nuclear age into a serious discussion within the counsels of the ecumenical movement: "The whole period from 1950 to 1958, when Bell acted as chairman of the Central Committee and as Honorary President, shows a strong emphasis on the consideration of the nature and use of nuclear devices."[23] It was with "a

21. For the whole speech see Debates of the House of Lords, vol. 167, cols. 1158-64 (28 June 1950).

22. For the available overviews in English see Owen Chadwick, *The Christian Church in the Cold War* (London: Penguin Books, 1993); Dianne Kirby, ed., *Religion and the Cold War* (London: Palgrave, 2002). But scholarship in this area is still gathering momentum.

23. Jaakko Rusama, *Unity and Compassion: Moral Issues in the Life and Thought of George K. A. Bell* (Helsinki: The Finnish Society for Missiology and Ecumenics, 1986), p. 172.

burning conviction" that the World Council of Churches must issue a statement about the new hydrogen bomb that Bell turned up at the little study center at Bossey for a meeting of the Central Committee in February 1950 — and he carried a none-too-certain Central Committee with him. The upshot was a declaration that deplored unequivocally such a development as a "perversion" of the universal moral order and a sin against God. This was not merely a matter for the calculations of statesmen and scientists, but for the conscience of every man and every woman: "We appeal for a new gigantic effort for peace."[24]

Bell had no illusions about the state that had been established by the Bolshevik revolution of October 1917. This totalitarian power was utterly dangerous to its own people, and any expansion of its influence must cause any Christian who cherished freedom to tremble. The Cold War historian Dianne Kirby is clearly uncomfortable that Bell's resolve to work against such a state and such an ideology showed an incautious readiness "to embrace a state-engendered consensus that promoted the Cold War as a crusade against the forces of evil, when in fact it was a traditional power struggle between rival states."[25] A lecture at Chatham House in June 1949 had found Bell in uncompromising form, and Kirby points to a meeting of the Executive Committee of the World Council of Churches in the summer of 1951, in which he put about a paper on "Peace and Soviet Policy" produced by the British Foreign Office.[26] Far from showing Bell to be a dissenting voice, did such occasions show him to be little more than an instrument of the state — even its "spiritual auxiliary"?

Bell did not regard cooperation with the state as necessarily a compromise of ecclesiastical, or moral, independence. It depended on the particular question. His disagreements with government policy may have done much to define his public reputation, but many controversies found him convinced that British politics remained the expression of a basic integrity in high places. Kirby herself allows that even in the thick of his wartime campaigns he had friends, sympathizers, and allies in Whitehall, and he was prepared to prove himself an ally to them, too. Furthermore, he was likely to accept, and put about, information from any credible quarter.

As the Cold War now passed through one bleak phase after another,

---

24. Rusama, *Unity and Compassion*, p. 174.

25. See Dianne Kirby, "George Bell and the Cold War," in Chandler, ed., *The Church and Humanity*, p. 152.

26. Kirby, "Cold War," p. 160.

Bell maintained that Christians must frame a committed response to the challenge of communism. It is no surprise to find that the little group of Anglican thinkers who gathered around the Oxford thinker Donald Mac-Kinnon to publish *Christian Faith and Communist Faith* in 1953 did so under the aegis of the Bishop of Chichester. To this Bell contributed a concise introduction in which he allowed himself some broader reflections. "Communism," he wrote, "is, without doubt, the most powerful challenge to the Christian religion today. But its full force cannot be understood unless it is itself apprehended as a religion." This was by now familiar ground. But Bell could see that while Roman Catholics were wholly at odds with the communist states, in eastern Europe there were many Protestants who acknowledged some moral, progressive force in that new religion. In such a context it must be asked: Were these two faiths "fundamentally incompatible"? If that was true, what made them so?[27] In 1954 Bell accepted an invitation to speak to the Worthing Labour Party. Here he pronounced that communism and Christianity must be utterly at odds, but that they should also distinguish between the Soviet State and the Russian people.

The terrible power now paraded by governments in this nuclear age continued to preoccupy Bell. In 1955 he collaborated with John E. Roberts, a professor of physics at the University of London and a Methodist, on a pamphlet entitled *Nuclear War and Peace: The Facts and the Challenge.* Here the division of duties was a clear one: Roberts wrote of science while Bell discussed ethics. There was a flutter of interest in the newspapers, and the instrument of the Communist Party, *The Daily Worker,* gave him a headline: "Bishop condemns H-Bomb. Deterrent idea is 'Delusion.'" Bell sent a copy of the pamphlet to the Foreign Secretary, Selwyn Lloyd, emphasizing that he was not a pacifist and that he was no supporter of the National Peace Council, which had published it. This received a thorough inspection in Whitehall, and Bell himself earned a courteous, even sympathetic, reply. But here the historian Gerhard Besier has shown how official opinion managed not only to blunt the force of his arguments but even to wring from them some shades of endorsement for the policies of the state.[28]

Political crises now tumbled into view almost by the week. These could unite and give ecumenists a reason for their labors. But they could

27. D. M. MacKinnon, ed., *Christian Faith and Communist Faith: A Series of Studies by Members of the Anglican Communion* (London: Macmillan, 1953), pp. ix-xii.

28. Gerhard Besier, "'Intimately Associated for Many Years': The Common Life-Work of George Bell and Willem Visser 't Hooft in the Service of the Universal Church," in Chandler, ed., *The Church and Humanity,* pp. 189-90.

also divide. They could show the relevance of the World Council to a world in travail, but also show cruelly the limits of its influence. Already, when the Central Committee met at Toronto in 1950, the agenda was full of the defense of religious liberty, the emergence of official racial discrimination in South Africa, and the outbreak of war in Korea. The last of these provoked the first resignation from the Presiduum: T. C. Chao resigned as "a patriotic Chinese."[29] Meanwhile, the retreat from empire threw up another landscape of costly change. As a Dutchman, Visser 't Hooft found himself in the very thick of mounting controversies in Indonesia. But decolonization could also find a ready, positive echo in the churches. For, as the 1950s unfolded, many sensed that the work of Western missionaries was now effectively done and that the "new" churches must find their own leaders and their own place in the great ecumenical opportunity. In such a way the idea of a World Council of Churches matched the mood and the need of the day and saw an obvious way to grow and flourish.

In the Cold War Bell had found a role that showed lines of continuity with his public career before 1945. But the world of political power looked, if anything, still more massive and less amenable to the interventions of an English bishop than ever before. Significantly, the period inspired very few intense new friendships with men and women caught behind the Iron Curtain, for these confinements made such things impossible, and without them he lacked his old eloquence. Was the figure of the Bishop of Chichester now a receding one?

Ecumenical Doubts and the Apotheosis of Evanston

In the summer of 1951 Bell was invited to Cambridge to give the final lecture in a series devoted to "The Approach to Christian Unity." Such an occasion might well have drawn from him a merely dry, workaday response, or a conventional exercise in predictable rhetoric. But his words now showed a very sharp measuring of ecumenical realities indeed. Parts of the lecture come almost as a shock. Drawing from words of Charles Péguy that this would be a century of war, and from others by his friend Otto Dibelius that this would be the century of the church, Bell acknowledged that ecumenism had in many ways shown a "halting" history. There had been pioneers; the scandal of division was acknowledged. But, for the most part,

29. See Jasper, *Bell,* p. 328.

the churches at large had been "untouched": "The thing with which we are faced is not only the fact but the temper of isolation. . . . In all our churches, there is too little movement, and too much circumspection." When he looked back over thirty years he saw a new spirit, a new generosity, and a new friendship. "But when it comes to the expression of that new spirit in the more concrete form of church relations, there is little, if any, advance at all." In their own country they were "no further forward in 1951 than we were in 1920. Indeed, in some ways, the reports of earlier conferences were more hopeful than their successors."

Where then to look? There was only one "outstanding" achievement, and that had been in South India. What Christians there had achieved had come because they possessed what the British churches lacked: a motive, "powerfully held," to preach the gospel to a non-Christian world. Bell warned, "Is not the isolation of individual denominations and congregations, and their concentration on themselves and their traditions, the result of blindness to the needs of the world?"[30]

There were new speeches to be made — in London, in church meetings across the diocese, in towns and cities where the view of the Bishop of Chichester was called for. In 1952 Bell the diocesan bishop published another charge to his clergy, reflecting on his secondary visitation of the diocese at large. Much had altered since his first, fourteen years before. In *The Word and the Sacraments* he acknowledged, "Amid all the confusion of the modern world, with its babel of tongues and its following of false idols, the old Christian order suddenly puts its head above the surface of life, and claims a share of men's attention for a passing moment."[31] The "spiritual call" that he now proposed for the year 1953 showed a determination to stir up a religiosity that he believed still rested in the English people at large. This charge has not the eloquence of its predecessor of 1938; it shows effort, purpose, and high resolve, but somehow these properties do not quite yield that elusive quality, inspiration.

Surveying the still-rising edifice of the World Council of Churches in October 1953, Bell remarked, "What worries me is the almost complete lack of any organisation for getting the World Council into the mind of the Church of England."[32] The doubt would not go away. In the following

---

30. G. K. A. Bell, *The Approach to Christian Unity: Sermons Preached before the University of Cambridge, 1951* (Cambridge: W. Heffer & Sons, n.d.), pp. 57-63.

31. G. K. A. Bell, *The Word and the Sacraments* (Diocese of Chichester, 1952), p. 9.

32. Jasper, *Bell*, p. 331.

year Bell became a president of the WCC. This gave him a central position, if not quite clearly a role. When the second General Assembly of the movement grew near in 1954, Penguin asked him to write a second book, this time on ecumenism. This came as a superb opportunity, not least to influence the mind of his own church, and he dashed it off in only a few weeks. Yet, when it appeared, some were left feeling that *The Kingship of Christ* somehow lacked the urgency, the idealistic force, which had ignited *Christianity and World Order* fourteen years before.[33] Essentially, this new book was a briskly efficient survey. But was it also the work of a man whose vision was beginning to wane?

The great gathering at Evanston took "Christian Hope" as its theme and certainly made much of it. (A janitor was heard to remark dryly, and perhaps wearily, "They sure is givin' hope a good goin' over!")[34] The consequent volume of reports bore the title *Evanston Speaks,* and certainly there was a great deal of speaking.[35] By Evanston few ecumenists could have many illusions about what happens when theologians set to work excavating a single word. As a foundation for unity "hope" proved to be anything but innocuous. It was soon clear that the ecumenists had run straight into a frowning brick wall of eschatology and then into a dispute about the significance of Israel.

A photograph of Bell at Evanston captures him in a lounge suit and tie, looking benign and relaxed. But by the time of the General Assembly the criticisms of some constituents were indeed mounting. A number of Anglicans, in particular, were looking frankly skeptical. The Bishop of London, Henry Campbell, grumbled that this General Assembly had been the work of "German theology, American money and Dutch bureaucracy."[36] Visser 't Hooft did not much care for this description, but, even if it is allowed, a historian may still be impressed by the combination of such formidable forces. Surely what was more important was whether such things were put to work vigorously on behalf of a bold idea and a wide constituency. Bell saw clearly that the integrity of the World Council of Churches lay in its power to show itself to be rooted in the many landscapes and lives

33. The generally sympathetic Kenneth Slack observed, "It is sad to reflect that the author of that dull book once had the felicitous pen that wrote Randall Davidson." Kenneth Slack, *George Bell* (London: SCM Press, 1971), p. 117.

34. Jasper, *Bell,* p. 336.

35. *Evanston Speaks: Reports from the Second Assembly of the World Council of Churches, August 15-31, 1954* (Geneva: World Council of Churches, 1954).

36. See Visser 't Hooft, *Memoirs,* p. 252.

of the Christian church across the world. Almost as soon as he returned to Chichester he convened a special conference of the Sussex Council of Churches to draw the experience of Evanston into a meaningful local context. There is more than a hint of anxiety in all this. Bell saw how quickly the great ecumenical movement might simply drift into its own bustling dimension, one barely connected to local life, but instead vastly busy with the higher politics of its own committees, conferences, memoranda, and resolutions. It was no easy task for an international movement to make headway in an age of nation-states. It would be no easier for a World Council of Churches to prosper in a continuing age of denominations. Building bridges had once been an exciting task. But very few choose to live on a bridge for long. At some point most will return to what they know as home.

CHAPTER ELEVEN

Toward the End . . . 1958

Although Mary Balmer found him still brimful of vigorous life and ambitious plans, the passage of time was now beginning to tell against the Bishop of Chichester. Bell surely knew it. Many of those refugees he had sought to settle in Britain had remained, and now he watched their children grow up. When he trooped off to address a gathering of "elderly people" in September 1952, he owned, almost plaintively, "Like you, my dear friends in West Sussex, I am an elderly person."[1]

Time altered even the steady patterns of life at the cathedral. Duncan-Jones, for so long a formidable presence in its precincts, was now growing deaf; sometimes he could be heard shouting at those who came to confess their sins before communion to speak up. A new dean came: Walter Hussey. Bell viewed his arrival with enthusiasm. Hussey had cultivated all manner of connections with artists and musicians, and had shown the courage of his convictions by commissioning a cantata (which became *Rejoice in the Lamb*) from the young Benjamin Britten and a monumental sculpture of the Madonna and Child from Henry Moore, both for the church of St. Matthew's in Northampton. Hussey, like Bell, saw himself as an instrument of a new creative relationship between the church and art.[2] And Bell could still show the strength of his convictions in this sphere. In 1954, when Hans Feibusch got into trouble with a commission to paint a mural in the church of St. Mary's, in Goring-by-Sea, the bishop was there firmly to overrule all objectors in his own consistory court. "Unless the Church is to be sterile in the fostering

1. Public address, Bell Papers, vol. 350, fol. 52.
2. See, at large, Walter Hussey, *Patron of Art: The Revival of a Great Tradition among Modern Artists* (London: Weidenfeld & Nicholson, 1985).

of creative art," he wrote, "it must be prepared to trust its chosen artists to begin their work and carry it through to the end as the fulfilment of a trust, the terms and circumstances of which they respect and understand."[3] Such words were significant, even bold. In January 1957 Bell attended a service at the cathedral to bless a new mural by Hans Feibusch, the baptism of Christ by John the Baptist. The artist, he again insisted, "must be *free*, and yet know how to commit the fruits of his vision to a discerning church."[4]

In these years he was no more simply the Bishop of Chichester than he had ever been. He was still often to be seen in Parliament. He was there to play a long, and ultimately pivotal, role in working for the abolition of the death penalty in the House of Lords. Doughty abolitionists, who clustered around men like the progressive publisher Victor Gollancz and the reforming lawyer Gerald Gardiner, had for years persevered in steady pursuit of their goal. But it proved hard going, and the Bishop of Chichester was not one of their number. After the Second World War, however, he became a conspicuous episcopal ally, not on public platforms but in Parliament. Archbishop Fisher would have none of this — and, at first, it was Fisher who represented the views prevalent on the bishops' bench. But obstinate, enduring Bell would see this campaign almost through to final accomplishment. By his retirement it could be seen clearly that opinion was altering by fractions. It was he who now spoke in Parliament for the majority of bishops, and Fisher who now looked isolated and beleaguered there.

Bell remained ever the internationalist, and the great, troubled realm of foreign affairs still absorbed him. The later 1950s found successive Conservative governments struggling to maintain British power abroad and in conflict with new movements for change there. Bell registered his opposition to the invasion of Egypt in 1956, taking the government to task for setting aside the United Nations and concealing much behind barricades of disingenuous language.[5] In this he was stoutly supported by Archbishop Fisher, who later distinguished himself by harassing the government spokesman, Lord Kilmuir, with an avalanche of interjections in the House of Lords.[6] When Britain resisted the claims of a growing popular

3. See R. C. D. Jasper, *George Bell, Bishop of Chichester* (London: Oxford University Press, 1967), pp. 131-33.

4. See Bell Papers, vol. 350, fol. 6.

5. *Hansard*, Debates of the House of Lords, fifth series, vol. 199, cols. 748-53 (13 September 1956).

6. *Hansard*, Debates of the House of Lords, fifth series, vol. 199, cols. 1293-1354 (1 November 1956).

nationalist movement in Greek Cyprus, Bell stirred to defend the Cypriot Archbishop Makarios against the criticisms of politicians who alleged that this turbulent prelate had become implicated in violence. In this Bell found less to admire in the Archbishop of Canterbury, and he had to work hard to bridge a gulf between Fisher in London and Visser 't Hooft in Geneva, for they were soon firmly, even bitterly, at odds.[7]

In ecclesiastical affairs there was one last, great task in hand. By this time Bell was working vigorously as joint chairman of the burgeoning conversations between Anglicans and Methodists. The church bureaucrat Kenneth Grubb saw him now and then and found himself a critic of the bishop, whom he alleged to be purposeful only in pursuit of his own enterprises. More sympathetic was Eric Kemp, a younger colleague, who still found the bishop a hard task master. Indeed, such labors showed clearly how heavily Bell depended on his own powers of endurance, and also how he assumed the stamina of his collaborators. But now and then it could be seen that he was continuing to rely upon things that were beginning to wear out. His own health, which had supported him stoutly for so many arduous years, was now faltering. One morning during the Anglican-Methodist Conversations he failed to appear at breakfast. Kemp made his way to his room and found him lying on the floor, his pale blue eyes staring, unseeing, at the ceiling. It was almost too clear and stern a warning.

The world was ever with him, and there were still many letters to read and write. Joseph Mutharaj writes of Bell's warm friendship with the Indian philosopher and statesman D. S. Radhakrishnan. They met, often in Oxford or at the Athenaeum in London, and their relationship came to possess some of the qualities of an intellectual rapport. Radhakrishnan would later remember Bell as "a liberal Christian: friendly to all religious men and gentle and refined in his behaviour."[8] The last striking intervention in international politics came in October 1956, when Soviet tanks rolled into Budapest to extinguish brutally the independence of a reformist communist government. Only that August Bell had been in the country for a meeting of the Central Committee of the WCC. Some then had been perplexed by the hospitality that was shown to them by a communist state.

---

7. For this see Gerhard Besier, " 'Intimately Associated for Many Years': The Common Life-Work of George Bell and Willem Visser 't Hooft in the Service of the Universal Church," in *The Church and Humanity: The Life and Work of George Bell, 1883-1958*, ed. Andrew Chandler (Farnham: Ashgate, 2012), pp. 190-92; also Jasper, *Bell*, p. 343.

8. Joseph Mutharaj, "An Indian Scholar Looks at Bishop Bell," in Chandler, ed., *The Church and Humanity*, p. 75.

Bell himself had no illusions but that this was a cruel dictatorship ruling by terror. When the national uprising had come he thought it "marvellous"; when the suppression followed he saw it to be "savage."[9] He wrote in protest to the Hungarian president, István Dobi, and also to the president of the office for church affairs, Janos Horvat, who had evidently given his earlier interventions on behalf of church people genuine attention, warning, "The trouble is that violence breeds violence."[10] On 4 July 1957 Bell returned to the House of Lords. His speech there showed him more than ever the Christian internationalist, setting out the interweaving lines of ecumenical diplomacy and material aid across closed borders and between free and oppressed nations, looking firmly to the United Nations, affirming the duty of the church to "raise the moral tone of international conduct, and also make a definite and valuable contribution to the building up of a responsible international society."[11] He continued to write letters, public and private. It was, again, to no avail. The Hungarian uprising showed the brutal immovability of the now settled truths of the Cold War in Europe. Perhaps to sound a noble strain of solidarity with those who endured in oppression was sometimes all that an English bishop could do? One year after the revolt Bell broadcast to Hungary over the BBC:

> You are not forgotten by the world outside, however ashamed we may be of the little, if anything, we have been able to do to show our fellow-feeling. There is a spiritual solidarity amongst men of all nations, races and religions, who care for truth, justice and freedom. For many of us it finds its expression in prayer, and for all of us in admiration, love and hope.[12]

What was the value of such words in a world like this? Perhaps almost nothing — perhaps far more than can be known.

There were still many more miles to be traveled, and travel tells on older men. In August the British Methodist Kenneth Slack came across the figure of the Bishop of Chichester at three o'clock in the morning in the strike-bound Idlewild Airport in New York. Slack found the context a "sordid" one. As the two men found they were both attending a meeting

---

9. *Hansard,* Debates of the House of Lords, fifth series, vol. 204, cols. 728-29 (1957).

10. Jasper, *Bell,* p. 341.

11. For the whole speech, see *Hansard,* Debates of the House of Lords, fifth series, vol. 204, cols. 727-32 (1957).

12. Jasper, *Bell,* p. 342.

of the Central Committee of the WCC at Yale, they traveled together in the motor car that had been provided for the bishop, who enjoyed such a favor as an Honorary President. This time Bell was looking not forward, but backward. He had begun to reflect on his plan to write his memoirs. Should it be an Anglican or an ecumenical autobiography, he wondered? Slack was perplexed by such a distinction and urged that it be both.[13] The story, and the distinction, remains suggestive.

By then the Bishop of Chichester had announced his retirement. Work went on, almost regardless. He gave a lecture to the Artworkers' Guild and found the audience — which included Hans Feibusch — appreciative. But in Chichester it was time to face the upheaval of departure. The new home would be in Canterbury. For several weeks a friend from the County Record Office, Patricia Gill, fluent in German, came to help him sort out the mountains of papers that had accumulated in the Bishop's Palace. Sometimes he joined in the task, sitting with her on the floor as she made her way through a new box or pile, or eating lunch. There followed a succession of official farewells. "Not for me a fugitive and cloistered Church," he told his diocesan council on 24 October 1957. Instead, Christians must meet the challenges and crises of the world by building bridges and striving for justice and peace. For himself, "I am conscious of many failures and faults. But I have never given up hoping or trying."[14] These were surely the words of the idealist in public life who has learned what it is to strain every nerve and yet still to falter.

Soon after his retirement, he began to travel. First he and Henrietta went to Greece, and made a particular point of visiting Delphi, to see in person the imagined landscape of antiquity that had brought him his youthful triumph in poetry at Oxford so many years before. He also traveled to Rome and was received by Pope Pius XII. A fourth, doughty volume of his series *Documents on Christian Unity* duly appeared. In the autumn of 1957 he traveled to Göttingen to give a lecture on "The Church and the Resistance Movement in Germany." The story of the Bonhoeffer family was now widely known, and not only in Germany. Time and context — and the unfolding Cold War — had yielded more mature perspectives on the tremendous affair in Sweden fifteen years before. For this Göttingen lecture Bell had prepared thoroughly. It represents his final, cumulative reflection on the matter. By now historians were beginning to record their

---

13. Kenneth Slack, *George Bell* (London: SCM Press, 1971), p. 7.
14. Jasper, *Bell*, p. 378.

own verdicts, and in Britain these looked far from sympathetic. It is likely that John Wheeler Bennett's study of the German army in politics, *The Nemesis of Power,* was much in Bell's mind, for he was offended by the book. He knew how the critics of the German resistance argued against it; he heard it called "vacillating, rash and disunited." "Nevertheless," he concluded firmly, "my own strong conviction is that the negative attitude of the Allies was wrong; that the sound and statesmanlike policy would have been to offer a positive response to the approaches made at such terrible risk; and that the failure to do so was tragic." Above all, this resistance had been driven by a "moral force":

> I do not dispute that there were different elements in it, not all on the same level of moral and religious inspiration. But the leaders were men of high ideals, to whom Hitler and all his works were an abomination. . . . I count it personally a high honour to have been with these two German pastors who came to Sweden in 1942 in the cause of truth, justice and freedom.[15]

Now the future of the world would depend on whether statesmen and leaders of nations would be led, not by the calculations of their predecessors in politics, but by the costly example that had been shown by these brave, doomed men. In these words Bell had brought what had so often been abandoned on the margins of diplomacy, politics, and history into the very heart of a righteous understanding of the age. He never ceased to hold his own government at least partly responsible for the tragedy.

In August 1958 Bell traveled to Denmark for another ecumenical gathering, this one to mark the tenth anniversary of the creation of the World Council of Churches. This time Henrietta was with him, to reassure and to instruct against unnecessary exertion. He preached at Odense Cathedral on Luke 17:10: "So likewise ye, when ye should have done all those things which are commanded you, say, We are unprofitable servants: we have done that which was our duty to do." And in this he recalled his great inspiration, Archbishop Söderblom. Many there were troubled to see how tired he was. It must have occurred to some of them, at least, that this might be their last meeting.

Once George Bell had looked upon the death of William Temple

---

15. G. K. A. Bell, "The Church and the Resistance Movement in Germany," *The Bridge,* November 1957, pp. 3-17.

with words adapted freely from the seventeenth-century divine, Richard Hooker: "Ministers of good things are like torches, a light to others, waste and destruction to themselves."[16] Now there was nothing left to give. It was in Canterbury that Bell died, on 3 October 1958. "I cannot grieve for his going," his widow told a young friend, Peter Walker; "he felt so much for all that was happening in the world."[17]

16. Memoir in A. E. Baker, *William Temple and His Message* (Harmondsworth: Penguin Books, 1946), p. 46. In the form in which Bell offers it, the quotation makes powerful sense. Other versions make it less appropriate to his meaning.

17. Andrew Chandler, "The Death of Dietrich Bonhoeffer," *Journal of Ecclesiastical History* 45, no. 3 (July 1993): 459.

CHAPTER TWELVE

The Place of George Bell

"Chichester is dead," pronounced Franz Hildebrandt from the pulpit of the chapel of Drew University on 8 October 1958; "Did you notice this in the papers a few days ago, and do you comprehend what it means?"[1]

Bell had once been gratified by an invitation to join a London dining club, equally clerical and lay, called *Nobodies Friends,* duly accepting his status as a Nobody with a wry, rhyming speech setting out his qualifications.[2] Indeed, what place had this man come to occupy in the world? In Britain civil honors are often awarded to those who have done recognizable duties bravely and well — or, perhaps, to those who once attracted admiration for individualism, and even controversy, but whose challenge has safely faded to a point of gracious irrelevance. When in Bell's later years Lord Woolton and a few allies had quietly proposed that the Bishop of Chichester be made a Companion of Honour, or something comparable, they encountered only silence. In the eyes of the Methodist Kenneth Slack, this spoke of "an implacable refusal to forgive the man who has betrayed the 'establishment' from within. That was Bell's offence, and it was to the end unpardonable."[3] But, in a sense, it was difficult for both church and state to know quite what to do with Bell. He himself sensed that a higher preferment would represent a vindication of his wartime speeches, and even hoped for one for that reason.[4]

1. Address by Hildebrandt in the chapel of Drew University, 8 October 1958, sent by Hildebrandt to Henrietta Bell, October 1958, Bell Papers, vol. 367, fols. 101-3.

2. To be found in *George Bell, Poems 1883-1958* (Brighton: privately published, 1960), p. 302.

3. Kenneth Slack, *George Bell* (London: SCM Press, 1971), pp. 123-24.

4. As observed by Bell's chaplain, Lancelot Mason, in Paul Foster, ed., *George Bell, 1883-1958: A Prophetic Bishop* (University of Chichester, Otter Memorial Series No. 17), p. 123.

If this was known it could not have helped. It might be argued that to have left Bell as an undecorated Bishop of Chichester represented a greater compliment, for it showed that his explosive properties had never been safely defused. Although he was certainly a part of the Establishment, however that phenomenon may be defined, he did not quite belong to it. He belonged to his age and still has the power to belong to another.

In the wake of his death, Henrietta Bell found telegrams and dozens of letters of tribute tumbling through the Canterbury letterbox, from priests and ministers at home and abroad, from old friends and allies across the world. She kept them almost reverently and even annotated one or two as they were carefully collected. One was marked, simply, "Friday." It had come from Archbishop Fisher in Lambeth Palace: immediate, hand-written, stark. The end, however anticipated, he found "abrupt, harsh — so final, and leaving such a terrible emptiness. I feel it here: how much more you."[5] This note matters. Fisher, the administrator, and Bell, the prophet, have too often been set beside each other as opposites, as they were surely both contenders for Canterbury in 1944. But there was more of Bell in Fisher than his critics allowed, and more of Fisher in Bell, too. Fisher knew how to weigh the value of this bishop of Chichester and saw what was at stake in him. Fisher was not often glimpsed as a man of feeling — but these are the words of a man shocked by grief.

There were letters from great names and names unknown to posterity. There were telegrams from the president and chancellor of Germany (Heuss and Adenauer) and also from the president of the Bundeshaus, the old resister of Nazism, Eugen Gerstenmaier. The reforming campaigner and publisher Victor Gollancz wrote that Bell had been "a shining light of goodness in the darkness of his own age."[6] Imogen Holst, daughter of the composer Gustav Holst, wrote, "We all of us, all over the world, owe him so much for all that he has done for us and for all his struggles for the things that matter most. There are no words to tell you what we feel about him."[7] The composer Benjamin Britten wrote, "He was a very great man, a most important figure in our time . . . he will be sadly missed."[8] Henrietta Bell cherished local correspondence, too. Nodding to Archbishop Fisher's 1946 appeal to the men and women of other traditions, a Congregationalist minister in Chichester, John Grant, recalled how dire had been the relations

---

5. Fisher to Henrietta Bell, "Friday," Bell Papers, vol. 367, fol. 66.
6. Gollancz to Henrietta Bell, October 1958, Bell Papers, vol. 367, fol. 79.
7. Imogen Holst to Henrietta Bell, 6 October 1958, Bell Papers, vol. 367, fol. 106.
8. Britten to Henrietta Bell, 8 October 1958, Bell Papers, vol. 367, fol. 36.

of church and chapel when he had first known the city in 1911. Now it was all quite different. Of Bell he wrote, "He brought us together . . . and kept us together so that in our meeting, thinking and planning together, it was as though we were one Church already." As a principle, or a proposition in an assembly or synod, it had been difficult for many like him to adopt episcopacy. Yet in Chichester, in a manner, they had; "not from any recognition of an official status but because we had found a father in God in our midst."[9] (Within a fortnight, Henrietta noted, Grant, too, was dead.) And there was another local correspondent, the honorary secretary of the Uckfield branch of the National Union of Public Employees, who wrote, "As a member of the Trade Union Movement, Dr. Bell will remain ever fresh in the memory of Sussex Trades Unionists for his inspiration as such and his complete understanding of Trades Unionism in general."[10]

"In him," wrote the French pastor Marc Boegner, "I lost a friend, in the fullest sense of the word, of whom I can never think without feeling the warmest gratitude."[11] It is as well to pause and look about at those stray individuals who had become, across the long years, Bell's earnest friends and allies. The biographer inevitably creates an odd perspective in drawing a cast of characters around the single narrative of one life. As Bell appears as a passing character in studies of Dietrich Bonhoeffer, so does Bonhoeffer come and go in a portrait of George Bell. But the cast that performed in the drama of Bell's life is striking, for in it so much of the eloquence, and so much of the tragedy, of his age could be glimpsed. No scheme can organize them satisfactorily, and it is as well to let chronology speak for itself. Many died before him.

In Britain, Bell's friends in the arts came to know the vindication of a wider fame. Gustav Holst never ceased to experiment generously in his compositions, much of his work resting outside the conventional forms and patterns that so many of his contemporaries maintained. When he died in 1934 Bell preached at his memorial service and praised "this prince of friends, and a prince of men and of teachers, as well as a prince of musicians."[12] He made sure that Holst's ashes were interred in Chiches-

9. Grant to Henrietta Bell, 4 October 1958, Bell Papers, vol. 367, fol. 84.

10. Bryant to Henrietta Bell, 4 October 1958, Bell Papers, vol. 367, fol. 37.

11. Marc Boegner, *The Long Road to Unity: Memories and Anticipations* (London: William Collins, 1970), p. 239.

12. "Address Given by the Bishop of Chichester at the Memorial Service for Gustav Holst at St. John's Church, Westminster, on Tuesday 19 June 1934," copy in Chichester Cathedral Library.

ter Cathedral, where they are now found beside a memorial to the early seventeenth-century composer and organist Thomas Weelkes.

Cosmo Gordon Lang, who as Archbishop of Canterbury had stood so firmly beside Bell in one controversy after another, died on 5 December 1945, hurrying to catch a train into central London for an appointment at a museum before a session in the House of Lords on the relief of distress in Europe.

Gandhi, who had come to Chichester in October 1931, went on to lead India to independence and to become one of the greatest figures of the twentieth century. He was shot down by a fanatic in 1948.

The German pastor Hans Schönfeld never recovered himself and died a tragic death in 1954.

Bishop Velimirovic had written spiritual works that would make him famous in the Orthodox world. After the war, he moved briefly to England in the autumn of 1945, this time invited by the exiled royalist government of Yugoslavia, and then on to the United States. Bell saw him for the last time in 1954, at Evanston. Two years later Velimirovic died in exile, at a monastery at St. Sava, South Canaan. Bell preached eloquently at a memorial service at the Serbian Orthodox Church in London.

Oliver St. John Gogarty, the irreverent comrade of Oxford days, enjoyed mixed fortunes in high company, hiding Irish soldiers in the war of independence, winning an Olympic medal for a single poem, earning the praise of Yeats, quarreling with James Joyce, and getting entangled in a law suit with cousins of Samuel Beckett. He settled in New York and died there in 1957.

T. S. Eliot earned a growing public acknowledgment as a poet, a playwright, and a commanding literary presence throughout his life, with a Nobel Prize to boot. Like Holst — only more so — Eliot has now become a subject for scholarship in himself. He died in 1965.

John Masefield became Poet Laureate in 1930. His writings of all kinds remained popular with the broad public for most of his life, though critics often perceived that much in literature had moved on around him. He died in 1967.

Sarvepalli Radhakrishnan flourished in politics and became president of India in 1962. He died in 1975.

The theater director E. Martin Browne flourished, bringing a revival of the York mystery plays to the 1951 Festival of Britain. His collaboration with T. S. Eliot brought a lengthening list of new works by the poet to the stage. He died in 1980.

Martin Niemöller survived six years in prison and emerged into the bleak daylight of post-war Germany to lead his church into a new world order, becoming a pacifist, campaigning against nuclear weapons and America's war in Vietnam, and becoming, like his English friend, a president of the World Council of Churches. He died in 1984. His wife, Else, had died in a car crash in 1961.

Gerhard and Sabine Leibholz returned to Göttingen, and in the years that followed Gerhard Leibholz became one of the leading constitutional lawyers of the new Federal Republic. He died in 1982; Sabine Leibholz died in 1999.

And, at last, over a long life Hans Feibusch executed almost forty commissions in English churches, one of the last of which was a posthumous portrait of Bell himself, for the German church in Forest Hill. He died, a bare month short of his hundredth birthday, in 1998. It is suggestive that Feibusch, like his fellow refugee Ulrich Simon, found a Christian faith of his own in the example of Bell, but eventually lost such faith after he had gone, for Feibusch returned to Judaism and Simon remained a Christian but, in his last years, lost his faith in the Church of England. One of the last occasions on which Simon's voice was heard in an English church took place at Chichester Cathedral, on 20 July 1994. Here, in a great service commemorating Bell's relationship with those who died resisting Hitler in Germany, he declaimed words from the twentieth chapter of the Book of Jeremiah: "There is in my heart, as it were, a burning fire shut up in my bones, and I am weary with holding it in, and I cannot."

George Bell and Secrecy

Ulrich Simon wrote of George Bell: "When I met him, I loved him, but I was instinctively aware of the secrets which he carried about him and of which he must be silent. He wanted to know . . . but he did not let anything be known."[13] The historian must acknowledge that, however rich the archives may be, there is a history of suppression at work in the subject almost as much as the history that we catch, still visible, in expression. With the figure of George Bell this reality of suppression has come to matter. His apparent modesty concealed a firm sense of his own qualities and

13. Ulrich Simon, *Sitting in Judgement, 1913-1963: An Interpretation of History* (London: SCM Press, 1978), pp. 85-86.

ambitions, and a determination to put them to work. The long history of ecumenical diplomacy that became, in so great a measure, his life depended wholly on the preservation of outward appearances even when explosions had occurred behind closed doors. His persevering role in the history of the German resistance against Hitler was something that absolutely demanded his secrecy, for it had now come to be a matter of life or death. Certainly, Bell was a man familiar with the arts of confidentiality. Did they not suit the quiet character of his virtues and were they not the requirements of his duties as a priest?

But only his virtues and duties? Since the disclosure in October 2015 of an allegation that, more than half a century before, he had committed sexual offenses against an individual who was at the time a young child, the ground on which we meet the figure of George Bell has been, suddenly, altered. The Church of England once commemorated him in its Calendar. Now, overnight, it has given him a new place, not in the histories of dictatorships and wars, but in a quite different, still unfolding history that accumulates ominously in the popular mind; an unspoken history now becoming spoken—and spoken in words of accusation. This tragic coda presents many with a painful challenge, and almost too severe a paradox, for it seems wholly at odds with the qualities that have for so long been so widely accepted in Bell, whose record was not simply one of a pursuit of justice in public affairs, but of justice in private relationships, too. For many families across three decades had found in him, and in the home that he created with his wife, a principled place of refuge from the storms of the world. But who in 2015 is left to speak, from intimate knowledge, on behalf of a man who died in 1958? Roy Porter, Bell's domestic chaplain, who observed how Bell hated to see any evasion or deceit in a priest of the diocese, died in December 2006. Bell's long-serving secretary, Mary Balmer Joice, died in February 2007. From these years only one working member of Bell's household still lives. To Adrian Carey, who became Bell's new chaplain in 1950, this book will return.

The Church

Today we are more than ever inclined to insist on the drawing of distinctions. One reason that Bell has escaped conventional attention is that he so often refused to conform to categorical expectations. He was an Anglican who was deeply ecumenical; he was an English man who viewed events abroad as quite as important as affairs at home. His life presents an intense personal piety, but he was far too much rooted in a world of politics to satisfy an enthusiast for spirituality. Was there a divide between this world of public politics and the interior world of private devotion? In the Church of England distinctions are often observed (and affected) between "low" evangelicals (whose faith emphasizes the saving power of Jesus on the cross), "high" church parties and Anglo-Catholics (who affirm a place within the whole catholic church in their worship and look with great sympathy to Rome, adopting incense, bells, and high ritual), and a "broad" church (the great body landing somewhere between the two).[14] Although some sensed that his own outlook was in many ways a "high" one, Bell's churchmanship, his tradition of belief, ecclesiology, and worship, is hard to characterize neatly. Quite simply, he was not what Anglicans think of as a "party" man. He was profoundly affected by the vivid insistence on the Incarnation that Anglo-Catholicism preached. This Incarnation was no self-regarding, church-bound affair. It turned the eyes of the Christian out across the world and brought him to intervene in the social conditions of the poor, and participate actively in the whole state of society. This was a rich, lively Christianity that assumed that great works were there to be done and that individuals bore a responsibility not merely for their own welfare but even for the welfare of the world itself. His view of art and the artist was deeply sacramental.

The historian Adrian Hastings wrote of Bell as "a man of immense compassion and obstinate consistency in clinging to a cause, with a superb heart well in advance of his rather mediocre head, as Temple's never was."[15] This is certainly not flattery. Few in the church now turn to Bell's writings. His books, sermons, and speeches do not establish that he was that exceedingly rare thing, an original theologian. But then neither was John Wesley. Like Wesley, Bell gave a new, urgent form to what he inherited and found about him: he developed, enriched, and applied and, in so doing, made what he inherited into something greater than it had been, something that could be received by men and women at large in the world, and something that possessed the power to endure. If his books have never been regarded as works of devotional literature, perhaps they should?

---

14. For a thorough overview published shortly after Bell's death see J. W. C. Wand, *Anglicanism in History and Today* (London: Weidenfeld and Nicholson, 1961), pp. 95-148.

15. Adrian Hastings, *A History of English Christianity, 1920-1990* (London: SCM Press, 1991), p. 341.

In the English church Bell remains vaguely honored, but effectively undervalued. His intellectual claims may have been indistinct to a scholar like Hastings, but Bell certainly did present a distinctive and important theological presence both in the life of the church and in the world at large because few insisted more perseveringly and convincingly that they actually belonged together. Bell as a theorist did not resolve the tension between the two dimensions. Perhaps to have tried would have been far too glib? He never apparently found a theological sufficiency in purely intellectual exercises. What he did was to insist on that tension, indeed to inhabit it, with a creative integrity. He was, at root, ambivalent about the Establishment of the Church of England, but time and again he sought to use it. He set the faith of the church and the ways of the world at odds, but he must have known all too well how deeply they intermingled in the deeds of the individual and the strategies of institutions. For the church of Christ is indeed in the world, but not of it — and the riddle is there to be lived, not resolved.

George Bell lived most of his working life as a bishop, and doubtless became many of the things people expected a bishop to be. Evidently he was quite at home in what was, in so many ways, a deeply conservative church that had acquired a significant dimension of lay representation in parish church councils and synods, both local and national, but still would remain, essentially, governed by what was a clerical oligarchy. To his diocesan clergy he could be devoutly generous but also exceedingly firm. He was not always a model of patience, and he could insist on standards that many found beyond them. It must have been hard for a man who knew such luminaries as Dietrich Bonhoeffer and Martin Niemöller as ardent friends to bear patiently with the daily provincial insularities of English life and English religion. But, for the most part, he appears to have integrated these dimensions with at least an adequate fluency and to have achieved an impressive coherence. At the end, people found they knew how to cherish him, rejoicing in his stature even when they disagreed with his opinions. He showed how episcopacy itself might acquire a vivid, and even urgent, new eloquence in the eyes of all Christians.

Bell did not see himself as much of a church politician. But he played a valuable part in the commission on church and state that followed the rejection of the new Prayer Book by the House of Commons in 1927-1928, and he made himself useful in other ways, too. He was an effective maker of motions of all kinds in Convocation and in the Church Assembly. But he did not shine there. By the time Archbishop Lang was contemplating retirement in 1942, a sense hung in the air that the Bishop of Chichester had not come on as well as he might. That he did not become Archbishop of Canterbury on Temple's death two years later would provoke a restless, irresolvable debate in church circles, a debate that even now does not go away.[16] But much of the reason lies not merely in the attitude of an offended prime minister but in the mind of the Church of England itself.

It was in the context of international ecumenism that the Bishop of Chichester was assuredly a figure of considerable stature, and in his lifetime he was honored accordingly. In many committee and conference rooms across the world he proved himself to be a superb diplomat, holding together all manner of diversities, evidently without giving offence or provoking alienation. When he wrote his memoirs, Marc Boegner felt that Bell's death had created a void in the World Council of Churches that could never be filled. For Bell, the ecumenical vision encompassed not merely the ecclesiastical dialogues of churches that simply continued to preserve their differences, but the great idea that the church existed to show a divided humanity its essential unity. For it spoke to the whole inhabited earth.

A new generation of ecumenists were soon busy enough with their own enterprises, and in the 1960s and 1970s much of great worth was accomplished. Yet the dominance of the clergy was never much shaken, and the laity, who had once provided so much of its vital money and high purpose, simply turned away from a movement that offered them little to do. What William Temple pronounced to be the "great new fact" of the age became, with almost perplexing speed, a peripheral obscurity lodged, indistinctly, in the background of the denominational imagination. Fifty years later, most in the Church of England would barely notice the existence of the movement that dwelt in Geneva. This vivid vision of the Union of Christians, which defined so much in Bell's life and work, now appears before the historian only as the labor of an age. As an ecumenist Bell left no inheritor.

The Arts

On 25 February 1959 the BBC gathered together a number of those who had known Bell, to remember him and to pay tribute to a man to whom

---

16. This is weighed with clarity by Slack in *George Bell*, pp. 114-16.

they had owed much. Martin Browne, now the veteran of many theatrical productions, recalled, "Nothing was outside the scope of his interest and understanding, and everything was related to his master's will and work. He was the broadest-minded, and also the deepest, Christian I have ever known."[17] Now at the very height of his fame, T. S. Eliot remembered how the origins of his poem "The Rock" had lain in a weekend at the Bishop's Palace in 1930, and how the vision that would become his first play, *Murder in the Cathedral*, had come to him as he and Bell had walked together around the gardens there in 1934. Bell, he said, was "a loveable man":

> On reflection, I find that in applying this definition I'm making it a compendium of all the qualities for which I loved and admired him. These include a dauntless integrity; no ambition could ever have deflected him from whichever course he felt to be right; no fear of the consequences to himself could ever have prevented him from speaking the truth as he saw it. With this went understanding and simplicity of manner, the outward signs, I believe, of inward humility. A friendly man, and a man of genuine piety — in short, a good man, and an honest man.[18]

Artists knew Bell as a kindred spirit, and it is important to acknowledge his quiet presence in the world of art in the public landscapes of twentieth-century Britain. If British life and culture had indeed been insular before the age of the dictators, it may well be asked if the decades in which Bell played his part had disturbed the old *modus vivendi.* At large, and just as Bishop Bell and so many of the advocates of the refugees from dictatorship had prophesied, British life had benefited abundantly from its earlier investment in the men and women who scuttled across the channel to make a home on these new shores. Within a few years many of the ventures that had first taken off in the hands of emigres had become established national institutions in their own right: the Glyndebourne opera company, of which Carl Ebert and Fritz Busch had been the decisive artistic ingredients; the Amadeus string quartet, which had first met in an internment camp; the fine arts publishing house Phaidon. By the end of the century what could look more securely national than the figure of Nikolas Pevsner, who by then had dedicated his life to writing authoritative

---

17. Bell Papers, vol. 367, fol. 328.
18. Bell Papers, vol. 367, fol. 328.

descriptions of English buildings? As for the churches, they, too, found the task of rebuilding conducive to new architecture and a modest sprinkling of new art inside them. This would reach its apogee in that strenuous fusion of proclamation, forgiveness, and new artistic wisdom, Coventry Cathedral. It is natural to wonder how much it all owed to the deliberate work that Bell had undertaken in search of a new unity between religious faith and artistic expression, not merely for aficionados, but urgently alive and vivid in the context of contemporary experience. Influence is never easy to discern, however we may strain to match a cause and an effect. But the atmosphere certainly had altered, and Bell was at least a fraction of the reason why.

It is difficult to know what Bell would have made of himself as a character in a theatrical production. In 1967 the controversial German playwright Rolf Hochhuth conjured up an encounter between Churchill and the Bishop of Chichester in his play *Soldaten*.[19] Here the figure of Bell, complained Gordon Rupp, was translated into "something more like a Lutheran pastor in a play by Ibsen."[20] Donald MacKinnon found more in the play to provoke a creative, if critical, reflection.[21] At all events, Hochhuth's Bell now looks far more like the spectacle of a moment of theater than an enduring representation of a man and his world. What remains striking is the simple fact that it was a German writer who noticed Bell. No British writer of stature evidently has.

The Realm of Politics

The moral philosopher Donald MacKinnon wrote that Bishop Bell "tested the Establishment to destruction."[22] What, then, were the political consequences of this bishop of Chichester?

The historian Owen Chadwick once observed, "George Bell was the most Christian bishop of his age, but had little idea how to commend the points which he wanted to press; and this lack was important historically,

---

19. Rolf Hochhuth, *Soldaten: Nekrolog auf Genf. Tragödie* (Hamburg: Rowolt, 1967), pp. 144-80.

20. Gordon Rupp, *I Seek My Brethren: Bishop George Bell and the German Churches* (London: Epworth, 1975), p. 19.

21. Donald MacKinnon, "The Controversial Bishop Bell," in *The Stripping of the Altars: The Gore Memorial Lecture and Other Pieces* (London: William Collins, 1969), pp. 88-91.

22. MacKinnon, "The Controversial Bishop Bell," p. 85.

for his causes were always the best, and yet he could not make men listen unless they wanted to listen."[23] This is a sharp judgment. Bell was not a man to ignite the idealism of a crowd from a public platform. In assemblies, meetings, or conferences he pursued his chosen objects steadfastly, even obdurately. Evidently, few were galvanized. Yet Bell knew how to gather allies and orchestrate a campaign. Without Bell what became a formidable national and international church opposition to the ecclesiastical policies of the Hitler regime between 1933 and 1939 would have been notably weaker, and arguably far less significant altogether.

The public arena in which Bell committed his greatest efforts remained the House of Lords. After his death, two considerable, and not unsympathetic, peers were doubtful as to his influence there. Lord Woolton perceived that the House of Lords "held him in the greatest respect, in complete disagreement." The wartime interventions of the Bishop of Chichester had left government policy quite untouched. Woolton found Bell too rigid to prevail in debate. A second contemporary, Lord Pakenham, recalled, "There was no one whose speeches were followed with a closer, or at times, more painful attention, when he raised, as he almost inevitably did, a moral issue. That is not to say that he was a popular speaker; there were quite a number of excellent peers who really couldn't take his speeches at all . . . they could hardly bear to listen in silence." For Bell's "mild manner" was mixed with a sense of the "immensely assured"; he had "none of the mock diffidence with which the professional parliamentarian commends himself." Pakenham went on:

> But more fundamentally, I think, it was because the politician, even if he be a real statesman, is concerned so much with expediency, and reasons of state, and things like that seemed to play no part whatever in the Bishop's philosophy . . . his was a deeply disturbing voice, and the disturbance was likely to be the greatest where the conscience to which he appealed was most sensitive.[24]

Very likely Bell was essentially realistic about his contribution to the politics of the world. But he still maintained publicly that politics, even of the most desperate and headlong kind, must answer to principle and

23. Owen Chadwick, *Hensley Henson: A Study in the Friction of Church and State* (Oxford: Oxford University Press, 1983), pp. 255-56.

24. For these two tributes, see Bell Papers, vol. 367, fols. 325-26.

that a government must be honest to its own people. He recognized the significance of the House of Lords and in an age of democratic institutions did something to justify what in many ways was a questionable relic of unrepresentative government. Indeed, he placed it squarely in the arena of British democracy at large. He was often found to be an active ingredient in a modest fraction of opinion that could still manage to redefine the character, and even the direction, of a wider public debate. This, too, was no mean feat. His opposition to internment in 1940 found him to be busy on the winning side. When Vansittart castigated Germans it mattered that Bell was there to argue against him and to ensure that the world knew that a retired diplomat with a place in the House of Lords did not amount to more in the realm of national policy than he actually did. In a world of dictatorship, any evidence of the public vitality of democracy in Britain meant far more to opinion abroad than many at home realized. Bell demonstrated the possibilities of democracy and the place of a parliament as the court not of a dictator but of a free people. Frank Pakenham might well have been skeptical about the impact of these speeches, but he acknowledged that when Bell retired "the leaders of the parties, and others who had debated with him, vied with one another in saluting a man of God who had brought by common consent much honour to a House of Parliament, where he had often felt compelled to take up so lonely a stand." Many years later, when Bell had become a figure of history, Owen Chadwick would read all of the House of Lords sessions in which he spoke and acknowledge their weaknesses and well as their strengths. "But," he concluded, "no one can read those debates without being grateful that, on all the most difficult moral issues of that difficult time, the Christian voice was represented in the highest counsels of the nation."[25]

This much was done in the foreground of national life. Bell attempted at least as much behind the scenes. International affairs are the province of diplomats as much as of politicians. Bell was one of a handful of church leaders who became actively involved in this barely glimpsed, often inglorious realm, and he must have sensed sharply how credible principles endure far more safely when they keep their distance from the precarious — and even dubious — entanglements of diplomacy. In seeking ameliorations, or improvements, he took upon himself at least a shadow of the taint of compromise in a number of his dealings abroad. Was he a good

25. Owen Chadwick, "The English Bishops and the Nazis," *Annual Report of the Friends of Lambeth Palace Library*, 1973, p. 28.

judge of character? Gordon Rupp certainly thought so; Donald MacKinnon was less sure, feeling that Joachim von Ribbentrop made rather too benign an impression on him when the two first met in November 1934.[26] Bell was prepared to cultivate a man like Rudolf Hess when others might have preferred to leave the room altogether. Later he intervened on behalf of a handful of defendants at the Nuremberg trials whose guilt would be firmly established. Was he, as Karl Barth gently chided, simply too much the English gentleman to be sharply alive to the presence of evil?[27]

Bell tried hard to carry off his diplomatic adventures as well as possible. After the meetings with Bonhoeffer and Schönfeld in Sweden in 1942, the Foreign Office was initially respectful, but soon it began to doubt that Bell was as discreet as he should be. Meanwhile, he had arguably run a grave risk in passing on the names of those involved in active resistance against the Hitler regime, clearly assuming that such information could not escape through the doors of Whitehall to another power.[28] How close did Bell actually come to doing the bidding of the state in pressing for a firm stand against communist power in the forums of the ecumenical movement? Did such things show him to be a more pragmatic, more questionable figure than his admirers allowed — even a plain amateur, who was too self-confident in his own independence to acknowledge how he, too, might be drawn into the service of those in power? About the Bishop of Chichester the opinions of diplomats, like those of politicians, divided. Some had little time for him; others thought well of what he did. A handful, like Alan Leiper, became genuine friends. Others came to acknowledge the weight of Bell's arguments only later in life. A Foreign Office mandarin who was most firmly set against any official reply to a German resistance movement in 1942, Sir Frank Roberts, was one of those who purposefully attended the service in Chichester Cathedral that marked the fiftieth anniversary of the 20 July 1944 conspiracy.

At all events, Bell was sure that such enterprises were utterly demanded of him in the world as he found it. Righteousness was something

---

26. MacKinnon, "The Controversial Bishop Bell," pp. 86-87. Bell's record of the meeting may be found in Andrew Chandler, ed., *Brethren in Adversity: Bishop George Bell, the Church of England and the Crisis of German Protestantism, 1933-1939* (Woodbridge: Boydell & Brewer, 1997), pp. 89-92. Here Bell is thorough but detached.

27. See Barth's letter to Bell of 28 January 1940, Bell Papers, vol. 74, fol. 12.

28. The British politician Frank Field, an admirer of Bell, regards this as something very near to folly given the presence in the British Intelligence service, MI6, of a man like Kim Philby, who was an agent for the Soviet Union.

pursued in the real conditions of life: it required not simply a devotion to moral law, something in which he devoutly believed, but the practical arts of calculation, negotiation, and compromise. He knew that the weighing of information and advice was, in itself, an art as to whether one should trust and adopt or doubt and avoid. He sought not merely to be right, but to exert an actual influence where he could. He always held in his mind the likely consequences of an act and sought to measure what he did in light of them. He knew that there must be a time to speak and a time to hold silence, a time to intervene and a time to desist. If he believed that a palpable good could be pursued in dubious company, Bell was prepared to be found in it. Above all, he saved many lives — though it is difficult to calculate how many. He knew that all of this must be fragile and vulnerable, but it was what came with taking one's place responsibly in the affairs of humanity. If he was criticized easily by those familiar with the conditions of democracy, it is significant that those who labored to resist the Nazi state in Germany itself knew the Bishop of Chichester to be a man who inhabited the same world as them. That this was so remains a cornerstone of his achievement as a man in the world, as a moralist, and as a Christian.

Reputation

The public achievement of George Bell, as it accumulated over half a century, remains almost startling in its breadth and weight. Yet if there is a single legacy that lay in this it was not one of great success and influence, but one of costly failure. For Bell committed himself to the cause of peaceful internationalism in a world that descended into two great wars; he worked tenaciously to serve a resistance movement against Hitler inside Germany that would fail to make common cause with governments abroad and that would be rooted out and destroyed; by the end of his life political power was no nearer the model of arbitration that he favored, but was asserting itself in the midst of nuclear calculations. Against these things may be set reasons for vindication. He proved effective in opposing the internment policy that the British government hastily adopted in 1940; his decision to speak against the Anglo-French invasion of Egypt in 1956 was duly justified. Often he was successful in keeping a particular strain of political idealism alive when it might not have been glimpsed at all. He was, and remains, one of the few British public figures to see a real moral power in the idea of European union. Politics of any kind, plied for its own sake, evidently interested him hardly at all. He was a principled, compassionate idealist, one of a generation who believed that a life given to the church was a life given to the world. There had to be a vision at the heart of every endeavor if it was worth anything at all.

That Bell was a Christian who labored unsparingly and devotedly need not be doubted. But the world still knows him very little. As a figure of history he is neither vivid nor impressive. Part of this is doubtless because his public personality lacked the striking qualities that lend themselves to a Christian historical memory all too often fashioned around charismatic presences. Bell inhabited a succession of controversial landscapes with dogged persistence, but he seldom made an issue merely of himself. He was not a great speaker or memorable wit; he could appear reticent, even shy. In public life he did not attach himself to the themes that still fascinate Christians who like to own an identity or explicit tradition. He remains a name invoked by ecumenists in search of patron saints, or controversialists leaning toward self-justification of one kind or another. But the backward references of the former are sometimes rather lightly done, and the latter hold him hostage to all kinds of fortunes and misfortunes. Bell remains a background figure in landscapes dominated by other presences. Many scholars recognize him, often indistinctly, as the friend and patron of Dietrich Bonhoeffer. Across fifty years the study of Bonhoeffer's life and thought has indeed become a scholarly industry in its own right, and few recognize the extent to which Bell played a significant part in making it so. It is Bell, still, who connects Western Christianity to the great drama of Nazism and fortifies our sense that it does indeed speak directly to us all.

So much of Bell's presence in the midst of the turmoil of his age was intangible because it lay, not in public pronouncements, but in a daily *modus vivendi* that our sources, however ample, hardly touch. What Ulrich Simon had observed was a man who preferred to listen rather than to talk; one who knew that he had much to learn and set out eagerly to do so. In this, too, lay something of his democracy; evidently he set store by the opinions and experiences of people who enjoyed no celebrity or status at all. As one who worked in the bosom of the British establishment he might well have gathered its assorted privileges to himself alone: there is something so very flattering in possessing easeful entry into private quarters like the Athenaeum Club, or Grillions, or a bishop's palace for that matter. If Bell did not quite fling open these doors to Everyman and Everywoman, he at least drew into such premises a motley succession of people whose ideals he sought to advance there. He made a consistent effort to exploit his position on behalf of those who needed him. These days patronage possesses a dubious reputation, as something of an affront to the workings of meritocracy. But Bell saw its value in absolute terms. In a world where a refugee needed a guarantee from a private citizen in one country in order to escape from his own, patronage was integral to a way of life. It was a method of virtue.

Bell approached the drama of Nazism, not as an issue over which he could exercise his capacity for righteous indignation, but as a fire that threatened to consume men and women he had come to know and love. The archives allow us to trace a pattern of other relationships with many whose names are hardly recognized by posterity at all, people whose dramas were quite as intense, who found in Bell not simply the reality of friendship in an inhospitable world, but even the kind of father in God they might never otherwise have known. In retrieving Bell we find ourselves left with this rich pattern, a dense interweaving of public and private worlds. For all the writings, public and private, that remain on paper, we may reflect on how much more was carried in the silence of the mind.

Bell belongs to British history as he belongs to German history and to international history. He is not wholly contained by ecclesiastical categories and is not fundamentally a man of secular politics. He turns up now and then in a context crowded with professionals, in Parliament or on a public platform alongside other fleeting worthies. He is, perhaps, only an arresting distraction from the main business. The very language that he voiced, heavy with Christian responsibility and imagery, and now more remote than ever, finds no obvious place in the foreground of practical politics. In a vast study of the morality of warfare, the British historian Michael Burleigh only nods at him, merely suspecting him of a certain clerical vanity for being there at all. Burleigh's brief discussion shows again how easy it is simply to regard Bell as an English bishop who was little better than a dilettante in morality, in politics, in the world at large.[29] For their part, German historians do him greater honor, perhaps because those who study the solitary travails of the German resisters against Hitler often know how vital moral legitimacy and justification was to them, and how precious was a sign of solidarity in foreign places.

---

29. Michael Burleigh, *Moral Combat: A History of World War II* (London: Harper-Collins, 2010), pp. 503-5.

The World

If Bell has endured in the background of the Christian imagination, he has at least persisted there. The redemptive language of patronage and friendship that he fashioned so freely spoke of a courageous determination to encounter a world whose evils lay hardly at all within his power to remedy. This remains at stake in Christian life. We are less and less encouraged to follow the integrity of our relationships into the turmoil, more and more to identify the right postures of the moment and to fashion our course accordingly. This lacks integrity because we are not being true to ourselves, or to each other, but only to the politics of the corporations to which we belong. This becomes too quickly a world of mere calculation, not love. Indeed, if today we do not find that Bell stands at the heart of our understandings, we might do well to ask what this suggests about our own perspectives and priorities. Benjamin Britten had insisted that Bell had been "a very great man, a most important figure for our time."[30] What had Britten seen in this man that he should write such words to his widow? And when Imogen Holst wrote to Henrietta Bell, "There are no words to tell you what *we* feel about him," for whom did she speak?[31]

"George Bell," affirmed Martin Niemöller, "was a man of the ecumenical movement, not because he had plans, not because he made church politics, but because he was a Christian who was led and driven by the love of Christ Jesus himself. He couldn't see somebody suffering without suffering himself. He couldn't see people left alone without becoming their brother."[32] This is surely crucial. Bell spoke directly to the individual before the crowds and to the people before the corporation. It was his genius to look a man or woman clearly in the eye, to make that person's world a part of his own, and to leave him or her with a sure sense that it was truly and lastingly so. It is arguable that the much overlooked legacy of George Bell is a real and precious one because it urges upon us the command to do all that is humanly possible to stand by those who yearn to speak new and bold words to a world in disarray. To such as these the regimenting world of the twentieth century so often offered only alienation, dispossession, and destruction. It was Bell's decision to stand by them and to extend

---

30. Britten to Henrietta Bell, 8 October 1958, Bell Papers, vol. 367, fol. 36.
31. Imogen Holst to Henrietta Bell, 6 October 1958, Bell Papers, vol. 367, fol. 106.
32. A transcript may be found in the Bell Papers, vol. 367; here see fol. 328.

generously the friendship, solidarity, and support that were his to give. In this there lay courage, as well as compassion.

Eberhard Bethge wrote that Karl Barth and George Bell were the only two personalities whom Dietrich Bonhoeffer held to have "real authority" over him.[33] It was Bonhoeffer who wrote that the church was only truly the church when it existed for others.[34] This provocative flash of costly wisdom gives some clue as to what the young German pastor and the English bishop found in each other. A church that lives only for itself will lose itself and be lost to all others; a church that lives for the world will find itself — and be found. It was, arguably, a vision of the Christian life that fused high spiritual longing with the everyday realities that became known in the experience of all men and women, in the vulgarity of politics and power, in patched-up bargains and elegant accommodations, in the mean streak of betrayal that so often lies somewhere beneath the surface. This is a costly piety that insists upon provocation, for against all reasonable objections it will maintain the unreasonable wisdom that it is in losing oneself that one finds oneself; that a man is his brother's keeper; that it is not in success as the world knows it that Christian integrity is at last to be found, but in crisis, loss, and grief. If Bell achieved a true measure of greatness as a Christian at large in the world of the twentieth century, it was not merely because his opinions were found to be right, or even righteous, but because he acknowledged fully those who knew the cost of such discipleship. To some, perhaps only a few, this particular significance will be understood devoutly, and cherished. By prodigious efforts across many years George Bell toiled to make the church more present and more credible in the lives of such men and women — and to make a belief in the God of Christianity more possible in a world of horrifying hatred and destruction. When in disappointed old age Heinrich Grüber published his memoirs, he dedicated them to his own courageous wife, Margarete, and to four men he had known and whose influence he had felt: George Bell, Martin Buber, Martin Luther King, and Albert Schweitzer.[35] Who is to suggest that a man like Grüber, who knew what it was to experience everyday life as a

33. Eberhard Bethge, *Dietrich Bonhoeffer: Theologian, Christian, Contemporary* (London: Fountain, 1970), p. 49.

34. See Dietrich Bonhoeffer, *Letters and Papers from Prison,* enlarged edition (London: SCM Press, 1971), p. 382.

35. Propst Heinrich Grüber, *Erinnerungen aus sieben Jahrzehnten* (Cologne/Berlin: Kiepenheuer & Witsch, 1968).

concentration camp prisoner at Dachau, did not know what he was doing when he placed Bell in such company? Yet our reckoning with the figure of this man has still barely begun.

It is this that makes the little blue book with which this study began something profoundly important for the Christianity of the twenty-first century. For this is a piety of a distinct kind. It opens a door on a greater, more vivid, and more dangerous sensibility and reveals a spirituality that is always restless, always straining and striving, searching for God in all things, yearning to know him in all things. For Bell saw in the Christian revelation the clear invitation to seek the Kingdom by doing the work of the Kingdom, not merely to observe the labor of others in the fields but to roll up one's sleeves and join in the task of gathering in the harvest. It is not simply a faith for the individual, or even for ecumenical conferences and movements. It defines the very idea of the universal church.

Those who encountered Bell often thought him very much an Englishman, very much an Anglican, very much a bishop. But if he was in some measure gladly defined by these properties, he was not contained by such categories. He put them to work in the world and grew, as great men do, into something far more nearly universal. In the midst of the many tasks and burdens that he took upon himself he became, truly, a great *pontifex,* one who built many bridges that would otherwise not have existed at all: between nations in wartime and in peacetime, between the powers of church and state, between faith and endeavor, between high — often impervious — public authority and the experience of the barely observed private citizen. He was, loyally, a presence within an establishment and yet he was also, devoutly, an embodiment of dissent, even resistance. As Donald MacKinnon observed in 1967, Bell achieved the transition between the Lambeth Palace of Randall Davidson, the Stockholm of Archbishop Söderblom, and the Flossenbürg of Dietrich Bonhoeffer — and he bore the cost. His was a Christianity rich in paradox: at times reckless and even improvident, at others almost painfully entangled in calculation; often rejoicing in the greatest of company and, so often, left utterly bereft. This, certainly, is a piety of the twentieth century. We may well wonder what the twenty-first century can hope to be without it.

The place where George Bell's ashes were interred remains suggestive. A week after his death they were moved beside St. Richard's altar in Chichester Cathedral. Here they remain, at the very center of the great church, but unobtrusive, rarely noticed by the wandering eye. But his memorial plaque can be seen by those who have come in search of it, particularly if they are prepared to step onto the platform itself and set off the cathedral alarm bell. Perhaps, after all, this is as it should be.

Henrietta Bell survived her husband by ten years, determined to see his life set before the world in an authoritative biography even as her remaining years were worn away by disease. That book was published in 1967, the same year in which the first edition of Eberhard Bethge's great biography of Dietrich Bonhoeffer appeared in Germany. It was said that in the accomplishment of this final task Henrietta Bell saw her own *Nunc Dimittis*.[36]

36. Adrian Carey, "The Pastoral Bishop," in *Bell of Chichester, 1883-1958: A Prophetic Bishop*, ed. Paul Foster (Chichester: Otter Memorial Papers No. 17), p. 47. Henrietta Bell died on 10 March 1968.

Piety

For Jews and "Non-Aryans"[1]

O pray for the peace of Jerusalem;
They shall prosper that love thee.

Pray for the Jews,
Pray for the Jews in Stepney, and Whitechapel, and Bethnal Green;
Pray for the German Jews;
For all those suffering pain, suffering disgrace,
Because of their race.

Pray for those who have a Jewish parent or grandparent,
And are Christians by faith.

Pray for the older people, who have laboured all their days,
Who have struggled bravely for Germany,
Who have lived nobly for Germany,
Whose sons have died for Germany,
Who are now spurned and despised,
Because they come of the Saviour's race.

Pray for the young men and women,
Who had begun to work for Germany,

1. By George Bell. Published in the Chichester Diocesan Gazette, 1936; reprinted in Paul Foster, ed., *Bell of Chichester, 1883-1958: A Prophetic Bishop* (University of Chichester, Otter Memorial Paper No. 17), pp. 82-83.

Following honest callings, honourable professions,
Eager to serve their country, as their fathers served it,
Who are now flung out, and denied all share in the national life,
Because they come of the Saviour's race.

Pray for the children,
Who yesterday were happy and free from care,
Happy in their schools, happy in their games,
Happy with other German boys and German girls,
With the same lessons, the same toys,
The same hopes, the same troubles and joys,
Who are now persecuted by their teachers,
Persecuted by their schoolfellows,
Pilloried in the classroom,
Expelled from the playground,
Because they come of the Saviour's race.

Pray for the Non-Aryan Christians,
Who have rejected Judaism,
And have accepted the Cross.

To the Jews, the Jews from the whole world
Give succour and sympathy.
But to these Non-Aryan Christians
Who speaks a word of comfort?
Who clothes them, or feeds them?
Who visits them in prison?
Who shares with them the Cross of Christ?

Pray for all Non-Aryan Christians,
Pray for them, and help them!
And remember the Saviour's word —
Inasmuch as ye did it not to the least of these,
Ye did it not to me.

Christis the King[2]
Written for *Songs of Praise*

Christ is the King! O friends upraise!
Anthems of joy and holy praise
For his brave saints of ancient days,
Who with a faith for ever new
Followed the King, and round him drew
Thousands of faithful men and true.

O Christian women, Christian men,
All the world over, seek again
The Way disciples followed then.
Christ through all ages is the same:
Place the same hope in his great Name,
With the same faith his word proclaim.

Let Love's unconquerable might
Your scattered companies unite
In service to the Lord of Light:
So shall God's will on earth be done,
New lamps be lit, new tasks begun,
And the whole Church at last be one.

2. By George Bell, the version published by Henrietta Bell in *George Bell, Poems 1883-1958* (Brighton: Printed for private circulation, 1960). The more widely known version is now to be found in many hymnals, set to Vulpius.

Provocation

A SINGLE CHRISTIAN FRONT[1]

Usher Hall, Edinburgh, 2 December, 1941

Evil's Bid for the World's Soul

Four years before the outbreak of war I was in the house of Rudolf Hess at Munich. I had gone to see him about the position of the Evangelical Church in Germany in the Church struggle. I also wanted to secure his interest in the attendance of a delegation from that Church at the Oxford Conference on Church, Community, and State in 1937. I tried to explain the general purposes which the Conference was intended to fulfil. After some unsuccessful attempts I said at last, 'Do you not see, Herr Hess, that there are so many evils in the world, and the Christian Churches must unite to do battle against them?' I shall never forget the immediate reply of Hess's wife, who was also in the room, as she said, 'Ah, now I understand why foreign Churches take such an interest in our German Church struggle.'

The Hess conception of the evils in the world was different from mine, as the whole subsequent history of the Third Reich has made plain. But the important thing to notice is that once the target of evil is seen, the fitness of a common action on the part of the Churches to attack it is acknowledged without the slightest hesitation.

To-night we are here to give our emphatic witness to the need for unity amongst those who profess and call themselves Christians in the British Isles, to do battle against the evil in the world. But the cause which brings us together — Scotland's Week of Witness to the World-Wide

---

1. From G. K. A. Bell, *The Church and Humanity, 1939-1946* (London: Longmans, Green & Co., 1946), pp. 58-66. The original text in Bell Papers in the Lambeth Palace Library contains the subtitles here retained.

Church — is much bigger than this. We meet here to declare that the Church is larger and greater than any national Church, or denominational Church — a Church which includes men and women of all countries and races, of all classes and cultures, a Church that is suffering in the battle, and yet is above the battle, a Church that can reconcile enemy with enemy through the Cross of Jesus Christ, and a Church with a mission to mankind.

It is, I think, extraordinarily important that we should keep the conception of the Church with a mission and the Militant Church in the very centre of our thinking. The Church is not a sort of universal boudoir where people meet and take their ease and keep their minds away from serious things. It is militant here in earth. It has a terrific work to do, to fight against the evil things. There is an intensity in the conflict with evil of which men have seldom been aware before. The whole world is a theatre of battle. I see the evil in the blindness and selfishness of all nations, including our own, between the two wars; I see it in the idolatry of wealth; I see it in the passive acceptance for years of the unemployment of millions, of the ill-housing of millions, of the starvation of millions all over the world; I see it in the bitter nationalism which sets people against people, and makes sheer power and domination the be-all and end-all of government; I see it in the totalitarian State; I see it in the brutality and cruelty employed by the Nazis against the Jews; I see it in the outrages inflicted on the Poles, unbelievable in quality and quantity, on the Czechs, on nearly all the peoples in the occupied territories. And while I see it in all these forms, I cannot fail to see it, concentrated in a special form, in the war, which is not a war of the British and the Russians against Germany, conceived as an imperial or national war, but is a war between God and the spirit of evil for the possession of the soul of Germany, sick and maddened Germany, and the soul of Britain and of Russia, and the soul of Europe and of the whole world.

The evils are rank and vigorous and full of power. They can only be defeated by an even more vigorous concentration of spiritual forces against them. They have so terrifying a strength that the whole Church must be in arms and not a single member in any nation wanting.

Our Limited Outlook

We have often asked in the past few years, Why has the League of Nations failed to stop war? An interesting book by Harold Butler, Warden of Nuffield College and for many years Director of the International Labour Office at Geneva, has just been published under the title of *The Lost Peace.* The man in the street, he says, has been taught at school to look on the world as a collection of perfectly separate states, each of which runs a lonely and selfish race against all the others. Even if some devil did occasionally catch the hindmost, every runner felt that all was well as long as he escaped. The average citizen of every nation had never been taught to think of himself as a member of a world society, with obligations to it similar to those which he owed to his town or his country. And he adds that it has now been made tragically clear that in the last resort the combined action of the world as a whole is necessary to stifle a major conflict once it has broken out. The world is too small nowadays for peace to be divisible.

Now the Church is a world society, created by God, and composed of men and women called to follow the ways of Christ. Why have its members in all nations, why have the different bodies of so many kinds contained within it, failed to prevent war? The Church is not, as numbers go, an insignificant society. There are millions who give it their allegiance. Is not the reason here again, partly at least, that the man in the pew, the average churchman, has likewise been taught to look on the Church as a collection of perfectly separate Churches, each of which runs a lonely and selfish race against the others? We have not recognised our unity. We have not seen the indispensable need for combined action. We have not observed that evil is too vast, too dangerous, too powerful nowadays for the Church to be divisible. We have got to make a revolution in our thinking.

Steps towards Unity

Something has already been done in a small degree by way of commencement. Two aspects of this commencement are connected with Edinburgh: it was here in 1910 that the World Missionary Conference met and gave its first impetus to the Ecumenical Movement. It was here that a further famous World Conference on Faith and Order met in 1937.

There are roughly two forms in which the movement for closer world-wide Christian unity has found expression in Europe and the United States. In the first instance, there are those whose aim is directed to organic unity or, at the least, inter-communion between the Churches. They desire one great Church in which agreement on doctrine is a *sine qua non,* and the ministers of every section are recognised universally. This part of the movement is known as *Faith and Order.* It was founded before the last war, and much scholarship has been expended on the cause. A large number of Churches sent their delegates to two great conferences: one at Lausanne in 1927; and the other here in Edinburgh ten years later.

The second form leaves organic unity entirely on one side. It aims at securing unity in Christian practice on the basis that while each Church remains loyal to its own tradition and religious experience, all the Churches can stand together on a common ground in social and international affairs. Those whose interest is along this line (and there are many who follow both lines) would bring the Christian conscience to bear on current problems with a united witness. This part of the movement is called *Life and Work.* It was founded as a result of the last war, for the very purpose of bringing the Churches together as they are, and persuading them to create a united Christian front to grapple with the demons of unemployment and war and all the other urgent social questions. It owes its origin to a great Swedish Churchman, Nathan Söderblom, and has gathered delegates from most of the non-Roman Churches to two great conferences at Stockholm in 1925 and at Oxford in 1937.

Both these movements are now working as partners in a permanent body called the *World Council of Churches,* in process of formation, whose object it is to carry on their discussions and facilitate common action by the Churches, and to help all the Churches to regard themselves as elements in the Church Universal.

But the World Council, Faith and Order, and Life and Work represent movements in which Roman Catholics play no part.

There is now a third movement which is only just commencing, dealing again with the international and the social field. It is a movement in which the Roman Catholics in England and in certain other countries, Holland amongst them, have joined, with the encouragement and sanction of the Pope, showing for the first time a readiness to co-operate on equal terms with Christians of other communions. I ask you to recognise this new Roman readiness for co-operation. But in order that the co-operation may be carried through without later disappointments, I also ask you to observe that all issues relating to organic unity, or dogmatic questions of worship, creed, and ministry are excluded. It is co-operation, not unity that is sought. This new movement is young, and it has its anxieties; but it is full of promise, and may lead to things which were quite beyond our dreams when this war began.

I mention these facts as some evidence that there is already a breeze stirring in different quarters within the Church. Driven by the events of world history, compelled by the experience of the new anti-Christian forces assailing us on all sides, Christians are slowly beginning to see that wherever they are, and to whatever Church they belong, they are all engaged in the same campaign, and that the field is the world.

We Must Unite in Our Witness

A thousand years in God's sight are but as one day. So with a thousand Churches. God sees them as parts of a single world-wide Christian front. Are they giving their witness to the Gospel, and proclaiming the truth of God as fully and as bravely as they can? Of course there are differences between them, but if they are to be effective in their witness to the world, the missionary Churches, the younger Churches, and the older Churches must stand together on their common ground. The enemy is everywhere. The false gods are everywhere. Lust, cruelty, violence, pride, nationalism, class hatred, race fever, worship of power, idolatry of the State, love of mammon. They are bound to dominate the world, and enslave it to anti-God, unless we Christians everywhere stand up, and stand up together, for God. Chaos and anti-Christ are before us. Are we awake to the horror they bring?

I am convinced, with Karl Barth, that the enterprise of Adolf Hitler, with all its clatter and fireworks, and all its cunning and dynamic energy, is the enterprise of an evil spirit, allowed its freedom for a time to test our faith. I am convinced that it is our duty to defeat it on the military field. But I am also convinced that while it must be defeated by military weapons, it cannot be really vanquished unless we possess and employ spiritual forces as well. But I am further also convinced that the enterprise of anti-God with which we have to contend, the anti-God that seeks to overwhelm mankind, is not confined to Adolf Hitler, but is attacking us everywhere and in every nation.

The Church is called under God to proclaim a new and living Christ, more powerful and creative than His adversary. Right across the national barriers Christian speaks to Christian. The Word of God is here; everywhere the Christian listens. In country after country its echo is heard. In Holland, in Norway, in Belgium, even in Germany itself, a Synod, a body of bishops, a cardinal, a pastor, with hundreds of thousands — nay, millions behind them, dare to give their witness and speak out for God. We must unite in our witness to the living God, and ask Him to grant mankind a re-creation of hope and life.

We are but a fragment of the whole. We know that we have given but a fragmentary witness to God. But at this tremendous testing time every single Christian has a contribution to make. God alone can rebuild the waste places; and it is through His Church that the regeneration will come. If Christianity is going to survive in Germany, it will be only as a Church. This does not mean that it will have the title and property and security of an official Church. But it does mean that it will have to be a living, confessing, witnessing Church. If Christianity is going to survive in Scotland or England, it will be only as a Church. This does not mean that it need have the prestige and tradition of an established Church. For the Church is not the Moderator, or the Bishop, or the Presbyter, or the Elder, but you and I and all of us who are baptised and believe in Christ. From Church to Church, from believer to believer, in Scotland, in France, in Germany, in Russia, the Word of God goes. I see the Universal Church steadily unfolding, not as a great totalitarian society, with its officers and its organisation, but as an innumerable company of living human things. I see them speaking to one another in the spirit, linking up with one another, however distant in space, through waves of prayer; I see them supporting one another across the frontiers with spiritual forces. The Universal Church is a life-giving Church; it is a reconciling Church; the Church of the Spirit; the Church of the Word of God.

Do you want this vision to be realised under God? Then do not lose it — keep it constantly before you, and, above all, in your own town, in your own street, in your own home, speak of the things of God with your fellow-believers of whatever Church. Listen to the Word of God in company with others. Meet in the Spirit of God, and pray together with all your heart that men living to-day may receive God's truth, and that God's Kingdom may come.

Postlude: History and Allegation

The substance of the allegation that George Bell sexually abused a child in the late 1940s and early 1950s today remains deliberately a secret. What is the responsibility of the historian under such circumstances? For history cannot be written on the basis of allegations any more than societies at large should seek to live and work by such things. Accusations and cases for a defense are, of course, the business of lawyers. Yet it is not inappropriate for a historian to question what it must be to allow, and indeed to publicize, the former without establishing clearly, and in a form that is recognizable to the public, an equal place for the latter.

It is important to acknowledge that George Bell was a historical figure and that to seek to understand him is something that calls upon the craft of the historian. What can we really feel that we know about his beliefs, his character, and his practices; about the culture that formed him, the spaces in which he was found, and the contexts through which he moved? At the outset we may be struck that no other English bishop of the twentieth century left behind so much evidence of his own patterns of behavior. The 368-volume archive that Bell left to the Church and to the world of scholarship contains not only his correspondence and papers but also his personal notebooks, in which he committed private thoughts and the content of conversations, and all of his pocket diaries from 1919 to 1957, in which he wrote down his appointments and engagements. It is a very great treasure indeed, and to judge it as a whole requires many years of work and reflection.

It is important to place the allegation published in 2015 within at least four firm, defining historical contexts: that Bell was a bishop of his church who took a conspicuously high view of the standards required by his office; that he was a public servant whose self-understanding was deeply fashioned by the standards of a particular culture and era; that his daily patterns of life and work were meticulously documented by himself and almost constantly observed by those who lived and worked with him; that the various properties of his character were widely observed, and recorded, by his contemporaries, by those who knew him intimately and those who encountered him in a variety of places and situations.

Bishop Bell lived and worked as a man "under authority." We know that his was an intense, high understanding of episcopacy, and there is no evidence that this ever relaxed in him, or suffered and weakened under strain. It is difficult for a skeptic to believe in the power that a sense of the sacred might exercise over the behavior of a man just as it is difficult for a pious mind not to accept the profession of a principle as the whole truth of a life. As Bell himself once observed, "Men are in danger (to use a phrase of Dean Church) of 'putting or dropping out of sight the supreme value of the spiritual part of man.'"[1] But for Bell the piety of a bishop was not simply a state of mind. It was a craft and a discipline, and one that he exercised with a rigor that was, even in his own day, conspicuous.

In 1946 the bishops of the Church of England received on "absolutely confidential" terms a compendium of the codes and practices of episcopacy. Drawn from the official minutes of the Bishops' Meetings, this presented a selection of decisions on a variety of matters agreed by the bishops across the first half of the twentieth century, and it allows the historian to understand more clearly how the episcopacy understood itself, not in public but behind closed doors. Here, for example, among the sections listed in the table of contents is one on "Clergy: Discipline and Disability." Over this it is worth pausing, not least because it is perhaps the only official, printed acknowledgment that there existed in the Church of England a Caution List. (The Archbishop of Canterbury: "To the outside world there is no such thing as the Caution List.") This named priests known to have been guilty of criminal or moral offenses or viewed with "grave suspicion." In fact, there were national and diocesan caution lists, and each diocesan bishop was advised to keep his own up-to-date, to consult it before making any appointment, and to pass any new name directly to Lambeth Palace. This significant, secret manual of episcopal practice was no ordinary labor, and it required no ordinary editor. A prefatory note by Archbishop Fisher

1. G. K. A. Bell, *The Modern Parson* (London, 1928), p. vi.

announced, "We owe the revision of a record first compiled in 1912 to the industry of the Bishop of Chichester."[2]

When Bell became chaplain to Archbishop Davidson he would have taken the minutes of these important, but private, meetings of bishops. After he became a bishop himself he never rested content merely to accept the official minutes now provided by his successors. He made his own. It is interesting to compare his notes with the official record from which the 1946 compendium was drawn. Discussions of clergy discipline seldom occurred, for they were regarded as diocesan matters. But when the revision of the Caution List was raised in January 1939 Bell's notes, though abbreviated, become strikingly firm. "Act promptly," he writes in bold handwriting, underlining the words not once but twice. This stands out on the page because Bell seldom drew a single line under a word in these meetings, and in all the notes that he made across almost thirty years it is indeed one of the very few times that any phrase or word was emphasized not once, but twice. The word "proofs" follows clearly, though further words are obscure.[3] By the late 1940s and early 1950s Bell was in age and experience a very senior bishop indeed, one whose authority was called upon by both archbishops if they were poorly placed, or unable, to execute a confidential duty themselves. The author knows of one case of clergy discipline in which Bell was asked to intervene. Indeed, by now a working relationship with the Caution List had been a part of almost Bell's entire career.

The novelist L. P. Hartley once famously remarked, "The past is a foreign country: they do things differently there."[4] Bell was not a man of our time. He was very much a man of a particular generation and a product of a certain culture. He believed that a life given to service demanded constant self-denial and a resolute subordination of private emotions and interests to public duty. Today we find the post-Victorian world that formed him, his relationships, and his very movement through life remote and difficult to understand; indeed, we find it easier to suspect such a culture than think it possible. But a historian may recognize its existence and its distinctive

2. *Private Memoranda of certain matters discussed at the Bishops' Meetings of Bishops of the Three Provinces of Canterbury, York and Wales held at Lambeth Palace (1902-1945), together with certain Resolutions adopted by the Convocations of Canterbury and York* (1946), Bell Papers, vol. 306. Bell was clearly proud of this publication, writing his name and the exact date of issue (10 January 1946) on the flyleaf.

3. Bell Papers, vol. 301, p. 5.

4. L. P. Hartley, *The Go-Between* (London, 1953), p. 1.

properties in many public lives of that era. The figures of Bell's own church who were his closest friends and allies — among them the archbishops Lang and Temple, or the layman Sir Wyndham Deedes — shared these attributes. They trusted each other, and their trust was not found to be misplaced.

The routines by which Bell framed his day are well recorded. In what was so often observed to be a crowded daily life, Bell shared almost all of his time with his wife, secretary, domestic chaplain, and driver. His chaplain's office was located by the main door, and it was one of the chaplain's duties to answer when the bell rang. Adrian Carey, who served Bell as chaplain between 1950 and 1952, is firm, indeed emphatic, that "no child or young teenager ever entered during my two years as Chaplain, except on the day in January chosen for the parish Christmas party which he and Mrs Bell laid on every year for the children of the clergy." Carey found Bell "shy with children but his goodness and affection were strangely apparent."[5] He was, in physical terms, reserved and undemonstrative, and those who knew him found his affection palpable but wholly invested in other terms, not least his eyes, which were memorable. Another observer, his niece, Helen Livingstone, once wrote, "He endeared himself to young people by treating them with as much courtesy and grave interest as if they were adults."[6] Bell worked alone in his study, but the door was always open so that his secretary could be in earshot. It may be significant that private conversations appear often to have taken place not indoors, but in the garden. Even when Mary Balmer Joice left the palace at five o'clock in the evening Bell worked with his chaplain until late into the night. Carey finds it impossible to imagine a scenario in which an act of sexual abuse could occur. It is certainly exceedingly difficult to connect such a thing with what we know of these personalities and their constantly interrelating patterns of behavior.

If Bell documented his own life with a conspicuous assiduity, it is arguable that no other bishop of the twentieth-century church was so much observed, and recorded, by his contemporaries. What, in these terms, can we feel we know about the properties of his character? Adrian Carey was above all struck by the consistency of his bishop's integrity. In his years at the Bishop's Palace he observed no lapses. Indeed, Bell

5. Letter from Adrian Carey to Charles Moore, 6 January 2016, quoted with permission; also conversation with the present author. For all of this I am grateful.

6. R. C. D. Jasper, *George Bell: Bishop of Chichester* (London, 1967), p. 367.

appeared to him wholly devoted to the "Truth." He used the word itself often and even raised the pitch of his voice whenever he did so. Nothing at all in Carey's experience even suggested to him that Bell's character was in any sense self-contradictory. He appeared to intimates a man happy and fulfilled in his marriage. He was not austere in company, but he lived simply and owned few possessions. Much as he loved art, he acquired little for himself. We also know that it was a life lived with principled, and disciplined, generosity. This Bell did not record himself, but it was observed by others. On occasions it was simply spontaneous. When he encountered a young Indian visitor inadequately clothed for the English climate it was with no fuss at all that he gave him his own coat.[7] Bell must have made significant profits from his books, which sold well, and it is almost certain that he gave most of this money away, often to the refugees whose families he guaranteed or to needy people who simply crossed his path. When he died he left only £3,914 18s 6d behind.

The allegation of 2015 is anomalous. Indeed, it seems to exist in its own world, evidently uncorroborated by any other independent source. It also remains unique, for apparently no other such accusation has arisen. In sum, we are asked to invest an entire authority in one testimony and to dismiss all the materials by which we have come to know the historical George Bell as mere figments of reputation. The corollary of such a method may now be witnessed in the hasty removal of his name or image from public institutions and commemorations. It may simply be observed here that such iconoclastic activities are not unknown to historians of other, far darker, times and contexts.

---

7. As recounted to the author by E. C. John.

Bibliography

1. A Selective List of Bell's Published Writings

The Golden Anthologies (general editor). London: George Routledge, n.d.
The Golden Book of Ballads (general editor). London: George Routledge, n.d.
 [c. 1904-6].
The War and the Kingdom of God (ed.). London: Longmans & Green, 1915.
The Meaning of the Creed: Papers on the Apostles' Creed (ed.). London: SPCK, 1918.
Documents on Christian Unity, 1920-24 (ed.). Oxford: Oxford University Press, 1924.
The Modern Parson. London: SCM Press, 1928.
Documents on Christian Unity (Second Series) (ed.). Oxford: Oxford University
 Press, 1930.
Mysterium Christi: Christological Studies by British and German Theologians (ed.,
 with Adolf Deissmann). London: Longmans, 1930.
The Story of Chichester Cathedral (introduction), by A. S. Duncan-Jones. London:
 Raphael Tuck and Sons, n.d. [1933].
Randall Davidson, Archbishop of Canterbury. Oxford: Oxford University Press,
 1935; 2nd edition, revised, 1938; 3rd edition, with a new preface, 1952.
Humanity and the Refugees: The Fifth Lucien Wolff Memorial Lecture. London:
 Jewish Historical Society, 1939.
National Service: A Letter to the Clergy of the Diocese from the Bishop of Chichester.
 Diocese of Chichester, 1939.
Pastor Niemöller and His Creed (foreword). London: Hodder & Stoughton, 1939.
Christianity and World Order. Harmondsworth: Penguin, 1940.
The English Church. London: William Collins, 1942.
*With God in the Darkness, and Other Papers Illustrating the Norwegian Church Con-
 flict, by Eivind Berggrav, Bishop of Oslo* (ed., with H. M. Waddams). London:
 Hodder & Stoughton, 1943.
The Church and Humanity, 1939-1946. London: Longmans, 1946.

William Temple and His Message (memoir by Bell), by Canon A. E. Baker. Harmondsworth: Penguin, 1946.

Christian Unity: The Anglican Position. Olaus Petri Lectures at Uppsala University, October 1946. London: Hodder & Stoughton, 1948.

The Cost of Discipleship, by Dietrich Bonhoeffer (foreword). English edition, abridged. London: SCM Press, 1948.

Documents on Christian Unity (Third Series) (ed.). Oxford: Oxford University Press, 1948.

The Function of Chichester Cathedral: A Charge at His Primary Visitation of the Cathedral Church November 4, 1948. Printed for private circulation, 1948.

Kirche in der Welt: Reden und Aufsaetze des Bischofs von Chichester, Dr George Bell, edited and translated by Rudolf Weckerling. Berlin: Wichern-Verlag, 1948.

Mixed Marriages. London: SPCK, 1948.

The Approach to Christian Unity. Cambridge: Heffer, 1951.

The Word and the Sacraments. Diocese of Chichester, 1952.

The Kingship of Christ. Harmondsworth: Penguin, 1954.

Documents on Christian Unity (Fourth Series) (ed.). Oxford: Oxford University Press, 1958.

George Bell: Poems 1904-1958. Brighton: Printed for private circulation, 1960.

2. Archival

George Bell Papers, London, Lambeth Palace Library.

Bishop Headlam Papers, London, Lambeth Palace Library.

Archbishop Lang Papers, London, Lambeth Palace Library.

Archbishop Temple Papers, London, Lambeth Palace Library.

The Diary of Alan C. Don, London, Lambeth Palace Library.

Kirchliches Aussenamt Papers, Berlin, Evangelisches Zentralarchiv.

3. Unpublished Dissertations

Chandler, Andrew. "The Church of England and National Socialist Germany, 1933-1945." Ph.D. thesis, Cambridge University, 1991.

Hampson, Daphne. "The British Response to the German Church Struggle, 1933-1939." D.Phil. thesis, Oxford University, 1973.

4. Published Archival Literature

Bethge, Eberhard, and Ronald C. D. Jasper, eds. *An der Schwelle zum Gespaltenen*

Europa: Der Briefwechsel zwischen George Bell und Gerhard Leibholz (1939-1951). Stuttgart and Berlin: Kreuz Verlag, 1974.

Boyens, Armin. *Kirchenkampf und Ökumene: Darstellung und Dokumentation,* 2 vols. (1933-1939; 1939-1945). Gütersloh: Chr. Kaiser Verlag, 1969 and 1973.

Chandler, Andrew. *Brethren in Adversity: Bishop George Bell, the Church of England and the Crisis of German Protestantism, 1933-1939*. Woodbridge: Boydell & Brewer, 1997.

Dietrich Bonhoeffer Werke, 17 vols. Gütersloh: Gütersloh Verlagshaus, 1994-2013.

Dietrich Bonhoeffer Works, 16 vols. Minneapolis: Augsburg Fortress Press, 1996-2013.

Lindt, Andreas. *George Bell — Alphons Koechlin Briefwechsel, 1933-1954*. Zurich: EVZ Verlag, 1969.

Snoek, Johan M. *The Grey Book: A Collection of Protests against Anti-Semitism and the Persecution of the Jews Issued by Non–Roman Catholic Churches and Church Leaders during Hitler's Rule*. Assen Van Gorcum, 1969.

Selected Published and Secondary Works

Barns, Margarita. *India Today and Tomorrow*. London: George Allen & Unwin, 1937.

Bentley, James. *Martin Niemöller*. Oxford: Oxford University Press, 1984.

Besier, Gerhard. *Die Kirchen und das Dritten Reich*, vol. 3: *Spaltungen und Abwehrkämpfe, 1934 bis 1937*. Munich: Propylaen, 2001.

————. *"Selbstreinigung" unter britischer Besatzungherrschaft: Die Evangelisch-Lutherisch Landeskirche Hannovers und ihr Landesbischof Marahrens, 1945-1947*. Göttingen: Vandenhoeck & Ruprecht, 1986.

Bethge, Eberhard. *Dietrich Bonhoeffer: A Biography*. Revised edition. Minneapolis: Augsburg Fortress Press, 2000.

————. *Dietrich Bonhoeffer: Theologian, Christian, Contemporary*. London: Fountain, 1970.

Boegner, Marc. *The Long Road to Unity: Memories and Anticipations*. London: William Collins, 1970.

Brinson, Charmian. "The Anglican Bishop, the Methodist Minister and the Women of Rushen: George Bell, J. Benson Harrison and Their Work for Women Internees." *Humanitas: The Journal of the George Bell Institute* 7, no. 2 (April 2006).

Burleigh, Michael. *Moral Combat: A History of World War II*. London: Harper-Collins, 2010.

————. *Sacred Causes: Religion and Politics from the European Dictators to Al Qaeda*. London: HarperPress, 2006.

————. *The Third Reich: A New History*. London: Macmillan, 2000.

Carpenter, S. C. *Duncan-Jones of Chichester.* London: Mowbray, 1956.

Chadwick, Owen. *Britain and the Vatican during the Second World War.* Cambridge: Cambridge University Press, 1986.

————. "The English Bishops and the Nazis." The Friends of Lambeth Palace Library Annual Report, 1973.

————. *Hensley Henson: A Study in the Friction between Church and State.* Oxford: Oxford University Press, 1983.

Chandler, Andrew. *Brethren in Adversity: Bishop George Bell, the Church of England, and the Crisis of German Protestantism.* Woodbridge: Boydell & Brewer, 1997.

————. "The Church of England and the Obliteration Bombing of Germany in the Second World War." *English Historical Review* 108, no. 3 (October 1993).

————. "The Death of Dietrich Bonhoeffer." *Journal of Ecclesiastical History* 45, no. 3 (July 1994).

————. "Lambeth Palace, the Church of England and the Jews of Germany and Austria in 1938." *Leo Baeck Institute Yearbook* 40 (1995).

————. "A Question of Fundamental Principles: The Church of England and the Jews of Germany, 1933-1937." *Leo Baeck Institute Yearbook* 38 (1993).

Chandler, Andrew, ed. *The Church and Humanity: The Life and Work of George Bell, 1883-1958:* Farnham: Ashgate, 2012.

Chandler, Andrew, ed. *The Moral Imperative: New Essays on the Ethics of Resistance in Nazi Germany, 1933-45.* Boulder: Westview, 1998.

Clements, Keith. *Faith on the Frontier: A Life of J. H. Oldham.* Edinburgh: T&T Clark, 1999.

Conway, John S. *The Nazi Persecution of the Churches, 1933-45.* London: Weidenfeld & Nicholson, 1968.

Cresswell, Amos, and Max Tow. *Dr Franz Hildebrandt: Mr Valiant-for-Truth.* Leominster: Gracewing, 2000.

Duncan-Jones, A. S. *The Struggle for Religious Freedom in Germany.* London: Victor Gollancz, 1938.

Edwards, David. *Leaders of the Church of England, 1828-1944.* London: Oxford University Press, 1971.

Ehrenberg, Hans. *Autobiography of a German Pastor.* London: SCM Press, 1943.

Foster, Paul, ed. *Bell of Chichester, 1883-1958: A Prophetic Bishop.* University of Chichester, Otter Memorial Papers No. 17, 2004.

Grubb, Sir Kenneth. *Crypts of Power: An Autobiography.* London: Hodder & Stoughton, 1971.

Grüber, Heinrich. *Erinnerungen aus sieben Jahrzehnten.* Cologne and Berlin: Kiepenheuer & Witsch, 1968.

Gutteridge, Richard. "The Churches and the Jews in England, 1933-1945." In *Judaism and Christianity under the Impact of National Socialism,* ed. Otto Dov

Kolka and Paul Mendes-Flohr, pp. 353-78. Jerusalem: The Historical Society of Israel and the Zalman Shazar Center for Jewish History, 1987.

Haselock, Jeremy. "George Kennedy Allen Bell, Bishop of Chichester and Pastoral Liturgist." *Studia Liturgica* 35 (2005): 192-203.

Hastings, Adrian. *A History of English Christianity, 1920-1990.* London: SCM Press, 1991.

Heiene, Gunnar. *Eivind Berggrav: Ein Biografie.* Göttingen: Vandenhoeck & Ruprecht, 1997.

Hein, David. "George Bell, Bishop of Chishester, on the Morality of War." *Anglican and Episcopal History* 58 (1989): 498-509.

Hildebrandt, Franz. *'And Other Pastors of Thy Flock': A German Tribute to the Bishop of Chichester.* Cambridge: Cambridge University Press, 1942.

Hobbs, Mary. "Books in Crisis in Barchester." *The Book Collector* 44, no. 1 (Spring 1995).

Huttner, Markus. *Totalitarismus und Säkulare Religionen.* Bonn: Bouvier Verlag, 1999.

Iremonger, F. A. *William Temple, Archbishop of Canterbury: His Life and Letters.* London: Oxford University Press, 1948.

Jasper, R. C. D. *Arthur Cayley Headlam: Life and Letters of a Bishop.* London: Faith Press, 1960.

―――. *George Bell, Bishop of Chichester.* London: Oxford University Press, 1967.

Jehle-Wildberger, Marianne. *Adolf Keller (1872-1963). Pionier der ökumenischen Bewegung.* Zurich: Theologischer Verlag Zürich, 2008.

Kettenacker, Lothar, ed. *Das 'Andere Deutschland' im Zweiten Weltkrieg: Emigration und Widerstand in internationaler Perspektiv.* Stuttgart: Ernst Klett Verlag, 1977.

Klemperer, Klemens von. *The German Resistance against Hitler: The Search for Allies Abroad, 1938-1945.* Oxford: Oxford University Press, 1992.

Koenigswald, Harald von. *Birger Forell: Leben und Wirken in den Jahren 1933-1958.* Witten and Berlin: Eckart Verlag, 1962.

Lange, Dietz. *Nathan Söderblom: Brev-Lettres-Briefe-Letters; A Selection from His Correspondence.* Göttingen: Vandenhoeck & Ruprecht, 2006.

―――. *Nathan Söderblom und Seine Zeit.* Göttingen: Vandenhoeck & Ruprecht, 2011.

Lawson, Tom. *The Church of England and the Holocaust: Christianity, Memory and Nazism.* Woodbridge: Boydell, 2006.

Lockhart, J. G. *Cosmo Gordon Lang.* London: Hodder & Stoughton, 1949.

Ludlow, Peter. "The Refugee Problem in the 1930s: The Failures and Successes of Protestant Relief Programmes." *English Historical Review* 90 (1975).

MacKinnon, Donald. "The Controversial Bishop Bell." In *The Stripping of the Altars: The Gore Memorial Lecture Delivered on 5 November 1968 in Westminster*

Abbey, and Other Papers and Essays on Related Topics. London: William Collins, 1969.

———. *The Stripping of the Altars: The Gore Memorial Lecture and Other Pieces:* London: William Collins, 1969.

Nash, David. *Christian Ideals in British Culture: Stories of Belief in the Twentieth Century.* Basingstoke: Palgrave Macmillan, 2013.

Raina, Peter. *Bishop George Bell: The Greatest Churchman — a Portrait in Letters.* London: CTBI, 2006.

Rieger, Julius. *The Silent Church: The Problem of the German Confessional Witness.* London: SCM Press, 1944.

Robbins, Keith. "Dorothy Buxton and the German Church Struggle: Church, Society and Politics." *Studies in Church History* 12 (1975).

———. *England, Ireland, Scotland, Wales: The Christian Church, 1900-2000.* Oxford: Oxford University Press, 2008.

———. "Martin Niemöller, the German Church Struggle and English Opinion." *Journal of Ecclesiastical History* 21, no. 2 (April 1970): 149-70.

Roggelin, Holger. *Franz Hildebrant: Ein Lutherischer Dissenter im Kirchenkampf und Exil.* Göttingen: Vandenhoeck & Ruprecht, 1999.

Rouse, Ruth, and Stephen Neill, eds. *A History of the Ecumenical Movement, 1517-1948.* London: SPCK, 1954.

Rupp, Gordon. *I Seek My Brethren: Bishop Bell and the German Church Struggle.* London: Epworth Press, 1975.

Rusama, Jaakko. *Unity and Compassion: Moral Issues in the Life and Thought of George K. A. Bell.* Helsinki: The Finnish Society for Missiology and Ecumenics, 1986.

Schlingensiepen, Ferdinand. *Dietrich Bonhoeffer, 1906-1945: Martyr, Thinker, Man of Resistance.* Translated by Isabel Best. London: T&T Clark, 2010.

———. *Vom Gehorsam zur Freiheit: Biografien aus dem Widerstand.* Munich: Deutscher Taschenbuch Verlag, 2014.

Scholder, Klaus. *The Churches and the Third Reich.* Translated by John Bowden. 2 vols. London: SCM Press, 1987 and 1988.

———. *A Requiem for Hitler and Other New Perspectives on the German Church Struggle.* Translated by John Bowden. London: SCM Press, 1989.

Simon, Ulrich. *Sitting in Judgement, 1913-1963: An Interpretation of History.* London: SPCK, 1978.

Sinclair, Margaret. *William Paton.* London: SCM Press, 1949.

Slack, Kenneth. *George Bell.* London: SCM Press, 1971.

Smith, Graeme. *Oxford 1937: The Universal Christian Council for Life and Work Conference.* Frankfurt am Main: Peter Lang, 2004.

Studdert-Kennedy, Gerald. *British Christians, Indian Nationalists and the Raj.* Delhi: Oxford University Press, 1991.

Sundkler, Bengt. *The Church of South India: The Movement towards Union, 1900-1947*. London: Lutterworth Press, 1954.

———. *Nathan Söderblom: His Life and Work*. London: Lutterworth Press, 1968.

Visser 't Hooft, W. A. *The Genesis and Formation of the World Council of Churches*. Geneva: World Council of Churches, 1982.

———. *Memoirs*. London: William Collins, 1973.

Walker, Peter. *The Anglican Church Today: Rediscovering the Middle Way*. London: Mowbrays, 1986.

Walsh, Michael J. *The Westminster Cardinals: The Past and the Future*. London: Continuum, 2008.

Wasserstein, Bernard. *Britain and the Jews of Europe, 1939-1945*. 2nd edition. London: Leicester University Press, 1999.

Wilkinson, Alan. *Dissent or Conform? War, Peace and the English Churches, 1900-1945*. London: SCM Press, 1986.

Zimmermann, Wolf-Dieter, and Ronald Gregor Smith. *I Knew Dietrich Bonhoeffer: Reminiscences by His Friends*. London: William Collins, 1966.

Index

Index